Human Resource Management

Human Resource Management

ANUPAMA AWASTHI

Orange Booooks International
NEW DELHI-110002

ISBN : 978-93-83263-52-3

Published in 2018 in India by

Orange Boooks International

Contact Us
113A, Prakasha Scout,
Ansari Road, Daryaganj,
New Delhi - 110 002
INDIA
Phone:- 011-43046297,
011-43522777
Email:- Info@obipd.com

Preface

As HR strives to gain greater strategic influence, human resource and business leaders must look beyond the HR profession. They must learn how the strategic "decision sciences" of finance and marketing evolved from the professional practices of accounting and sales.

Human resource management is all about increasing employee performance to their highest level corresponding to their role in the organization. Since every organization is made of people, HRM is all about acquiring services of people, developing their skills, motivating them to the foremost level and making sure that they continue to maintain their commitment towards the organization.

The goals and objectives of HRM are aligned with the strategic objectives and plans of the organization. The role of HRM is to determine the human resources needed to support strategic objectives and to ensure that employees are selected, trained, evaluated, and rewarded in ways that further the achievement of business objectives. Strategic HRM is frequently described as a linear, balanced process that begins with the identification of goals that will guide human resource practices. The integration of the HR programs with the goals of the organization will result to the organization's increased value. The recruitment, compensation, performance appraisal, promotion, training and other functions are designed and managed so that they work towards the strategic objectives of the firm Strategic HRM has the purpose of improving the way that human resources are managed within firms.

Human resources planning is a process that identifies current and future human resources needs for an organization to achieve its goals. Human resources planning should serve as a link between human resources management and the overall strategic plan of an organization. Aging worker populations in most western countries and growing demands for qualified workers in developing economies have underscored the importance of effective Human Resources Planning.

Strategic human resource management is the proactive management of people. It requires thinking ahead, and planning ways for a company to better meet the needs of its employees, and for the employees to better meet the needs of the company. This can affect the way things are done at a business site, improving everything from hiring practices and employee training programs to assessment techniques and discipline.

Today's HR is focused mainly on its professional practice, which, like accounting and sales, is important but incomplete. Full strategic partnership requires a "decision science" that enhances decisions about talent resources; finance and marketing enhance decisions about money and customers. We describe the historical lessons from finance and marketing, and how they reveal the elements of a new decision science for talent resources, and a logical framework to support the decision science.

Job evaluation is the systematic process for assessing the relative worth of jobs within an organization. A comprehensive analysis of each position's tasks, responsibilities, knowledge, and skill requirements is used to assess the value to the employer of the job's content and provide an internal ranking of the jobs. It is important to remember that job evaluation is a measurement of the internal relativity of the position and not the incumbent in the position. This analysis can also contribute to effective job design by establishing the organizational context and value of the job, and to hiring and promotion processes by providing job analysis on skill and competencies required to successfully meet job requirements. All the matter is just compiled and edited in nature. Taken from the various sources which are in public domain.

This is a reference book. All the matter is just compiled and edited in nature, taken from the various sources which are in public domain.

This book requires no pre-requisite and assumes no particular area of concentration, yet provides a strong and solid foundation for any one who wish as to specialise in human resource management.

—Editor

Contents

1

Introduction

Human Relations is called HR also known as Human Resources. Managing HR is called Human Resources Management (HRM). Developing HR is called HRD. HRM is a philosophy, while HRD includes the activities and processes undertaken to promote the intellectual, moral, psychological, cultural, social and economic development of the individuals in an organization, in order to help them to achieve higher human potential as a resource for the community. It is a continuous process by which the employees are assisted in a planned way to develop capabilities.

Trends in HRM

An organization's labour force comes from its external labour market - individuals who are actively seeking employment. HRM helps organizations find and keep the best possible fit between their social system and technical system. Organizations need employees with broad skills and strong motivation. Recruiting and selection decisions are especially important for organizations that rely on knowledge workers. Employees' responsibility and authority are given to make decisions regarding all aspects of product development or customer service. HR professionals can support organizational strategies for quality growth and efficiency. Organizations with international operations hire employees in foreign countries, where they operate, as they need knowledge of differences in culture and business practices.

Now-a-days, information system has become a tool for more HR professionals, and often, these systems are provided through the Internet. The widespread usage of the Internet also includes HRM applications. Organizations search for talents, and screening candidates online. Employees may receive training online. The employment relationship takes the form of a psychological contract that describes what employers and employees expect from the employment relationship. The employees are looking for flexible work schedules, comfortable working conditions and greater autonomy, opportunities for training and development, and performance-related financial incentives. For HRM, the changes require planning for flexible staffing levels. Organizations seek flexibility in staffing levels through alternatives to the employment relationship. They may use outsourcing as well as temporary and contract workers.

Strategic HRM

It is that set of managerial decisions and actions that determine the long term performance of a corporation. It includes environmental scanning, strategy formulation, implementation, evaluation and control. The biggest benefit that strategic HRM offers is competitive advantage by building critical capabilities of HR in an organization. Strategic HRM facilitates in strategy formulation by making an organization's SWOT analysis, and also in policy implementation by providing competent human resources and competitive intelligence.

We can divide HRM into seven sections, i.e., HRM - Environment and Strategies, HRM - Acquisition and Absorption, Development, Maintenance and Retention, Control, Miscellaneous, HRM Practices.

HRM Environment and Strategies includes objectives, scope and functions, evolution and development of HRM. *Acquisition and Absorption includes* HR planning, job analysis and design, recruitment, selection, placement, induction and socialisation. *Development section includes* career planning and development, employee training, executive development, organization development and internal mobility and separation.

Maintenance and Retention section includes job evaluation, wage and salary administration, incentives and benefits, motivation, employee empowerment, workers participation in management, employee health and safety, social security, employee discipline, employee grievance, industrial relations, industrial disputes, trade unions, collective bargaining, performance & potential appraisal. *Control section includes* personnel research and audit, human resource audit and human resource information system. *Miscellaneous section includes* HRM in a changing environment, IHRM, HRM in virtual organizations. *The final section is HRM Practices* in various organization levels.

CONCEPT AND MEANING OF HUMAN RESOURCE MANAGEMENT (HRM)

Human resource management was previously known as personnel management which was concerned with the activities of a single department.

It was typically concerned with the administration of human. The functions carried out by the department were recruitment and selection, reward, appraisal, development, grievance handling, retirement,registration and so forth. It was introduced and developed in the bureaucratic set up in which importance was given on organization and administration of manpower.

Now, human resource management may be defined as a process in which human resources are recruited and mobilized in such a way that it helps in achieving the objective of the organization. HRM is concerned with the people dimension in management under which the consideration is given towards recruitment and selection, development, motivation and maintenance of human resources in an organization. It is one of the main functions of management, which is related with the management of human energies and competencies. Human resource management helps to ensure the right man,for the right position and at the right time in a changing environment. The organizational performance depends on the efficiency of human resource working in the organization. Hence, a proper set up should be taken for manpower planning, recruitment, motivation, training and development, performance evaluation, remuneration management and industrial relation.

Moreover, human resource management is concerned with the development of human skill, knowledge and ability to perform the organizational tasks effectively and efficiently. It is a field of study consisting of four functions- acquisition, development, motivation and maintenance of human resources. The acquisition is related with getting people,development is with preparing them for work, motivation refers to activating them and finally maintenance refers to keeping them retained in the organization. Therefore, human resource management is an art of managing and mobilizing people in the organization. It is done through the application of different practices and policies which ultimately values human resources as major asset of an organization. It integrates personnel function into strategic management.

Functions of Human Resource Management

Human resource management is all about increasing employee performance to their highest level corresponding to their role in the organization. Since every organization is made of people, HRM is all about acquiring services of people, developing their skills, motivating them to the foremost level and making sure that they continue to maintain their commitment towards the organization.

In short, HRM is concerned with the management of employees from recruitment to retirement. Although there are many functions of human resource management, following is the list of five major functions.

Recruitment and selection

Recruitment is the process of captivating, screening, and selecting potential and qualified candidates based on objective criteria for a particular job. The goal of this process is to attract the qualified applicants and to encourage the unqualified applicants to opt themselves out.

Before starting the process of recruitment, the companies must execute proper staffing plans and should grade the number of employees they are going to need. Forecasting of the employees should depend upon the annual budget of the organization and short-term and long-term goals of the organization.

Recruitment and selection process is very important to every organization because it reduces the costs of mistakes such as engaging incompetent, unmotivated, and underqualified employees. Firing the unqualified candidate and hiring the new employee is again an expensive process.

Orientation

Many organizations do not provide a thorough orientation to the new employees. This is the fundamental step to help a new employee to adjust himself with the employer and with his new job. Employee orientation program should include the objectives and goals of the organization and how the employee can help to achieve the long-term and short-term goals of the organization.

Giving intensive orientation to the employee is one of the major functions of human resource management. The program should help the employee to know his assigned duties and his exact job description, job role, and the relationship of position to other positions in the organization. It gives clarification to the employee to take an active role in the organization.

Maintaining good working conditions

It is the responsibility of the human resource management to provide good working conditions to the employee so that they may like the workplace and the work environment. It is the fundamental duty of the HR department to motivate the employees. The study has been found that employees don't contribute to the goals of the organization as much as they can. This is because of the lack of motivation.

Human resource management should come up with a system to provide financial and non-financial benefits to the employee from the various departments. Employee welfare is another concept which should be managed by HR team. Employee welfare promotes job satisfaction.

Managing Employee relations

Employees are the pillars of any organization. Employee relationship is a very broad concept and it is one of the crucial functions of human resource management. It also helps to foster good employee relations. They have the ability to influence behaviors and work outputs.

Management should Organize activities which will help to know an employee at the personal and professional level. Well-planned employee relations will promote a healthy and balanced relation between the employee and the employer. It is the key for the organization to be successful.

Training and development

Training and development are the indispensable functions of human resource management. It is the attempt to improve the current or future performance of an employee by increasing the ability of an employee through educating and increasing one's skills or knowledge in the particular subject.

Roles & Responsibilities

With advancement in technology, conventional methods are being replaced by new-age techniques. Globalization is on the rise and companies are spreading out all around the world, no longer restricted by geographical barriers. Economies are rising and falling and evolving continuously. Adding to the turmoil are stringent laws and regulations passed, leading to a constant void waiting to be filled with effective policies that follow all the legal guidelines and at the same time are not compromising on the organization's survival. In the midst of all this, is a function necessary, but minimally looked upon – the human resource function. In a quest to integrate the operations and strategies of a business across a wide array of products, services, ideas, and cultures, the role of human resource managers is constantly evolving. HR managers, who were once confined to handling basic data work and routine record keeping amongst employees, are now exposed to an evolving nature of diverse workforce complexities, legal obligations, and strategic management of the organizational goals.

With that background, first let's shed some light on the conventional HR functions and the traditional role of HR managers:

Recruitment

This is the one function which is hand in glove with HR. Recruitment has been one of the major responsibilities of the HR team. It is the job of HR personnel to plan and devise strategic campaigns and guidelines for recruiting suitable candidates for a required job description. They also have to serve as a mediator between the employer and the candidate and communicate company policies and terms of the contract to the candidate before he is hired. This is the first pillar of HR management that every HR manager starts with. It's probably one of the most important aspects of any HR professional's career. The recruitment function comprises 2 main objectives:

Attract Talent: Attracting talent starts with first planning the requirement of manpower in the organization. Gauging needs of the organization's human resource requirements, and accordingly putting a plan of action to fulfill those needs with placement of "talented professionals". That's followed by creating an "employer brand" which will be representative of the organization's good image and portray an attractive impression in the minds of potential candidates.

The employer branding aspects have become very important owing to the new-age media and awareness of employee rights. Putting the best foot forward is no longer enough, it needs to be followed through with honest actions in favor of the employees. And finally... the HR manager needs to them create detailed recruitment strategies carry out the hiring process.

Hire Resources: This is where the recruitment strategies are put in action. In the current age, there's ton of competition vying for the attention of the best talent in the market. The HR manager needs to run all possible engines to go out there in the market and find that one suitable gem.

This part of the role includes things like finding relevant locations to look in, reach out to maximum potential candidates using mass communication mediums, aggregate all responses, filter out irrelevant applications, judge suitable incumbents and coordinate internally to get them interviewed. Once the finalists are decided, the HR manager turns into a 'negotiator' of sorts, working as a mediator between the company and the candidate to find that win-win ground.

Training

Not all is done once you've recruited a suitable candidate for the job. Many organizations perform tasks a tad differently. Training employee is important to help the new hires get acquainted with the organization's work pattern. It is imperative for the HR department to incorporate a training program for every new employee based on the skill set required for their job. It will further also contribute towards employee motivation and retention.

For the training to be effective, every new employee can be subjected to an on-the-job training for the initial days to get him in sync with the work guidelines of the organization. This training will not only be of assistance to the employee but also give the HR team an insight into the employee's workmanship. On completion of the training, HR plays a significant role in assessing the results of the training program and grading employees on the same.

Professional Development

Closely related to training, developing your employees professionally is an added bonus for the employee as well as the organization. Enrolling the employee to attend conferences, trade shows, seminars etc that may be in his personal interest will make the employee feel cared-for and a vital part of the organization, thus increasing employee engagement. It will be beneficial to the organization by way of the employee's added skill set.

In short, it is a win-win. It is the HR head's job to get to know the employee's hobbies and areas of interest and look out for opportunities that will help them build onto those hobbies. For example, if an employee wants to master the technique of SEO, the HR could enroll him for seminars and conferences that talk on the same. However, this should not turn out to be a selfish attempt that benefits the organization only.

Appraisals

Since HRM is a body meant for the employees, carrying out timely performance appraisals is a given. Performance appraisals help in employee motivation by encouraging them to work to their fullest potential. It also enables to give them feedback on their work and suggest necessary measures for the same. This helps employees to have a clear view of what is expected of them and what they are delivering. They can thus, work better towards improving their performance and achieving targets.

The role of HR (especially the HR manager) in this would be to have a policy of generating timely appraisal reports and a review of the same by the authorities. The HR team should communicate individually with employees and give a clear feedback or suggestion on their performance. A system to reward employees excelling at their work would help in employee motivation and thus garner a higher degree of productivity and employee engagement.

Maintaining Work Culture

It is the duty of the HR to maintain a healthy, safe, and fun work environment to ensure a level of comfort amongst the employees and eliminate any stressful or awkward atmosphere that may hinder the performance of the staff. It is vital to have an efficient work atmosphere, because an individual's performance a largely dependent on the surrounding he's working in.

It would be great to have an open-door policy up to some extent wherein employees can freely communicate and voice their opinions to be given consideration. The HR department's role is to be a friendly body with an open attitude. By communicating and treating every employee as equal, the HR can build a rapport with the employees. This goes a long way in increasing employee engagement and gives a higher job satisfaction.

Resolving Conflicts

Where different people have different views, conflicts are almost inevitable. Whether the dispute is amongst two or more employees or between the employee and the management, an HR manager has the right to intervene and help map out a solution.

The HR should be available at the disposal of the conflicting parties and hear out their issues without being judgmental. Prior investigations are a must before passing any judgment. The HR head is not expected to discriminate or play favorites in this matter and always deliver an unbiased and practical decision. A reimbursement in case of any loss caused and strict actions against the defaulter should be practiced for effective conflict resolution by the HRM.

Employee Relations

The Human Resources is called so because its major responsibility is dealing with the human part of the organization and this involves having great interpersonal skills. An HR manager who sits in the office all day will not turn out to be good at building connections with the employees and thus fail to serve the purpose of being an HR head. As an HR person, employees should feel comfortable coming up to you with their problems and for that, it is important that the HR team builds a good public image within the organization. The HR team has to be proactive and know their employees. An HR personnel's job is not a desk job altogether. The HR head's role is to establish the trust and confidence of the employees and not have a "don't mess with me" demeanour. He should be looked upon as both an HR expert and an employee advocate.

Rewards and Incentives

Rewarding the employees for a work well done imparts motivation and at the same time induces a desire to excel at tasks in hope of obtaining rewards. It serves as bait for inculcating a healthy competitive environment amongst employees to achieve targets and meet deadlines. A reward need not be materialistic always. It could just be a word of appreciation in front of all coworkers for a menial task done with complete honesty.

However, with globalization and evolving trends, compensations like holiday packages, pay incentive, bonuses, and promotion are taking a backseat. If as an HR manager you are wanting to reward your employees efficiently, it's time you adapt new ways of awarding benefits such as flexible work times, paternity leave, extended holidays, telecommuting etc. These non-traditional rewards will prove fruitful not only in engaging existing workforce but also as an added benefit to attract new talent to your organization.

Legal Knowledge

This may seem the least glamorous of all, but is an important aspect of the HRM. An HR manager should always be in compliance with the law. Whether it's drafting new policies or writing terms of a contract, it is the HR department's job to build guidelines keeping the laws in mind. This ensures an organization's continued growth and existence. While drafting policies, the HR should always ensure to be at an upper hand legally and keep the organization's practices in tune with the labor laws, tax laws, permissible working hours, minimum wages, and a no-discrimination policy.

Organization

An HR head is responsible for organizing all functions of the organization. To start with, it includes employee on-boarding, i.e. welcoming new employees. It is a must for every HR head to carry out an induction for every new hire, and give them an orientation regarding the company policies and rules.

The HR personnel should also introduce the new employees to their colleagues and assign them a mentor. It also involves listing out job expectations and defining roles and responsibilities, thus getting the new employees in tune with the working of the organization. The HR personnel are also responsible for organizing and storing all employee data efficiently and keeping it secure.

Management

Management is the most important job of an HR manager. It is what defines a good HR manager. Management extends right from managing employees to managing the employers and the whole HR department as well.

The role of an HR manager is to manage, create, implement and supervise policies/regulations, which are mandatory for every employee and also have knowledge of its appropriate functioning.

Monitoring attendance and tracking leaves forms a major chunk of the HR management function. There should be a proper management of the clock-in/out time to avoid late arrivals and track overtimes and half-days. As mentioned before, the HR as a department should also be well managed by the HR head. If the HR department itself is in a state of chaos, it cannot serve as a peacemaker for the other departments.

Payroll Management

Once all the attendance monitoring, leave tracking, clock in/outs etc is tracked and monitored, it's time for the most important aspect–calculating the payroll. Efficient calculation of salaries, wage-cuts, reimbursements, and generation of pay slips amounts to the role of HR managers in payroll management.

The HR manager should maintain transparency and provide the employees with information as and when asked. The HR should ensure not only accurate calculations of salaries but also timely transfer of the same. They also have an obligation towards exiting employees in settlement of dues and compensations.

Essential HR Manager Skills and Competencies

Human resource management responsibilities require an overlapping set of skills and competencies. If you're looking for an edge in today's competitive job market, understanding and developing these skills is the key to success. Let's count down six core competencies for HR professionals.

Human Resources Knowledge

Today's job seekers have access to more information than ever before. Therefore, the best HR professionals must be prepared to meet these informed candidates with industry expertise of their own. According to "Leading Now, Leading the Future," a report from the Society for Human Resources Management knowledge tops the list of contemporary HR manager skills and competencies.

Understanding how and why individuals enter and move within an organization is at the core of everything else you will do in human resources. HR managers who truly add value are always attuned to "the big picture" of how HR practices relate to a successful business.

Your knowledge in this area needs to be greater than anyone else's to support the objectives of employees and employers alike. After all, HR management is not just about talent acquisition, but also about retention.

A Commitment to Ongoing HR Learning

Today's business landscape is complex and in a state of constant flux. The field of HR is dynamic and our ability to process and understand it needs self-motivation.

Growing in your job means being receptive to new ideas, wherever they may come from. Have you demonstrated a commitment to ongoing learning by taking advantage of conferences, other colleagues in HR, or graduate studies?

HR professionals who never stop learning are well-positioned to translate well thought out industry trends and data into actionable insights.

Communication Skills in Human Resources

The primary function of the typical HR professional's job involves facilitating discussion between employees and employers. If a human resources manager can't communicate clearly they will not be successful. Both oral and written skill are required to effectively relay information.

One aspect of communication that gives people an edge is a strong ability for conflict resolution. Even in the most agreeable workplaces, problems arise that need a diplomatic ear, an eye for assessment, and a hand for getting the problem settled. This particular skill is invaluable when negotiating solutions and keeping things on track.

Critical Thinking Skills

Critical thinking is in the "sweet spot" of less common/more desired employed traits, according to an analysis of the skills gap by Bloomberg. HR professionals, in particular, frequently need to balance complex situations and take their time to think with a combination set-in-stone processes and outside-the-box thinking. Employees come from a breadth and depth of backgrounds and experiences. HR professionals need to strategically cultivate an environment in which all can work together toward the improvement of the business.

An Ethical Approach for Human Resources

The importance of ethics as an HR core competency cannot be overstated. Every day, HR professionals face ethical challenges related to everything from managing private employee information to protecting the reputation of their organizations. Adopting an unwavering and unilateral commitment to ethics not only helps attract top talent while safeguarding your organization, but also fosters a culture of trust and loyalty.

Part of being ethical is truly caring about people. Empathy for tough situations and "real life" goes a long way to setting you apart from those who just do it "by the book."

Some ethical principles are enshrined in law. Making sure your company's policies and practices are in legal compliance is a mainstay in the world of human resources. Avoiding discrimination in regard to ethnic background, disability, religious belief, and many other factors is important because of the hurt it will avoid and to foster a better, more diverse work environment.

Laws are always changing, sometimes incrementally, sometimes as part of a great cultural shift. Therefore, staying up to date on national news, trends, and laws is particularly important; ignorance of the law is not a winning defense. Legal compliance, of course, also protects the company and its officers.

Human Resources Organizational Skills

HR management is a juggling act. The more organized you are, the better you'll be able to stay ahead of what you need to do and have time for things you would like to do. If you think organization is something you either have or you don't, think again. Organization can be honed by understanding where you work, and doing a few things the same every day to build a routine.

CORPORATE STRATEGY IN HUMAN RESOURCE MANAGEMENT

Today, there is an urgent need to link human resource management, inextricable, to the business of the organization, at both the strategic and practical levels. The HR manager has the task of being on a constant lookout for the right choice of employees, fine-tuning the job mix and compensation package to benefit the individual and the organization, devising a flat organization structure and organizing training programmes for continuing the education at different levels in the organization.

Best Practices in HRM

A best practice in HRM has invoked a great deal of interest among HR professionals. Companies that are currently under-performing in the HR area can learn and adopt some of the best practices from organizations that have acquired some mastery over the good practices in HR. In the era of liberalization, the competitive scenario in the business environment has changed a lot. Consequently, HR practices have also changed phenomenally.

The performance of the employees determines the failure or the success of an organization. There are four stages of integration between HR functions and the strategic management functions: -

- Administrative Linkage
- One-way Linkage
- Two-way Linkage
- Integrative Linkage.

HR experts are having the opinion that, though "best practices in HRM" cannot be uniformly applied to all the organizations, they have a kind of uniform applicability in some functional areas, where psychological factors play an important role. Such areas are broadly classified as follows: -

- Process of selecting and recruiting the best talent.
- Allotment of work and responsibility, as would be appropriate to the employees natural talent and skill.
- System of initial training for new employees and specialized training for the experienced and skilled employees.
- Inculcation of a sense of team spirit.
- System of healthy and transparent communication, intra and extra company.
- System of periodic appraisal of the performance of employees.
- Suitable policy for career advancement of employees.
- Suitable policy for placement and transfer of employees.
- Suitable policy of recognizing and rewarding merit.
- Provision of security in service, to the deserving employees.

HRM in Cross-Cultural Context

Multi-cultural workforce congregations have become today's workplace realities. The cross-border market terrorism spared by MNCs evoked counter-insurgency and strategic warfare from domestic businesses. Partnering people in this race is vital for success in the market place. Workplaces have increasingly symbolized multi-cultural villages, resulting in a growing need for cross-cultural intelligence.

The future competitiveness of corporations will depend on their ability to attract and manage diverse talents effectively. Cross-cultural training will give managers on international assignments the cultural understanding essential to accomplish their tasks.

Cross-cultural differences are the cause of failed negotiations and interactions, resulting in losses to the firms. The strategic role of HRM in strengthening and sustaining corporate growth has assumed paramount significance, the world over.

Employee Engagement

Products and process alone can't help organizations to sustain loyal customers. They also need highly-motivated, dedicated and involved employees who are very passionate about their work and their organization; in short, they need "engaged employees". But, nurturing engaged employees requires a lot of effort and skill on the part of HR managers and calls for a different HR philosophy in the organization.

We need employee engagement to serve as a core competency of an organization that would provide sustainable competitive advantage. We know employee engagement towards their work, throw few test "symptoms", i.e., feeling of creating value, having a direction to follow, an air of trust, creating engaged employees through top management endorsement, a work environment to cherish, innovative leadership and clear growth trajectories, 'one step up from commitment'.

Employee engagement is the new buzzword. A successful business is directly linked to the commitment of its employees. Employee engagement ensures the successful execution of any business strategy.

HUMAN RESOURCE PLANNING

Need for Human Resource Planning

Human Resource Planning is the process by which a management determines how an organization should move from its current manpower position to its desire manpower position. This way a management strives to have the right number and the right kind of people at the right places at the right time. Human Resource Planning consists of a series of activities:

1. Forecasting future manpower requirements
2. Making an inventory of present manpower resources.
3. Anticipating manpower problems by projecting present resources into the future.
4. Planning the necessary programs of requirement, selection, training & development to ensure that future manpower requirements are properly met.

Human Resource Planning is necessary for one or more of the following reasons:

1. Effective manpower planning is required for every organization to carry on the work efficiently.
2. There is a constant need for replacing personnel who have grown old or who retire so that the work doesn't suffer.
3. Human Resource Planning is essential because of frequent labour turnover that arises from social & economical factors like voluntary quits, marriage, promotions etc.
4. Due to rising standards of living large quantities of goods are required because of which human resource planning is unavoidable.
5. The present workforce has to be changed in relation to the challenging needs of technology & production.
6. Manpower planning is needed in order to identify areas of surplus personnel or areas in which there is shortage of personnel.

Process of Human Resource Planning:

1. Deciding goals or objectives
2. Estimating future organizational structure & manpower requirements
3. Auditing Human Resources
4. Planning job requirements & job descriptions
5. Developing a human resource plan.

Assessment of Available HR in the Organization

The assessment of available HR in the organization is an important step to human resource planning. This assessment of manpower requirement depends on the manpower assumptions and the organizational corporate strategy.

1. Zero Budgeting – The total operation begins from zero where the objective of the managers is to lay importance on their current activities.
2. Ideal Approach – Decision like off-loading, sub-contracting, maintenance, production, technology is kept in mind while assessing human resource in the organization.
3. Realistic Approach – Based on existing information manpower assessment is determined.

Work Load Analysis

It's the method of studying & analysing a job to prepare the manning norms. Work load analysis is used to understand the methods & processes of doing a particular job. It thus helps in improving the productivity of an organization.

Gender Development Index of India

The human development index (HDI) compiled by the UNDP, is a summary measure of a country's human development. It measures the average achievements in a country in three basic dimensions:

- a long and healthy life, as measured by life expectancy at birth;
- access to knowledge, as measured by the adult literacy rate and the combined gross enrolment (sic) ratio in education; and
- a decent standard of living, as measured by GDP per capita in purchasing power parity (PPP) US dollars.

These three dimensions are standardized to values between 0 and 1, and the simple average is taken to arrive at the overall HDI value in the range 0 to 1. Countries are then ranked on the basis of this value with a rank of 1 representing the highest HDI value. India ranks 134 among 182 countries and is classified as a medium HDI country.

Between 1980 and 2007, India's HDI increased by about 1.3% every year. Many African countries show even higher growth rates in HDI, reflecting the very low levels they were at in 1980. Most high income countries show growth rates between 0.25 to 0.5% per year over this period.

The ranking clearly showed India has slipped in comparative terms in ensuring a better quality of life for its citizens as in the previous index, compiled together for 2007 and 2008, it ranked 128, while the position the year before was 126. Norway, Australia and Iceland top the HDI while Afghanistan, Sierra Leone and Niger are the bottom of the HDI.

Gender Development Index of India

In terms of the Gender Development Index, India ranks 113 out of 157 countries. Gender Development Index is calculated with the use of 3 variables:

- Life Expectancy
- Education
- Estimated Earned Income.

Government Expenditure in Social Sector

The government to improve these parameters that affect the HDI and GDI has increasingly been spending higher on social services as a proportion of total expenditure and was 22.5% for 2008. Expenditure on education and health care has also increased.

Poverty Index of India

There are concerns about vulnerability of people who have crossed the poverty line (PL) and are at present above it. Vulnerability is a relative term and could be gauged from the consumption pattern in the absence of a better available alternative. The average per capita consumption expenditure for rural and urban population as per 61st Round (2004-05) is Rs. 558.78 and Rs.1052.36, respectively. NSSO data also reveals that rural population on an average spends about 55% of its consumption on food and the remaining 45% on non-food items.

POLICIES OF HUMAN RESOURCE MANAGEMENT

Human resource policies are systems of codified decisions, established by an organization, to support administrative personnel functions, performance management, employee relations and resource planning. Each company has a different set of circumstances, and so develops an individual set of human resource policies.

Purposes

HR policies allow an organization to be clear with employees on:

- The nature of the organization
- What they should expect from the organization
- What the organization expects of them
- How policies and procedures work
- What is acceptable and unacceptable behaviour
- The consequences of unacceptable behaviour

The establishment of policies can help an organization demonstrate, both internally and externally, that it meets requirements for diversity, ethics and training as well as its commitments in relation to regulation and corporate governance.

For example, in order to dismiss an employee in accordance with employment law requirements, amongst other considerations, it will normally be necessary to meet provisions within employment contracts and collective bargaining agreements. The establishment of an HR Policy which sets out obligations, standards of behaviour and document displinary procedures, is now the standard approach to meeting these obligations.

HR policies can also be very effective at supporting and building the desired organizational culture. For example, recruitment and retention policies might outline the way the organization values a flexible workforce, compensation policies might support this by offering a 48/52 pay option where employees can take an extra four weeks holidays per year and receive less pay across the year.

Developing the HR Policies

HR policies provide an organization with a mechanism to manage risk by staying up to date with current trends in employment standards and legislation. The policies must be framed in a manner that the companies vision and the human resource helping the company to archive it or work towards it are at all levels benefited and at the same time not deviated from their main objective.

Procedure in Human Resource Management

If an organization has to move towards excellence, maintenance of harmonious and cordial relationship is a vital condition. Similar to organization' expectations from the employees. The employees do have more expectation in terms what they have contributed to each other. Failure to meet with each others expectation or the deviations from what has already been accepted may lead to indiscipline, grievance and stress are of continuing in nature and often judicial-legal process may not be of much help in resolving them.

Managing Discipline

In the modern management process, discipline should be viewed as a behavioural modification process. Although there may be many norms fixed for desirable behaviour wherever there are deviations. Appropriate corrective measures should also be taken for overall effectiveness, of an organization. Promotion, maintenance and strengthening of discipline will be a continuing affair, only if some of the following conditions are fulfilled.

They are normally:

- A shared culture
- Inculcation of positive attitudes
- Scope for problem-solving and
- A feeling of satisfaction.

Approaches to Deal with Indiscipline

This approach tends to emphasize the coercive and punitive methods that fall with in the legal-constitutional framework. It may not always be realistic.

Judicial Approach

This is only an after effect approach. It follows the law of natural justice and provides the offender all possible opportunity to bring out his side of the case. This is a time consuming process and conducive climates are not often restored.

Humanistic Approach

It lays emphasis on a healthy inter personal relationship between the employer and employee. Corrective steps are taken in helping the employees to get over their difficulties and to the extent possible, punitive actions are avoided in spite of some perceived inconsistency that may exist among other workmen.

Human Resources Development Approach

Keeping in mind the Theory Y and its implications, organizational goals have to be enhanced through adequate training, motivational patterns and personnel policies. Groups are used as influences and often made to act as catalysts to emulate norms of behaviour.

Likewise, the effectiveness in maintaining discipline is also possible through the process of leadership. A leader has to exhibit mutuality of interaction, persuation, highly interpersonal in his relationships and get himself involved and should expect participation from others to achieve the organizational goals and bear in mind not to indulge in favouritism while taking appropriate actions.

To avoid displeasure among the employees while enforcing discipline, it would be a desirable course of action if only one employees his diagnostic skills and intervention skills. If a change is to be expected in an individuals behaviour, some amount of influence had to be exercised in order to create a congenial atmosphere.

Managing Grievance

In a democratic set up any employee should be in a position to express his dissatisfaction, whether it be a minor irritation, a serious problem, or a difference of opinion in the work assignment or in the terms and conditions of employment.

The feeling of discontent or dissatisfaction becomes a complaint when:

- It has not assumed
- The matter has been presented in a highly informal way.

A complaint turns into a grievance when:

- There is a feeling of injustice
- Expressing the feeling formally, either verbally or in writing and
- It is related to policies, procedures and operations of the organization.

The National Commission on labour (1969) for example defines grievance in the following way:

> *"Complaints affecting one or more individual workers in respect of their wage payments, overtime, leave, transfer, promotion, seniority, work assignment and discharge would constitude grievance. Where the points at dispute are general applicability or of considerable magnitude they will fall outside the scope of this procedure."*

Nature and Causes of Grievance

In an organization a grievance may be presented by an employee or group employees, with respect to any measure or a situation that directly affects the individual or is likely to affect, the conditions of employment of many workers. If such a grievance is transformed into a general claim, either by the union, or by a group of employees, then the claim falls outside the scope of grievance procedure as it is a collective grievance and therefore it falls under collective bargaining. In 'Grievance Procedure, A survey of practices in industries in India', it's classified in to 19 causes of employee grievances have been outlined.

They are:

1. Promotions
2. Amenities
3. Continuity of service
4. Compensation
5. Disciplinary action

6. Fines
7. Increment
8. Leave
9. Medical Benefits
10. Nature of job
11. Payment
12. Acting promotion
13. Recovery of dues
14. Safety appliances
15. Superannuation
16. Suppression
17. Transfer
18. Victimisation and
19. Condition of work.

HUMAN RESOURCES MANAGEMENT TRENDS AND INFLUENCES

In organizations, it is important to determine both current and future organisational requirements for both core employees and the contingent workforce in terms of their skills/technical abilities, competencies, flexibility etc. The analysis requires consideration of the internal and external factors that can have an effect on the resourcing, development, motivation and retention of employees and other workers. The external factors are those largely out-with the control of the organization and include issues such as the economic climate, current and future trends of the labour market e.g. skills, education level, government investment into industries etc. On the other hand internal influences are broadly within the control of the organization to predict determine and monitor, for example the organizational culture underpinned by management behaviours (or style), environmental climate and the approach to ethical and corporate social responsibilities.

Major Trends

In order to know the business environment in which any organization operates, three major trends should be considered: Demographics the characteristics of a population/workforce, for example, age, gender or social class. This type of trend may have an effect in relation to pension offerings, insurance packages etc. Diversity the variation within the population/ work place. Changes in society now mean that a larger proportion of organizations are made up of "baby-boomers" or older employees in comparison to thirty years ago. Advocates of "work place diversity" simply advocate an employee base that is a mirror reflection of the make-up of society insofar as race, gender, sexual orientation, etc. Skills and qualifications as industries move from manual to a more managerial professions so does the need for more highly skilled graduates. If the market is "tight" (i.e. not enough staff for the jobs), employers will have to compete for employees by offering financial rewards, community investment, etc.

Individual Responses

In regard to how individuals respond to the changes in a labour market the following should be understood: Geographical spread how far is the job from the individual? The distance to travel to work should be in line with the pay offered by the organization and the transportation and infrastructure of the area will also be an influencing factor in deciding who will apply for a post.

Occupational structure the norms and values of the different careers within an organization. Mahoney 1989 developed 3 different types of occupational structure namely craft (loyalty to the profession), organization career (promotion through the firm) and unstructured. Generational difference different age categories of employees have certain characteristics, for example their behaviour and their expectations of the organization.

Framework

Human Resources Development is a framework for the expansion of human capital within an organization or (in new approaches) a municipality, region, or nation. Human Resources Development is a combination of training and education, in a broad context of adequate health and employment policies, that ensures the continual improvement and growth of both the individual, the organisation, and the national human resourcefulnes.

Adam Smith states, "The capacities of individuals depended on their access to education". Human Resources Development is the medium that drives the process between training and learning in a broadly fostering environment. Human Resources Development is not a defined object, but a series of organised processes, "with a specific learning objective" (Nadler,1984) Within a national context, it becomes a strategic approach to inter sectoral linkages between health, education and employment.

Structure

Human Resources Development is the structure that allows for individual development, potentially satisfying the organization's, or the nation's goals. The development of the individual will benefit both the individual, the organization, or the nation and its citizens.

In the corporate vision, the Human Resources Development framework views employees, as an asset to the enterprise whose value will be enhanced by development, "Its primary focus is on growth and employee development...it emphasises developing individual potential and skills" Human Resources Development in this treatment can be in-room group training, tertiary or vocational courses or mentoring and coaching by senior employees with the aim for a desired outcome that will develop the individual's performance. At the level of a national strategy, it can be a broad inter sectoral approach to fostering creative contributions to national productivity.

Training

At the organizational level, a successful Human Resources Development program will prepare the individual to undertake a higher level of work, "organized learning over a given period of time, to provide the possibility of performance change" (Nadler 1984).

In these settings, Human Resources Development is the framework that focuses on the organizations competencies at the first stage, training, and then developing the employee, through education, to satisfy the organizations long-term needs and the individuals' career goals and employee value to their present and future employers. Human Resources Development can be defined simply as developing the most important section of any business its human resource by, "attaining or upgrading the skills and attitudes of employees at all levels in order to maximise the effectiveness of the enterprise" (Kelly 2001).

The people within an organization are its human resource. Human Resources Development from a business perspective is not entirely focused on the individual's growth and development, "development occurs to enhance the organization's value, not solely for individual improvement. Individual education and development is a tool and a means to an end, not the end goal itself". The broader concept of national and more strategic attention to the development of human resources is beginning to emerge as newly independent countries face strong competition for their skilled professionals and the accompanying brain-drain they experience.

Recruitment

Employee recruitment forms a major part of an organization's overall resourcing strategies which seek to identify and secure the people needed for the organisation to survive and succeed in the short to medium-term. Recruitment activities need to be responsive to the ever-increasingly competitive market to secure suitably qualified and capable recruits at all levels. To be effective these initiatives need to include how and when to source the best recruits internally or externally. Common to the success of either are; well-defined organisational structures with sound job design, robust task and person specification and versatile selection processes, reward, employment relations and human resource policies, underpinned by a commitment for strong employer branding and employee engagement strategies.

Internal recruitment can provide the most cost-effective source for recruits if the potential of the existing pool of employees has been enhanced through training, development and other performance-enhancing activities such as performance appraisal, succession planning and development centres to review performance and assess employee development needs and promotional potential.

Increasingly, securing the best quality candidates for almost all organizations will rely, at least occasionally if not substantially, on external recruitment methods. Rapid changing business models demand skills of experiences which cannot be sourced or rapidly enough developed from the existing employee base. It would be unusual for an organisation today to undertake all aspects of the recruitment process without support from third-party dedicated recruitment firms.

This may involve a range of support services, such as; provision of CVs or resumes, identifying recruitment media, advertisement design and media placement for job vacancies, candidate response handling, short-listed, conducting aptitude testing, preliminary interviews or reference and qualification verification. Typically, small organisations may not have in-house resources or, in common with larger organisations, may not possess the particular skill-set required to undertake a specific recruitment assignment. Where requirements arise these will be referred on an adhoc basis to government job centres or commercially run employment agencies.

Except in sectors where high-volume recruitment is the norm, an organization faced with an unexpected requirement for an unusually large number of new recruits at short notice will often hand over the task to a specialist external recruiter to manage the end-to-end resourcing programme. Sourcing executive-level and senior management as well as the acquisition of scarce or 'high-potential' recruits has been a long-established market serviced by a wide range of 'search and selection' or 'head-hunting' consultancies which typically form long-standing relationships with their client organizations.

Finally, certain organizations with sophisticated HR practices have identified there is a strategic advantage in out sourcing complete responsibility for all workforce procurement to one or more third-party recruitment agencies or consultancies. In the most sophisticated of these arrangements the external recruitment services provider may not only physically locate, or 'embed', their resourcing team(s) within the client organization's offices but will work in tandem with the senior human resource management team in developing the longer-term HR resourcing strategy and plan.

Modern Concept of Human Resources

Though human resources have been part of business and organizations since the first days of agriculture, the modern concept of human resources began in reaction to the efficiency focus of Taylorism in the early 1900s. By 1920, psychologists and employment experts in the United States started the human relations movement, which viewed workers in terms of their psychology and fit with companies, rather than as interchangeable parts. This movement grew throughout the middle of the 20th century, placing emphasis on how leadership, cohesion, and loyalty played important roles in organizational success. Although this view was increasingly challenged by more quantitatively rigorous and less "soft" management techniques in the 1960s and beyond, human resources development had gained a permanent role within organizations, agencies and nations, increasingly as not only an academic discipline, but as a central theme in development policy.

HRM IN 2020

Now, we identify and discuss about five issues which are expected to affect the organizational HR in the future: (i) The corporations of tomorrow, (ii) Information age, (iii) Virtual corporation, (iv) Diversity, and (v) Social responsibility.

Corporation of Tomorrow

In future, there is a two-fold effect on Indian Industries, i.e.,(i) Generation of employment, and (ii) Industrial restructuring

We assume that in the future workplace, which may come true by 2020:

- A majority of people worldwide will be connected through the IT infrastructure.
- Connectivity is the new frontier on the information highway to connect with one another.
- There are various factors on which the growth and expansion of connective technology will depend.
- The basic organizing unit in the workplace will be one individual engaging in business through connective technology.
- A learning culture will be festered by the technologies that will serve, entertain, and help people do their work. It will be basic workplace skill.
- Power in the organization of 2020 will be in flat structure.
- Culture and language will still move between the poles of traditionalism and modernism.

Information Age

Information age has heralded a new way of doing business. IT has the power to change the most well-entrenched business paradigms. It has the power to link and connect people, and enable the exchange of products, services and capital, in an entirely different manner than in the past.

IT has increased the efficiency of the human resource functions and reduced the burden of administrative work in the HR department, at the same time, helping to increase productivity.

Virtual Corporations

A virtual company is usually a highly networked organization that extensively contracts out activities that were once performed in-house, allowing both speed and flexibility. The key to success in a virtual corporation is connectivity, i.e., the ability to network with a large number of independent companies.

Social Responsibility

Change in technology results in a change in the structure, design and environment of an organization. It has four stages: (i) Acquisition of technology, (ii) adaptation of technology, (iii) utilization of technology, and (iv) improvement and development of technology. Organizations of the future will operate in a workspace, which is likely to be much more broadly defined, than it is today. Connectivity within and outside the organizations, will create a world virtual reality organization.

Environmental problems fall into two broad categories, i.e., (i) Problems that arise out of poverty and inadequate development, and (ii) Problems that arise out of the process of development (threat of earthquake, deforestation, pollution of ground water).

The Impact of Strategic Human Resource Management

Strategic human resource management (SHRM) enhances productivity and the effectiveness of organisations. Research shows that when organisations employ such personnel practices as internal career ladders, formal training systems, results-oriented performance appraisal, employment security, employee voice/participation, broadly defined jobs, and performance-based compensation, they are more able to achieve their goals and objectives.

Using logistic regression analyses of data from a survey of North Carolina county social service professionals, this study examines the extent to which strategic human resource management is perceived to affect outcome assessments (or performance measurements) for welfare reform. While strategic human resource management practices are perceived to be present, they clearly are not a predominant feature in North Carolina counties. The results of the logistic regression analyses indicate an overall weak relationship between strategic human resource management and outcome assessments (accounting for fewer than 3 per cent of the explained variance in each model).

The performance of organisations is the focus of intensive research efforts. How well an organisation performs its mission and accomplishes its goals of programme service delivery is of paramount concern. Administrative capacity is a major component in this performance. Administrative capacity, a resource based view of organisations, focuses on those factors that are actually within our power to affect. Improving administrative capacity and, especially, those aspects dealing with human capital offer the most promise for improving organisational effectiveness.

Strategic human resources management practices enhance employee productivity and the ability of agencies to achieve their mission. Integrating the use of personnel practices into the strategic planning process enables an organisation to better achieve its goals and objectives. Productivity gains from the diffusion of technological innovations are now incorporated into both public and private sector organisations. Future productivity gains must focus on how people use these technologies.

Modern, knowledge based organisations are ideal settings for the application of strategic human resources management practices. Inasmuch as their competitive advantage is attributable to their people techniques which focus on people should prove to be directly linked to measures of organisational success. Civil service systems are designed to integrate the multiple values pursued by the public sector. While these rules can inhibit the adoption of progressive personnel practices, they are not the necessarily rigid barriers to change. The public sector has been the venue of many experiments and innovations in recent years. Social service agencies (such as those in studied here in North Carolina) are indeed knowledge-based organisations. According to Theodore Lowi's (1972) policy typology, social services represent an effort at redistribution. While the agencies possess a professional, social science knowledge base, their redistributive objective remains controversial. In addition, the beneficiaries of this redistributive transfer from the haves to the have-nots are a politically marginalized segment of society (Mosher, 1968; Meier, 1987).

Combining human resource practices, all with a focus on the achievement of organisational goals and objectives, can have a substantial affect on the ultimate success of the organisation. Resource-based theory posits that competitive advantage and the implementation of plans is highly dependent upon an organisation's basic inputs, including its human capital. Research on strategic human resource management offers empirical support for this thesis.

This study examines the perception of strategic human resources practices (e.g., internal career ladders, formal training systems, results-oriented performance appraisal, employment security, employee voice/ participation, broadly defined jobs, and performance-based compensation) held among North Carolina county social services professionals. The study examines the relationships among these SHRM perceptions and demographic characteristics (such as county population, change in unemployment, age, education, ethnic status, gender, and supervisory status) four measures of outcome assessments on how well welfare reform is achieving its goals.

Strategic Planning and Personnel Practices

For motivation and incentives to work, they first must be tied to a goal. An organisation must employ needs assessment and human resource development strategies in pursuit of its vision or mission. Needs assessment (of where an organisation wants to go) and human resources development (of those who are to get it there) focus on the specific organisational and individual needs whose satisfaction will lead to enhanced productivity. The vision and path for fulfilling it derived from strategic planning is put into practical perspective through the use of macro-tools such as Total Quality Management (at the group-level) and Management by Objectives (at the individual-level). Strategic planning is rational analysis. It takes "what is" and develops ideas of "what should be" along with plans for "how to get there." With a realistic organisational strategy focused on what the future should look like, strategic planning provides the "road map" for fulfilling that future. Strategic planning should also incorporate the human resources necessary for accomplishing its goals.

The foremost advantage derived from strategic planning is that it helps improve organisational performance. Strategic planning focuses on the future — what should be?

As such, it serves as a guiding star by which to steer the organisation's development. Individual and team effort can be devoted to accomplishing the organisation's goals (Keen, 1994).

Strategic planning also helps to concentrate individual efforts into a team effort. It can assist in developing total quality management and objective-based performance appraisal systems. Accountability for results can be assigned. The strategic planning process itself can serve as a team-building exercise. Finally, the process itself transforms perceptions away from separate and distinct projects and towards systemic viewpoints.

In addition to leadership support, those engaged in strategic planning need be aware of other potential problems. As occurs with all management techniques, individuals will need extensive training and refresher training (to answer unforeseen questions that arise in response to implementation). Conflict, confusion, and chaos will prevail initially and for some time thereafter. Only as individuals learn how to do it and see its value will the benefits of strategic planning be realized.

In the modern, knowledge-based organisation strategic planning is quite clearly strategic human resources planning. In an empirical study noting the impact of strategic human resource management on organisational performance, John E. Delery and D. Harold Doty (1996) identify seven general employment practices:

1. Internal career ladders
2. Formal training systems
3. Results-oriented performance appraisal
4. Employment security
5. Employee voice/Participation

6. Broadly defined jobs
7. Performance-based compensation

These personnel practices form the basis upon which the concept of strategic human resource management is constructed for this study. While other and similar personnel practices are left out, this enables the findings here to be compared with those of Delery and Doty (1996). While these specific personnel practices are discussed below, research has established linkages between SHRM and various measures of organisational effectiveness.

Whereas much of this research has concentrated on private sector organisations, this study focuses on the provision of public social services. The general hypothesis underlying this study is that each practice does indeed matter and individually (and collectively) contributes to organisational success.

Strategic Human Resources Practices

Internal Career Ladder

A career system is necessary to focus individual attention on the strategic issues facing an organisation over the long term. Objectives and reward systems tied to the short-term lead to dysfunctional behaviour and goal displacement. Government with its 2- year, 4-year, and 6-year electoral cycles has always suffered from this myopia. A longterm perspective induces organisational commitment and loyalty. It enables individuals and organisations to invest in training and productivity improvements knowing that they will reap the benefits from that enhanced knowledge and technique.

County social service professionals generally perceive the existence of career ladder. However, this ladder is seen as rather narrow within their organisations. Hence, career or promotional opportunities may lead outside of the organisation.

Formal Training Systems

It can no longer be taken for granted that employees will arrive at work with all the requisite skills. Too much of what goes on in today's organisation requires specific adaptation. The most knowledgeable and skilled worker still requires training so as to fit into the organisation and become a valuable contributor to the team (Quinn, Anderson, and Finkelstein, 1996).

The chief function of the supervisor is the development of the people in their unit. Managers who have often been promoted from a technical position must remember that they are now the coaches; others have the responsibility of caring out the plays on the field. The manager/coach can have the greatest effect only by assuring that the employee/player is truly prepared for action. While the importance of training and development is now recognized, it remains a neglected area. Beginning Employees like the buildings and equipment of government are allowed to depreciate through an under investment in maintenance (Elmore, 1991; Gray, Hall, Miller, and Shasky, 1997).

North Carolina social service employees generally perceive that training is available. However, training is focused on current job skills and not on employee development for future advancement.

Results-Oriented Performance Appraisal

Performance appraisal is used as an aid in making judgment decisions pertaining to promotion, demotion, retention, transfer, and pay. It is also employed as a developmental guide for training needs assessment and employee feedback. Performance appraisal also aids with a number of more general organisational functions as a means for validating selection and hiring procedures, promoting employee-supervisor understanding, and supporting an organisation's culture.

The environment in which welfare reform has occurred extensively involves measurable goals and objectives. Employees perceive that these have been transferred from the organisation to individual performance appraisals.

Employment Security

Employee rights and the mechanism for enforcing them (i.e., the grievance process) serve as a safeguard for assuring that employees are accorded the basic dignity that every human being is entitled to. Like similar safety devices, we hope that we never will really need to use them. While most organisations would prefer to do without such legal and formal systems, reality requires them. If there were no past abuses, there would be no need for laws prohibiting such practices. Job security remains a hallmark of public employment in the counties. This is actually an advantage in that it allows the professional employees to devote their attention to doing the job rather than worrying about having the job.

Employee Voice/Participation

In Exit, Voice, and Loyalty Albert O. Hirschman (1970) proposes a typology of responses to dissatisfaction. A theory of individual self-interest, which not only operates in terms of the economic market but with respect to socio-political values, is primarily an attempt to explain an organisation's survival. Although Hirschman=s theory focuses on decisions regarding the acceptance/rejection of an organisation's products or services, it can also be interpreted with regard to similar decisions by an organisation's own personnel vis-a-vis the organisation itself.

Efforts to change a perceived negative situation give rise to voice. Voice is seen to represent a political dimension that can encompass a gamut of behaviours ranging from grumbling through participative management to full scale democracy. It represents a viable, non-market means for assuring organisational survival. While voice focuses internally on the advocacy of reform, loyalty represents the employee's willingness to "stand up" for the organisation. In this instance advocacy is in response to outside criticism and is an expression of confidence in the organisation.

In a series of articles Farrell and Rusbult explicitly extend Hirshman=s concept to personnel matters. As a result of a multidimensional scaling of job dissatisfaction, Farrell (1983) was able to demonstrate support for a modified version of Hirschman=s typology. To the categories of exit, voice, and loyalty Farrell added one for neglect. Neglect indicates a condition in which employees' give-up but stay to draw a paycheck. Neglect may involve absenteeism and obstructionism or merely a passive "I don't care" attitude.

North Carolina county social services agencies appear as models of participation. The professional employees exercise a strong voice in the organisation and are responsible for making many of the decisions.

Broadly Defined Jobs

The "triumph of technique over purpose" is also evident here. The rigidity invested in the use of pay scales (and the commitant job analyses upon which they are based) denies organisations the flexibility to adjust to and meet change. Individuals cannot readily be reassigned duties. This is especially a problem if those duties are from jobs officially designated as having lower grades.

Even if pay remains constant, a lower grade assignment might be seen psychologically as a career setback. Reward for exceptional performance is thwarted by the formal attachment of pay ceilings or maximum salaries to specific job grades. Broadbanding has been introduced as a means to cut through the Gordian knot of classification. The employee is seen to benefit from both more challenging and meaningful work assignments and the possibility of pay increases.

While broadbanding may not be the case here, position descriptions for county professionals are clearly state-of-the-art. It is evident that welfare reform's transformation of the job from eligibility determiner to job counselor may have witnessed a "triumph of purpose through technique."

Performance-Based Compensation

Strategic pay requires that all decisions relative to compensation and benefits are designed to attract, retain, or motivate employees. As such, the entire organisation's reward structure is designed to fully serve its mission or purpose. In reality, most organisations limit incentive pay to only a portion of the compensation package. All employees who perform satisfactorily are guaranteed a set base pay and benefits package. Even so, this guarantee serves to calm fears with regard to financial security and, hence, helps attract and retain individuals.

A wide array of extrinsic pay-for-performance schemes exists. The modern pay-for- performance scheme builds upon a base-pay system. The salary or wage put "at risk" is such to encourage or motivate the worker without jeopardizing his or her basic financial security. One can address overall individual performance or specific instances; focus can be on group performance at the organisational or team level. Individual systems based on merit pay step increases; annuities, bonuses, and suggestion awards as well as skill- or competency-based approaches abound. In addition group or organisation rewards are the focus of gain or goal sharing programmes. Performance appraisal systems are the trigger instrument for operationalizing pay-for-performance. The individual performance rating is used to determine which employees are eligible for individual and group awards as well as the amount of reward an individual is entitled to.

Pay for performance is not widely practiced in the public sector. Similar to most other public organisations, counties in North Carolina have not linked their missions to their compensation systems.

2

Human Resource Planning and Development

HR planning has traditionally been defined as "the process of anticipating and making provision for the movement of people into, within, and out of an organization" (Sherman, Bohlander, & Snell, 1998, p. 124). The purpose of HR planning is to effectively utilize the resources represented by these people in order to realize the organization's goals.

The traditional view of HR planning is that the organization should forecast, based on history, the head count needed to replace the people who leave the organization. HR planning as traditionally practiced focuses attention on quantity, the number of people, rather than the quality, or underlying characteristics (that is, the talents or competencies), of people.

In a different sense, it is also possible to understand HR planning as the strategic business plan that guides the HR department or function, which clarifies the mission and purpose of the department or function, its goals and objectives, current strengths and weaknesses, possible threats and opportunities, and long-term strategy (Rothwell & Kazanas, 2003).

HR planning serves as a guide for an organization's HR policies, programs, and procedures; it is an important part of the organization's overall business plan. Combining strategy and HR planning creates a greater capacity for change (Ulrich 1992). The challenge, however, as Brockbank (1999, in Kesler, 2000) pointed out, continues to be identifying ways in which to link HR plans and business strategy.

Interest in HR planning has increased greatly in recent years. Rothwell and Sredl (2000) suggest reasons such as the importance of people and their competencies to an organization, challenges created as people affect plans that apply to them; and the wide effect of HR plans on the entire organization. HR planning cannot effectively be accomplished if it is aligned or linked with the business, yet done in isolation as separate human resource efforts (Walker, 1994). Widespread downsizing has prompted growing attention to the qualitative difference in people, since some people are, for instance, simply more creative propuctive than others.

It should be emphasized, however, that HR leadership is essential no matter how HR planning is defined. The top HR official, usually a vice president, plays a role in ensuring that the organization adopts a proactive, rather than a reactive, stance in winning the war for talent (Rothwell, Prescott, & Taylor, 1998). Competency-based HR planning can play an important part in giving the HR leader what he or she needs in order to exert that important leadership role.

HR PLANNING : PURPOSE AND GOALS

The purpose and goals of HR planning are mainly:

1. To ensure optimum and effective use of human resources currently employed;
2. To research and reconfigure new skill sets to cope with organisational needs given depleting relevant skills population
3. To assess the employability of the human resource given changing skills and competencies
4. To draw specific outlines of competencies as they differ from today
5. To assess or forecast future skills requirement if organisation's overall objectives are to be achieved; and
6. To identify control standards to ensure that necessary resources are identified, available as and when required.
7. To fundamentally study the corporate strategy, the business mission and overall philosophy of recruiting VS systems, technology, outsourcing.
8. Analyze the people market environment and its changes as it affects the firm Vis a Vis competition.

Corporate goals for attaching importance to HR planning and forecasting exercises are:

1. to determine hiring pattern and specific action plans;
2. to anticipate redundancies;
3. to minimize downsizing, surpluses, early retirement;
4. to plan for optimum training levels;
5. to manage management development programmes;
6. new project forecasting and recruitment planning;
7. to cost the manpower in new project;

8. to assist productivity bargaining; and
9. to assess future accommodation requirements.

Human Resource Planning

In an early treatment of the topic, Vetter (1967) defined human resource planning as the process by which management determines how the organisation should move from its current manpower position to its desired position. Through planning, management strives to have the right number and the right kinds of people, at the right places, at the right time, doing things which result in both the organisation and the individual receiving maximum long-run benefits.

Contemporary human resource planning occurs within the broad context of organisational and strategic business planning. It involves forecasting the organisation's future human resource needs and planning for how those needs will be met. It includes establishing objectives and then developing and implementing programmes (staffing, appraising, compensating, and training) to ensure that people are available with the appropriate characteristics and skills when and where the organisation needs them. It may also involve developing and implementing programmes to improve employee performance or to increase employee satisfaction and involvement in order to boost organisational productivity, quality, or innovation. Finally, human resource planning includes gathering data that can be used to evaluate the effectiveness of ongoing programmes and inform planners when revisions in their forecasts and programmes are needed.

Because a major objective of planning is facilitating an organisation's effectiveness, it must be integrated with the organisation's short-term and longer term business objectives and plans.' Increasingly this is being done in leading organisations, although in the past business needs usually defined personnel needs and human resource planning, which meant that planning became a reactive process. The reactive nature of the process went handin- hand with a short-term orientation. Now, major changes in business, economic, and social environments are creating uncertainties that are forcing organisations to integrate business planning with human resource planning and to adopt a longer term perspective. For example, according to Kathryn Connors, vice president of human resources at Liz Claiborne, Human resources is part of the strategic (business) planning process. It's part of policy development, line extension planning and the merger and acquisition processes. Little is done-in the company that doesn't involve us in the planning, policy or finalization stages of any deal.

John O'Brien, vice president of human resources at Digital Equipment Corporation, describes an integrated linkage between business and human resource plans as one by which human resource and line managers work jointly to develop business plans and determine human resource needs, analyze the work force profile in terms of future business strategies, review emerging human resource issues, and develop programmes to address the issues and support the business plans. According to O'Brien, such joint efforts occur when human resource planners convince corporate business planners that "human resources represent a major competitive advantage" that can increase profits when managed carefully. This article describes some of the activities that industrial/organisational (I/O) psychologists are engaged in as they seek to improve the competitiveness of organisations through effective human resource planning.

Factors Underlying Increased Interest in Human Resource Planning

Undoubtedly, there are many factors that account for the increased attention directed to human resource planning, but environmental forces-globalization, new technologies, economic conditions, and a changing work forceseem particularly potent. These create complexity and uncertainty for organisations. Uncertainty can interfere with efficient operations, so organisations typically attempt to reduce its impact; formal planning is one common tactic used by organisations to buffer themselves from environmental uncertainty.

The changing characteristics of the work force, which is but one important environmental factor, make the need for planning evident. Between 1976 and 1980, the labor force grew an average of 2.8 per cent, but between 1991 and 1995, the rate of growth will drop to 1.1 per cent. Additionally, whereas more than 3 million people joined the labor force in 1978, less than 2 million people are projected to enter the labor force each year from 1987 to 1995. Comparatively, the proportion of younger people (aged 16 to 24) and older people (aged 55 and over) in the work force will decline. People aged 25 to 54 will constitute a greater percentage of the labor force, increasing from 61 per cent in 1975 to 73 per cent in 1995. The number of mothers in the work force with children under one year old incre ased from 42 per cent in 1980 to 55 per cent in 1989. The ethnic mix of the labor force is also changing. The Bureau of Labor Statistics estimates that ethnic minorities will account for 57 per cent of the growth in the labor force between now and the year 2000. Of the approximately 25 million workers added to the work force between 1985 and 2000, 42 per cent are expected to be native White women and only 15 per cent are expected to be native White men. Fully 22 per cent are expected to be immigrants. All of these demographic projections have significant implications for managing human resources, thereby increasing the importance of human resource planning.

The changing demographics mean there will be fewer entry-level employees, so competition among employers will increase. In addition, the changing demographics signal changes in the abilities, skills, interests, and values of tomorrow's work force. For example, shortages of many types of skilled workers are imminent, including tool-and-die makers, bricklayers, shipbuilders, mechanics, machinists, and engineers. Even if organisations are willing to train new employees, the task may be difficult, as the U.S. Navy has found. At a time when many of its training manuals required 12th-grade reading skills, nearly one fourth of the high school graduates who entered the Navy read below the 10th-grade level (National Alliance of Business, 1986). Such statistics are alarming when compared to projections indicating that the levels of various skills needed for new jobs are likely to increase in the future.

A consideration of how the values of workers who will soon make up the majority of the work force differ from those who will begin to leave it suggests additional changes on the horizon. There is already evidence of growing resistance from employees to relocation. Greater emphasis on self-evaluation and a reduction in loyalty and dedication to employers makes it more difficult for organisations to assume they can move employees around anywhere and anytime. A decline in organisational loyalty is occurring at the same time that workers are feeling insecure about their employment.

A recent study comparing the work values of those over 40 years old with those under 40 years old suggested other types of changes for which organisations must prepare. For example, employees from the younger generation, who grew up during the Vietnam war, do not trust authority as much as do members of the older generation, who are products of the World War II era. The younger generation thinks work should be fun, whereas the older generation sees work as a duty and vehicle for financial support. Younger employees believe people should advance as quickly as their competence permits, whereas older workers believe that experience is the necessary road to promotion. Finally, this study found that for the younger generation, "fairness" means allowing people to be different, but for the older generation it means treating people equally.

Changes in the work force are just one aspect of the environment stimulating the need for human resource planning. The demographic changes are somewhat predictable, but when they are considered in combination with changing technology and many of the other external changes described elsewhere in this issue, they pose significant challenges for human resource planning and contribute to its changing status during the past two decades.

Strategic HR Planning

Strategic HR planning is an important component of strategic HR management. It links HR management directly to the strategic plan of your organisation. Most mid- to large sized organisations have a strategic plan that guides the organisation in successfully meeting its mission. Organisations routinely complete financial plans to ensure they achieve organisational goals and while workforce plans are not as common, they are just as important.

Even a small organisation with as few as 10 staff can develop a strategic plan to guide decisions about the future. Based on the strategic plan, your organisation can develop a strategic HR plan that will allow you to make HR management decisions now to support the future direction of the organisation. Strategic HR planning is also important from a budgetary point of view so that you can factor the costs of recruitment, training, etc. into your organisational budget.

Strategic HR management is defined as:

Integrating human resource management strategies and systems to achieve the overall mission, strategies, and success of the firm while meeting the needs of employees and other stakeholders.

Introduction to Strategic HR Planning

The overall purpose of strategic HR planning is to:

- Ensure adequate human resources to meet the strategic goals and operational plans of your organisation - the right people with the right skills at the right time
- Keep up with social, economic, legislative and technological trends that impact on human resources in your area and in the sector
- Remain flexible so that your organisation can manage change if the future is different than anticipated

Strategic HR planning predicts the future HR management needs of the organisation after analyzing the organisation's current human resources, the external labour market and the future HR environment that the organisation will be operating in. The analysis of HR management issues external to the organisation and developing scenarios about the future are what distinguishes strategic planning from operational planning. The basic questions to be answered for strategic planning are:

- Where are we going?
- How will we develop HR strategies to successfully get there, given the circumstances?
- What skill sets do we need?

The Strategic HR Planning Process

The strategic HR planning process has four steps:

1. Assessing the current HR capacity;
2. Forecasting HR requirements;
3. Gap analysis;
4. Developing HR strategies to support organisational strategies.

Assessing Current HR Capacity

Based on the organisation's strategic plan, the first step in the strategic HR planning process is to assess the current HR capacity of the organisation. The knowledge, skills and abilities of your current staff need to be identified. This can be done by developing a skills inventory for each employee. The skills inventory should go beyond the skills needed for the particular position. List all skills each employee has demonstrated. For example, recreational or volunteer activities may involve special skills that could be relevant to the organisation. Education levels and certificates or additional training should also be included. An employee's performance assessment form can be reviewed to determine if the person is ready and willing to take on more responsibility and to look at the employee's current development plans.

Forecasting HR Requirements

The next step is to forecast HR needs for the future based on the strategic goals of the organisation. Realistic forecasting of human resources involves estimating both demand and supply. Questions to be answered include:

- How many staff will be required to achieve the strategic goals of the organisation?
- What jobs will need to be filled?
- What skill sets will people need?

When forecasting demands for HR, you must also assess the challenges that you will have in meeting your staffing need based on the external environment.

- How will the external environment impact on our HR needs?

Attrition - not replacing employees when they leave - is another way to reduce staff. The viability of this option depends on how urgently you need to reduce staff. It will mean that jobs performed in the organisation will have to be reorganized so that essential work of the departing employee is covered. Careful assessment of the reorganized workloads of remaining employees should include an analysis of whether or not their new workloads will result in improved outcomes.

It is important to consider current labour market trends (e.g., the looming skills shortage as baby boomers begin to retire) because there may be longer-term consequences if you let staff go. Sometimes existing workers may be willing to voluntarily reduce their hours, especially if the situation is temporary. Job sharing may be another option. The key to success is to ensure that employees are satisfied with the arrangement, that they confirm agreement to the new arrangement in writing, and that it meets the needs of the employer. Excellent communication is a prerequisite for success.

Your analysis may tell you that your organisation may have more resources in some areas of the organisation than others. This calls for a redeployment of workers to the area of shortage. The training needs of the transferred workers needs to be taken into account.

Training and Development Strategies

This strategy includes:

- Providing staff with training to take on new roles
- Providing current staff with development opportunities to prepare them for future jobs in your organisation

Training and development needs can be met in a variety of ways. One approach is for the employer to pay for employees to upgrade their skills. This may involve sending the employee to take courses or certificates or it may be accomplished through on-the-job training. Many training and development needs can be met through cost effective techniques. See the HR Toolkit section on Learning, Training and Development for more information.

Recruitment Strategies

This strategy includes:

- Recruiting new staff with the skill and abilities that your organisation will need in the future;

- Considering all the available options for strategically promoting job openings and encouraging suitable candidates to apply.

For strategic HR planning, each time you recruit you should be looking at the requirements from a strategic perspective. Perhaps your organisation has a need for a new fundraiser right now to plan special events as part of your fundraising plan. However, if your organisation is considering moving from fundraising through special events to planned giving, your recruitment strategy should be to find someone who can do both to align with the change that you plan for the future.

Outsourcing Strategies

This strategy includes:

- Using external individuals or organisations to do some tasks.

Many organisations look outside their own staff pool and contract for certain skills. This is particularly helpful for accomplishing specific, specialized tasks that don't require ongoing full-time work. Some organisations outsource HR activities, project work or bookkeeping. For example, payroll may be done by an external organisation rather than a staff person, a short term project may be done using a consultant, or specific expertise such as legal advice may be purchase from an outside source. When deciding to outsource to an individual, ensure you are not mistakenly calling an employee a consultant. This is illegal and can have serious financial implications for your organisation. To understand the differences between employees and self-employed people, visit the Canada Revenue Agency's website. Each outsourcing decision has implications for meeting the organisation's goals and should therefore be carefully assessed.

Collaboration Strategies

Finally, the strategic HR planning process may lead to indirect strategies that go beyond your organisation. By collaborating with other organisations you may have better success at dealing with a shortage of certain skills.

Types of collaboration could include:

- Working together to influence the types of courses offered by educational institutions
- Working with other organisations to prepare future leaders by sharing in the development of promising individuals
- Sharing the costs of training for groups of employees
- Allowing employees to visit other organisations to gain skills and insight

HRD OBJECTIVES

In the second article, Bates introduces the topic of HRD objectives by noting that the multidisciplinary and somewhat nebulous nature of the field of HRD implies a wide, complex range of objectives and activities. At the same time, HRD must be flexible enough to meet the needs of a rapidly changing economic and social environment. How can we visualize and make sense out of this broad scope of objectives?

A Conceptual Framework

Bates presents a framework to help capture and illustrate the dynamic nature of HRD objectives. He suggests two different kinds of HRD objectives, those related to change and those related to maintenance. Each type of objective encompasses four levels of objectives: individual, critical performance subsystem, process, and mission. The framework illustrates the interdependent and mutually reinforcing aspects of HRD objectives. By enhancing learning and human potential, we create high performance work systems, which in turn contribute to sustainable human development. Sustainable human development is a fundamental objective of HRD because it makes future improvements in learning, human potential and work system performance possible. The following is a brief summary of the elements of this framework.

First, change objectives focus on improving the functioning of work systems, including methods, processes, and system and sub-system interfaces, as well as developing new systems. Maintenance objectives, on the other hand, serve the purpose of preserving the functioning of the work system, and may include analysis of the operation of subsystems, interventions to control operations, troubleshooting to identify causes of malfunctions, and so on. Both change and maintenance objectives contribute to sustaining and improving work system performance. HRD objectives at the individual level are meant to enable individuals within a work environment to improve their contributions to the overall system performance. Critical performance subsystem objectives focus on work teams, production units and other internal sub-systems that contribute to the overall mission of the work system. At the process level, objectives focus on improving the way in which work gets done by considering sets of interconnected work activities or processes that produce a product or service. Mission level objectives focus on the relationship between HRD, work system goals, and the work system's external environment. All lower level objectives should be developed and carried out in ways that support these guiding objectives.

Level HRD Objectives

According to Bates, two mission-level objectives should guide HRD practice. The first objective emphasizes HRD as a strategic asset. HRD objectives should address the long-term performance goals of the organization and help ensure that those goals are met. The second mission-level objective is to enhance learning, human potential and high performance in work systems in ways that contribute to sustainable human development. These two objectives demonstrate that HRD as a field of practice is concerned not only with "what is", but more importantly, with "what should be," and as such, HRD is a normative endeavour. HRD, because of its unique capabilities, can and should play a leading role in solving human and organizational problems while also providing leadership for efforts to develop a sustainable future.

STRATEGIC PLAN OF HUMAN RESOURCE MANAGEMENT AND DEVELOPMENT

The following information highlights the activities that have been undertaken to achieve implementation of these strategies together with the ongoing operational requirements of the department. The establishment of project groups/problem solving groups has been a key feature in progressing identified human resource strategies.

The Human Resource Management Strategic plan implementation process identified 7 key strategies and 12 supporting strategies as priorities. A further prioritisation process identified three key strategies to be progressed over the next 12-18 months. These are:

- Assessment and determination of organisational communication requirements;
- Development of core leadership and corporate competencies;
- Organisational performance indicators that are developed and integrated with personal performance management systems.

Strategic of Leadership

Within the leadership strategic results area the following activities have been our focus:

Organisational Communication of Strategy

The assessment and determination of organisational communication requirements was identified as a priority strategy for progression by the Department. A Communication Liaison Group was established with representatives of Executive, Management and Staff. The group has:

- defined two key categories for communication [2] departmental responsibilities [2] audit responsibilities, each with various sub-categories;
- recorded issues and problems under each communication category;
- undertaken an analysis of the strengths and weaknesses of each key communication sub-category;
- determined potential solutions for each communication sub-category issue/problem where appropriate;
- made recommendations to Executive for implementation

The overall outcome of this activity is:

- Improved communication systems and processes that enhance organisational effectiveness.

Leadership and Competency Development

The development of leadership and corporate competencies was identified as a priority strategy for progression by the Department. A scoping session was facilitated for key parties within the Department to clarify the project, and to be clear about the competencies, their associated systems and how these will contribute to, and be used by, the Department. Preliminary work has been set for this project such as project outcomes, outlines and timeframes. Initial work will be applied to Audit Graduate positions and then gradually progressed throughout the Department. The overall outcomes of these activities are:

- to adopt a purpose [2] built competency [2] based approach as a basis for monitoring and measuring human resource and organisational effectiveness;
- that, once developed, the competency profiles are to be integrated with other systems, such as recruitment and selection, training and development and performance appraisal.

Strategic Capability

Within the capability strategic results area the following activities have been our focus:

Training of Professional Development

The Department attaches particularly high importance to the development and training of its employees in order to achieve the corporate goals. Training and development was identified as a key priority strategy in the Human Resource Management Strategic Plan. The 1998-99 Professional Development Program was based on the responses to the

Training Needs Analysis conducted during the year. The program emphasised a range of training, development and learning activities for the varied and changing needs of the Department and its employees. The courses included in the Professional Development Program. The training focused on three main areas;

- audit working papers module (1329 hours)
- audit methodology (1063 hours)
- information technology (863 hours)

As part of that program the Department presents a series of technical workshops which update all employees on technical issues and developments. The program was supplemented with employees attending external courses, conferences and seminars to assist the Department's business needs. To commence a more formal approach to management development training this year the Department provided the opportunity for senior managers to participate in a university-based comprehensive management development program. Six employees will be commencing this program in the next financial year. The Department, in addition, encouraged employees to maintain and enhance their skills through the application of self-paced learning by using CD ROM training packages and video tapes.

Professional Bodies/Institutions

As would be expected of a professional department, most of the employees are members of professional bodies and some employees are members of more than one professional body. The Department supports and encourages employees to attain professional accreditation with the Australian Society of Certified Accountants (ASCPA), CPA status and participate on special interest committees and working groups associated with the South Australian Division of the ASCPA.

Seventy-three employees are members of the ASCPA. Five of these employees hold the designation of Fellow of that Society and one holds a fellowship in the Institute of Chartered Accountants in Australia. In addition, eight employees are members of other professional bodies. During 1998-99 the Department continued to support the ASCPA Work Experience Program with the placement of four university students in the Department for a period of two weeks. The main objective of the program is to give students undertaking tertiary studies some experience of working in their field of interest. The names of all employees in the Department, their tertiary qualifications and membership status. The overall outcomes of these activities are that:

- training and development processes support, measure, motivate and develop staff capabilities;
- a high level of employee professionalism is maintained.

Job and Person Specifications

The Department completed a review of job and person specifications for all non-executive positions. All non-executive positions have outcome oriented job and person specifications that reflect any redefined roles and responsibilities. The overall outcomes of these activities is:

- that a complete review of the job and person specifications and classification levels of all positions below the Director level is undertaken;
- that the outcomes of the review are implemented throughout the Department providing links between effective job roles, responsibilities and required corporate objectives.

Capacity to Deliver

Within the Capacity to Deliver strategic results area the following activities have been our focus:

Employees and Recruitment

Employees are our most valuable resource and the Department has to compete with the wider public sector and the private sector for the best quality graduates. An integral part of the recruitment strategy is a Graduate Recruitment Program and one of the major drives for the program is extensive liaison with the three South Australian Universities.

The Department maintained a high profile at the universities by conducting a 'campus interview program' and attending a 'career fair'. The Department produced and distributed at the university campuses a careers booklet which outlines the departmental responsibilities and the rewarding and exciting career opportunities. This was coupled with its annual prize presentation to the universities for student achievements in auditing, public sector accounting, financial management, information systems and law. The Department's program is a separate initiative from the South Australian Government University Graduate Youth Recruitment Initiative Equal Employment Opportunity Program. However as the Department's program has some components similar to those of the South Australian Government Program, the Department received a subsidy of $79 000 for audit graduates.

Selected graduates usually commence duties during the second week of January each year. Graduates participate in an induction course during their first week of employment. The course is designed to provide them with an understanding of the role of the Department, public finance, auditing methodologies and specialised audit software used. The induction course is followed up shortly afterwards with a series of more detailed courses. As part of the conditions of employment, graduates are appointed depending on Departmental needs on a probationary basis or on a temporary basis for up to 12 months. During the probationary or temporary service, regular performance assessments are undertaken by supervisors to assess satisfactory performance before a permanent appointment may be conferred under the provisions of the *Public Sector Management Act 1995.*

Agreement of Enterprise Bargaining

The Department's second enterprise agreement, which was ratified by the Industrial Relations Commission of South Australia in February 1998, expired on 30 June 1999. During this time the Single Bargaining Centre established project groups and other Departmental employees have contributed to the development and implementation of change initiatives as defined in the enterprise agreement. In June 1999 the South Australian Government Wages Parity Enterprise Agreement was ratified by the Industrial Relations Commission of South Australia. Upon commencement of the term of this agreement, the Department's agreement was superseded.

However a number of clauses from the Department's second enterprise agreement were saved in the wages parity agreement which the Department continues to develop and implement. A range of human resource management and development policies was identified for review or development. To contribute to this process the Single Bargaining Centre implemented a policy formulation and consultation process. Organisational policies and procedures that have been developed or re-developed include part time policy, equal opportunity, sexual harassment, and family carers leave.

Workforce Profile

The Department collects a range of workforce statistics. These statistics provide the means of profiling our current workforce and comparing previous years' statistics.

Average of Employee Turnover and Movements

On average the employee FTE for 1998-99 was 93.6 (100.5 for 1997-98). The level of turnover has gradually decreased since 1996-97 from 21 to 16 percent. The graph above reflects this movement. Employees of this Department are still sought frequently by other public and private sector organisations.

Work Experience Profile

At 30 June 1999 the average work experience of employees in the Department was 8 years and 7 months compared to 8 years and 1 month at 30 June 1998. The slight increase can be attributed to the decrease in turnover and the relative stability of the workforce at the senior/middle management levels.

Age Profile of Employees

At 30 June 1999 the average age of the Department's employees was 32 years 11 months compared to 32 years 5 months as at 30 June 1998. Most of the Department's workforce falls in the 30-39 year old bracket, with this group accounting for 28 percent. Large proportions of employees are in the 20-24 year old group (23 percent) and the 25-29 year old group (27 percent).

Sick Leave

The average number of days sick leave taken per full time equivalent employee during 1998-99 was 6.2 days (6.2 days for 1997-98).

The overall outcomes of these activities are:

- that the Department consistently maintains the capacity to deliver audit functions through attracting and maintaining appropriately skilled people and developing effective human resource systems and processes;
- that an organisational environment exists where people are valued, diversity accepted and sound equitable policies are in place.

Benchmarking

The Department has participated in benchmarking exercises with other audit offices as part of its involvement with the Australasian Council of Auditors-General (ACAG).

Organisational Performance Measures

Through the Department's second round enterprise bargaining agreement the development of organisational performance indicators was identified as a project. Some background work and research has now been completed to enable this project to commence in 1999-2000. A range of initiatives under this strategy is documented in other parts of this operations report.

Relationships Focus

Within the Relationships Focus strategic results area, the following activities have been our focus: As part of the Human Resource Management Strategic Plan development an extensive employee survey process was undertaken. The results of this survey continue to contribute to the outcomes of organisational human resource management and development projects. A range of other initiatives under this strategy is documented in other parts of this operations report.

HUMAN RESOURCE PLANNING AND SHRM

Human resource planning is viewed as a process. As a process, human resource planning focuses on identifying an organization's human resource needs under changing conditions and developing the interventions and initiatives necessary to satisfy those needs. In HRM planning, planners analyze an organization's HRM needs in a dynamic environment and develop activities that enable an organization to adapt to change. The HRM planning process involves forecasting HRM needs and developing programs to ensure that right numbers and types of individuals are available at the right time and place (2000).

SHRM: Contingency Perspective

Proponents of the contingency perspective in SHRM argue that a firm can be effective if its HR practices and strategy are aligned with other aspects and strategies of the firm. Contingency perspective is also called 'fit-alignment' perspective. There are two forms of fit alignment – vertical and horizontal. The vertical alignment (external alignment) is the level of alignment between the components of the organization's human resource strategy and core features of its business strategy. Horizontal fit (internal alignment) measures the level of alignment among components of the organization's HR strategies such as recruitment, selection, training and compensation.

Perhaps, the most notable argument in favour of the fit perspective was presented by (1988). They argued that HR must be closely integrated into the planning process of the firm. In addition they also advocated the idea that a firm can achieve success if it is able to develop HR policies and practices that complement and support both other HR policies and practices and the other elements of the organization's strategic plan. Two types of fit were identified by these theorists. These are internal and external. Internal fit refers to the level of that human resource practices complement and support each other. External fit on the other hand, refers to the level of complement and support between HR practices and other elements of the strategic plan. The contingency perspective according to (2005) assumes that business performance will be improved when there is consistency or fit between the business strategy and HR policies. It has been argued that HRM practices that are not aligned and consistent with organizational strategy and which conflict with other HRM practices can restrain both individual and organizational performance.

There are several benefits that are attributed to the fit perspective on SHRM. (1989) suggested that firms that seek to pursue innovation as a strategy used HRM practices that will complement the strategy.

DEFINITION OF SHRM BASED ON FIT PERSPECTIVE

Based on contingency or fit perspective, SHRM can be defined as the integration of HR practices and policies to the overall organizational objectives with the aim of improving performance. (2006) defines SHRM as the process of linking the human resource functions with the strategic objectives of the organization in order to produce better performance. (1991) on the other hand defines SHRM as the linking of HRM with the strategic goals and objectives of the organization in order to achieve a progressive business performance and achieve an organizational structure that promotes innovation and flexibility. The goals and objectives of HRM are aligned with the strategic objectives and plans of the organization. The role of HRM is to determine the human resources needed to support strategic objectives and to ensure that employees are selected, trained, evaluated, and rewarded in ways that further the achievement of business objectives. Strategic HRM is frequently described as a linear, balanced process that begins with the identification of goals that will guide human resource practices. The integration of the HR programs with the goals of the organization will result to the organization's increased value. The recruitment, compensation, performance appraisal, promotion, training and other functions are designed and managed so that they work towards the strategic objectives of the firm Strategic HRM has the purpose of improving the way that human resources are managed within firms. The main objective of strategic HRM is to improve organizational performance as judged by its impact on the organization's declared corporate strategy (2004). Strategic human resources management means accepting the HRM function as a strategic partner in both the formulation of the organization's strategies and the implementation of those strategies through activities such as recruiting, selecting, training, and rewarding personnel (2002).

The contingency perspective of SHRM gives particular importance to HR planning. According to the contingency model, in order to achieve success, the HR policies and practices must be planned in such a way that they coincide with the company's business objectives and strategies. The contingency model highlights the importance of the HRM department as a strategic partner of the firm. In this regard, HR planning is placed at the centre of the formulation and implementation of the organization's strategies.

HR DEPARTMENT IN ORGANIZATION

New Functions of HRM

Different changes and challenges have caused a dramatic shift in the functions of HRM. Aside from its traditional functions such as human resource planning, recruitment and selection, job analysis, wage, salary and reward management, performance management, training and development, legislative compliance and labour relations, HRM has been called to serve other functions that create competitive advantage and ensure organizational success. Among these new roles are the following:

HRM as Human Capital Steward: As a Human Capital Steward, HR contributes to strategic capabilities by developing, leveraging, renewing, and nurturing a firm's stock of knowledge, skills, abilities, interests, and talents.

HR is there to help ensure that every individual is able to make value added contributions by identifying and cultivating individual competencies and capabilities. HR delivers people strategy by ensuring that renewal and rejuvenation are on-going activities. HR contributes to organizational success by initiating training and development activities and by creating a culture of continuous learning. HR shapes the values and provides the contextual backdrop that enables people to take initiative and use their judgment in a flexible and fluid business setting. The role of HR is not to create a dependency between the employee and the HR unit, but to forge a partnership that leads to increased intellectual capital, enhanced commitment, greater awareness of opportunities to make a difference, and adaptability (2004).

HRM as Relationship Builder: The role of Relationship Builder focuses on creating programs and practices that enable employees to encourage, facilitate, nourish, and sustain relationships among fellow employees, customers, suppliers, firms in complementary arenas, and at times, even rivals.

HR can deliver people strategy by contributing to a firm's ability to leverage its resources and develop strategic capabilities and core competencies by helping individuals build a strong web of relationships. Developing relationships between employees helps workers find jobs and creates a richer pool of recruits. It facilitates inter-unit resource exchange and product innovation. Social capital facilitates the creation of intellectual capital since people are more likely to share tacit information and take intellectual risks in a supportive social environment.

It facilitates cross-functional team effectiveness since social capital enables people to see situations from perspectives that are different from their own. It reduces turnover rates, since individuals are less likely to leave a firm if they have strong, positive social connections with their co-workers. It strengthens supplier relations, regional production networks, and inter-firm learning since social capital can be the foundation for multifaceted, multidirectional, mutually beneficial relationships that extend beyond transactional exchanges (1 2004).

HRM as Knowledge Management Facilitator: It is not enough simply to hire employees and put them to work. Strategic capability requires a firm to be able to create and disseminate knowledge among its employees.

HR can play a vital role in facilitating organization learning and knowledge sharing between employees, among departments, throughout the organization, and with external co-producers. An important aspect of human capital stewardship is identifying people who want to learn. Employees need to be able to learn and unlearn continuously, to teach and be taught.

The organization must tap into all employees' knowledge as sources of innovation. HR can make an important contribution by identifying sources of employee knowledge and eliciting that knowledge from employees. New knowledge must lead to new behaviours if it is to create strategic capability.

Knowledge is of little use unless a firm is bale to adjust its actions, decisions, and relationships to capitalize on the insight. Knowledge management facilitation includes developing organizational capabilities that enable individuals to apply knowledge more skilfully, quickly and creatively. Equally important, HR must help organizations strike a balance between productivity focusing efforts on critical tasks while constantly incorporating new ideas (2004).

HR as Rapid Deployment Specialist: The rapid pace and constantly changing environment that many organizations and industries confront creates another new challenge and new function for HRM: rapid Deployment Specialist. Strategic capability requires competence in rapidly assembling, concentrating, and deploying specific configurations of human capital in order to achieve mission-specific strategic goals. Rapid deployment of human talent requires adaptable employees. Workers need to be adaptable, versatile, and tolerant of uncertainty to operate effectively in the constantly changing global market (2004).

TRADITIONAL HR PLANNING

HR planning has its roots in military personnel planning. Initially, the U.S. military faced the challenge of ensuring stable staffing levels as some people concluded their tours of duty and left the military and others advanced through the ranks. The goal at that time was to determine the quantity of people sufficient to meet replacement needs and thereby maintain staffing levels in different job categories, at different levels of the organization, and in different locations.

Defense contractors adopted this military focus on head count. They carried over the philosophy of equating head count to production levels and, in turn, linking production levels to competitive success as measured by achievement of the organization's measurable strategic goals and objectives. This approach seemed to work well until the 1960s. At that time, three trends began to emerge that affected the success of traditional HR planning:

1. Changing technology: Technology is continuously changing. Organizations often undergo technological change in the hope of achieving breakthroughs in productivity. With cutting-edge technology, fewer people may be able to produce the same or greater outputs as were produced with traditional means.
2. Decreasing correlation of head count to outputs and success: A widening gap began to develop between the number of people employed by an organization, the output levels achieved by those people, and the organization's competitive success. There has never been an easy or particularly effective way to correlate the organization's head count with productivity and, in turn, with competitive success in a dynamic marketplace.
3. Increasing inaccuracy of labor forecasts: Labor forecasts based on historical ratios between head count and competitive success have been growing less accurate. Traditional forecasting bases predictions

of the future on the past or present. But as most businesspeople are now keenly aware, tomorrow's workplace may be radically different from the workplaces of yesterday and today. We should note, too, that individuals are not machines. One person's production level is not necessarily the same as another's. Hence, historical forecasts not only are often useless in predicting outputs or competitive success but may mislead decision makers by presenting them with inaccurate conclusions.

The traditional approach to HR planning begins with an assessment of the current supply of people at each level and of the current demand at each level and then proceeds to balancing supply and demand. The HR function performs balancing through such actions as recruitment, hiring, development, and reduction. The traditional focus of HR planning, however, has been on taking action with people rather than on achieving results.

To make the point more dramatically, and perhaps controversially, many organizations operate as if they were simply recruiting to "fill slots" or maintain the head count as vacancies occur. Recruiters concentrate on sourcing people whose perceived competencies appear to match the qualifications in job specifications and whose work experience and education make them appear qualified to carry out the work activities listed on a job description for a targeted job opening.

NEEDS ASSESSMENT

The first article deals with needs assessment for HRD. HRD needs assessment is an investigative process whose purpose is to connect an organization's performance problems or opportunities for performance improvement to specific HRD interventions. In simple terms it is a systematic process for identifying the gap between a current level of performance, or "what is", and a desired level of performance, "what should be".

What Are Needs? The term "need" can be somewhat ambiguous. What one person considers a need, another may consider a want or desire, leading to the terms "felt" and "actual" needs. In some cases, felt needs are actually symptoms of deeper actual needs. For example, a group of employees expresses a felt need for stress management training. Upon investigation, however, the actual need may be to ameliorate or eliminate the sources of stress, such as noise, inefficient work processes, or ineffective supervisory practices.

Needs Assessment

A comprehensive needs assessment provides a systematic way to research performance gaps, which can then provide substance and direction for strategic HRD planning, including the identification of performance improvement initiatives that are likely to provide the best return on HRD investments. Training needs assessments, for example, can determine levels of optimal performance and standards for excellence, evidence of individuals' actual performance levels, attitudes affecting performance, and root causes of performance problems. Although the needs assessment process is often skipped or cut short, for a variety of reasons, a well-researched needs assessment can help avoid wasted time, effort, and money. As Drucker has pointed out, "There is nothing so useless as doing efficiently that which should not be done at all." The type of information needed affects the focus of a needs assessment. Needs within an organization may be assessed at a high strategic level, a departmental or functional level, a team or group level, or at the individual level. The organization's performance within the context of the wider society might also serve as the focus of a needs assessment. Choosing an appropriate level of assessment is critical to the resulting analysis.

Methodologies

Berger provides suggestions for framing the needs assessment process, based on three elements: organization characteristics, decision-maker characteristics, and analyst characteristics. Numerous needs assessment models exist, and include steps such as the following:

1. Define the goals/objectives of the assessment.
2. Develop an initial plan.
3. Gain management commitment.
4. Identify the data needed.
5. Identify sources of data.
6. Select the most appropriate methodologies for the assessment.
7. Collect the data.
8. Analyze the results.
9. Resolve disagreements in interpretation of the results.
10. Prioritize the needs.
11. Compile and present your findings.

Techniques for data collection may include observation, surveys or questionnaires, one-on-one interviews, phone interviews, focus groups, tests, analysis of existing performance data, job and task analysis, critical incident surveys, and reviews of professional literature, conference reports and other benchmarking sources.

Link to Evaluation

Needs assessment is the first step of a planned performance improvement cycle. The results of the needs assessment can be used as the basis for evaluating the outcomes of the HRD initiative: Were the needs identified in the needs assessment satisfied as a result of the HRD initiative? Since evaluation frequently uncovers new needs that must be analyzed, the evaluation step often leads back to the beginning of the cycle, and so the cycle continues.

Need Assessment of Guidelines

Some of the guidelines for carrying out an effective needs assessment include:

- Use a performance model appropriate to the organization.
- Start as far up in the organization as possible when analyzing performance issues.
- Use a variety of techniques for gathering data.
- Keep the assessment short but complete.
- View needs assessment as an investment, not a cost, and market it that way to management.
- Be flexible.
- Consider timing.
- Consider the audience when reporting the results.

Finally, when assessing needs, consider not only performance as observed in the past, but also future performance needs.

THE ESSENCE OF HUMAN DEVELOPMENT

Human biology deals with the bodily processes. Understanding how our body works will help us take care of ourselves more. Human Biology was founded at the Stanford University in 1970. It is considered as an interdisciplinary field of medicine, nutrition, biological anthropology and biology, focusing in humans. It can be associated with primate biology as well as several other fields. Human development, on the other hand, deals with the process of growing to maturity. Biologically, this pertains to the growth from one-celled zygotes to adult human beings. The development begins, as we all know, with fertilization wherein the male gamete or sperm cell as well as the female gamete or the oocyte fuse actually gives rise to a diploid cell or the zygote. This would refer to the 3 stages such as the zygote, embryo and the fetus.

In modern medicine, pregnancy is characterized as the process wherein the fertilized zygote is implanted inside the woman's uterus, embedding on the endometrium or uterus lining. This will form a placenta, serving as the channel for the receiving of nutrients via the wall of the uterus. This is the umbilical cord of a newborn child, signifying the remnants of the implantation.

After this, the zygote will undergo rapid mitotic divisions having no significant growth (this process is referred to as cleavage) as well as cellular differentiation which will lead to the development of the embryo. Childbirth is a process wherein the baby is born. For many, it is regarded as the start of a person's life. In fact, in most cultures, the age is relative to this process.

There are different terms related to the age for the physical development. This would include the approximate age that ranges from many different terms. Prenatal is from fertilization to birth (from embryo to fetus stages). A child is that from birth to toddler years (from newborn or neonate to pre-pubescence or primary school age). Puberty and adolescence are the teenage years (from 13 up to 19 years old). An adult is from 20 years old to death (from young adult to senior citizen or advanced adult stages).

Death occurs at different ages, usually depending on the person (this is the stage of decomposition or the body's breakdown after death). The heart stops beating and all the other organs stop functioning. Most parents feel the urge to know the sex of their unborn child immediately. One good reason is so that they can already prepare themselves. This can range to the things they will be buying for the baby or to prepare themselves psychologically and emotionally on the child's future. Other reasons include conceiving accidentally, not planning to breastfeed, finding out the child's sex in a prior pregnancy, the influence of sex on futuristic childbearing plans, specific parental preference for the child's sex and the plans for renovation or moving associated with the wanting to learn the child's sex.

Studies show that both socioeconomic and demographic factors really affect a parent's desire to know the sex of their unborn child. The ones who prefer to know this are the ones with a lower socioeconomic status. Hence, at this point, the best way to determine the sex of an unborn child is through prenatal ultrasound examinations. Another common reason is to be able to come up with the baby's name. Parents think about it carefully, wanting it to be very meaningful, for the child will carry the name for the rest of his life.

Increasing mobility is not a new phenomenon. The process which started slowly with the developments in the fields of science and technology gradually evolved into lightning speed around the world. It had its repercussions both – good and bad. Alvin Toffler had conducted a detailed study on increasing mobility and shared the information with the readers in his widely acclaimed book "The Future Shock". Increasing mobility and migration are interdependent. No one is going to disagree with this truth. Immigration-its positive and negative aspects-has become a subject for study and research at the international level.

The other day there was a news item in 'The Hindu' by the noted journalist and correspondent Vidya Subramaniam on Human Development Reports (HDR) released simultaneously across the world by Deputy Chairman, Planning Commission: Montek Singh Ahluwalia and United Nations Co-ordinator Patrice Coeur Bizot: Overcoming Barriers: Human mobility and development and the salutary effects of migration between countries-from developing countries to developed countries, developing countries to other developing countries and migration within countries and the enormous potential, social, financial and cultural brought about by the latter.

The report is based on statistics and on going through it a citizen has much to feel cheerful about it. The report also mentions about certain areas of a country which are left behind in the field of education resulting in the reluctance of the inhabitants of these areas to emigrate to other parts of the country or to other countries. A country like India, where lack of adequate education facilities even 62 years after Independence has a lot to be ashamed of.

While feeling happy and elated about the positive aspects migration brings about in the world, we feel equally sad on going through news reports emanating from different countries on a regular basis – the harassment, hardships and torture the immigrants suffer at the hands of the citizens of a particular country.

The "Sons of the soil" policy and racist attacks escalate on a daily basis. Right below the news report on emigration, with a feeling of sadness I came across a news item on the racist attacks by Australians against the Indians who live and lead peaceful lives working as cabbies, bartendenders, such menial jobs and the students for the purpose of higher studies and dreaming of a bright future. These attacks on Indians even after government's strong protests and despite Australian Prime Minister Kevin Rudd's assurances to the Government of India on adopting a zero tolerance towards the attackers continue unabated. Recently Juliet Gillard, the

Education Minister of Australia on her visit to India also gave an assurance on these lines. All in vain. Now it is learnt that the Indian immigrants having lost their patience have started to hit back in the same coin. As somebody put it, "A confident resistance will make a thug flee".

Xenophobia has become a bane across world. More and more protectionist tendencies are the root causes. Even a few developed countries are prone to protectionist tendencies and intolerant towards the immigrants.

Nicholas Sarkozy, French President, was the Interior Minister under the regime of Jacques Chirac, before becoming President. Sarkozy was a pain in the neck of Chirac for his xenophobic policies. Jacques Chirac favoured Dominique De Villipine, the former Prime Minister according to the media reports to be his successor. Sarkozy could swing the mandate to his side, for he adopted a more protectionist policy and it had many takers then. The infamous racist attacks, the widely condemned electrocution of two African teenagers and his reported justification for the suppression of racist violence consequent upon it, his intolerance towards burqa-clad muslim women, even Sikhs sporting turbans following their religious beliefs during that period and even after that, was widely condemned.

Anyhow the highest position of President later somewhat made him show more maturity and he even played the role of a master diplomat in arriving at an amicable solution to the war between Russia and Georgia over South Ossetia, thus averting a catastrophe which would have reached an unimaginable dimension with USA intervening under the belligerent George Bush, the then President. Xenophobia still stares in the face of immigrants though. Economic recession across the world has a damaging contribution to this nagging problem.

Xenophobia and protectionist tendencies to a large extent are prevalent in various corners of the world. Not only between countries but even in a particular country itself. Take for example our own "Incredible Nation". The financial capital of India, "Mumbai" (sorry, not Bombay) is a glaring example of the "Sons of the soil". The emigrants from the States of Uttar Pradesh, Bihar, Orissa always live in perpetual fear of the "policy holders", the "Marathi mannoos". About a year ago, the North Indian inhabitants were brutally attacked, robbed of their belongings, their properties destroyed and forced them to flee to their States. Some even succumbed to injuries on being badly mauled.

Poor men, women and children leaving their beloveds in their respective native States catch trains and after three or four days of ardous train journeys reach the city not for leading a pompous life but for earning something to have atleast a square meal per day. They don't stay in flats, bungalows or five-star hotels but in slums, chawls and railway platforms. Mumbai is nobody's monopoly. It is a part of our nation and it should remain as such.

Directly Proportional to Economic Growth

Human rights is one factor that is much more instrumental than it is thought to be for the growth and development of a country. In the times when most of the countries in the world are democratic, human rights is a fundamental factor that needs to be addressed to.

These rights are not to be decided and written down in the constitution alone but they are to be equally implemented and practiced as they are the determinant and underlying factor behind another very important factor namely human development. Human resource is the aspect that is one of the most important in the overall condition of the concerned country. Human resource development should be and in fact is the most primary concern of most of the countries of the world. In some other countries democracy is just there for name, a decorative element to ordain the constitution. Some surveys conducted by the UN has showed that most of the countries that are low on human development and human rights are Muslim countries.

The interesting fact is however that this is not exclusive to the Muslim countries. Be it the Muslim countries or the non Muslim ones human development is imperative for the overall growth and development of any country. And it has also been noticed that the places where human development is poor and human resource is not as progressive as it ought to be, the issue of human rights was also in dire straits. Human rights are not practiced ideally as they ought to be in a democracy. This condition is very much prominent in the Muslim countries though there are a few non Muslim countries also included in the list. The bottom line is that Muslim or non Muslim growth is unattainable without appropriate human rights and subsequent development.

This trend is more common with the Muslim countries as they have a very arbitrary lifestyle. Gender inequality, fanaticism, religious, political and social bias are some the factors that have made the correct exercise of human rights very difficult in these countries. As a result human resource is at a very pathetic low in these nations. Economics, politics, society everything are man made. It is vital that human development is at an optimum for upliftment in these departments. Poor human resource results in low economy, disturbing politics and a society that cannot be called fit to survive in and these facts are not just bookish. The result can be seen in the current political and socio economic conditions of the countries that find a presence in this list.

When human resource is at the prime and in a good condition anything can be accomplished. The able, smart, and acumen friendly employees especially in the line of information technology have pushed the traders from the developed countries to hire the software company based in countries like India, China and Malaysia. These companies provide every solution from web application development to ecommerce solution and that too at extremely affordable rates.

HUMAN RESOURCES INTRANET

HR departments have been some of the most enthusiastic developers of intranet applications mainly because of the large amounts of paper-based processes that can be transitioned to the Web. Examples of possible content and applications

- Employee handbook
- Telephone/E-mail directory
- Interactive benefits information
- 401 K tracking
- Employee surveys
- Recruiting/job listings
- Candidate screening applications
- Organizational charts
- Newsletters
- New employee training
- Employee personalized home pages.

Operational HR Planning

All organisations engage in HR planning at an operational level even those that do not have a strategic plan. At the operational level, good HR planning is in part based on thinking ahead about the organisation.

At an operational level, organisations put in place HR management practices to support management and staff in achieving their day-to-day goals. Whether it's determining how many staff are needed to deliver services over the next year or how performance will be monitored, HR management practices and activities need to be planned to answer the question: "Where is our organisation going and how will it get there?"

The HR Toolkit has detailed information that you can use to develop an operational plan for your human resources practices and activities. Topics include:

- Employment Legislation and Standards
- Guideline to Developing HR Policy
- Getting the Right People
- Learning, Training and Development
- Compensation and Benefits
- Keeping the Right People.

If your organisation already has good HR management practices in place they should be reviewed on an ongoing basis, every two to three years, to ensure that they still meet organisational needs and comply with legislation.

At an operational level, organisations also need to be aware of the interdependencies between operational decisions and HR management practices. Decisions made on one aspect of human resources often have an impact on another aspect of HR management.

Succession Planning

What would you do in your organisation if a key employee resigned, fell ill or had to be fired tomorrow? Would you be prepared? Succession planning is not an issue that many organisations address in any systematic way. Because many organisations are small (with fewer than 10 employees) and because they may be facing other organisational challenges, thinking about who the next executive director might be or what would happen if the director of finance suddenly left is not high on their priority list.

There are many reasons why organisations need to be thinking about succession planning. The most important reason, of course, is that we rely on staff to carry out our missions, provide services and meet our organisation's goals. We need to think about what would happen to those services or our ability to fulfill our mission if a key staff member left.

Another reason to focus on succession planning is the changing realities of workplaces. The impending retirement of the baby boomers is expected to have a major impact on workforce capacity. Teresa Howe in "Succession Planning and Management" identified other emerging realities about the workforce in

- Vacancies in senior or key positions are occurring in numerous organisations simultaneously and demographics indicate there are statistically fewer people available to fill them

- Baby boomer retirements are on the rise just at the time when the economy is growing and increasing the demand for senior management expertise
- There is no emerging group of potential employees on the horizon as in past generations (i.e. baby boomers, women entering the workforce, large waves of immigration)
- Many organisations eliminated middle manager positions during restructuring in the 1980s and 90s and no longer have this group as a source to fill senior level vacancies
- Younger managers interested in moving up do not have the skills and experience required because they have not been adequately mentored This is because middle managers, who would normally perform this type of coaching role, were eliminated

With careful planning and preparation, organisations can manage the changes that result from a generational transfer of leadership as well as the ongoing changes that occur regularly when key employees leave an organisation.

Although the type and extent of planning will be different, organisations both large and small need to have some sort of succession plan. Effective succession planning supports organisational stability and sustainability by ensuring there is an established process to meet staffing requirements. Boards and executive directors can demonstrate leadership by having the strategies and processes in place to ensure that these transitions occur smoothly, with little disruption to the organisation.

What is Succession Planning?

A succession plan, simply put, is a component of good HR planning and management. Succession planning acknowledges that staff will not be with an organisation indefinitely and it provides a plan and process for addressing the changes that will occur when they leave. Most succession planning focuses on the most senior manager - the executive director, however, all key positions should be included in the plan. Key positions can be defined as those positions that are crucial for the operations of your organisation and, because of skill, seniority and/or experience, will be hard to replace.

Whenever size and resources permit, a succession plan should involve nurturing and developing employees from within an organisation. Employees who are perceived to have the skills, knowledge, qualities, experience and the desire can be groomed to move up to fill specific, key positions. Organisations should:

- Assess their current and future needs based on either their strategic plan, goals and objectives, or priority programmes and projects
- Match these to the capabilities of the existing workforce
- Develop a plan to manage the gaps that will arise when individuals in key positions leave or are promoted

The plan will generally include a combination of training and developing existing staff, and external recruitment.

Tips for Successful Succession Planning

Secure senior management and board support for a succession planning process. This gives employees and staff an understanding of how important succession planning is to the organisation. Review and update your succession plan regularly. This ensures you reassess your hiring needs and determine where the employees identified in the succession plan are in their development.

Develop procedure manuals for essential tasks carried out by key positions. Include step-by-step guidelines. Adequate time should be provided to prepare successors. The earlier they are identified, the easier it is on the individual to be advanced and on other employees within your organisation who will know whether certain options are available to them.

Understand that your succession plan will be a unique reflection of your organisation. Succession plans are as different from each other as the organisations for which they are developed.

Risk Management in HR

The only sure way to avoid risk in voluntary and non-profit organisations would be to lock the doors and put up a closed sign in the window. Risks are inevitable and organisations have a moral and legal obligation to attend to the safety and well-being of those they serve, those who work for them and others who come into contact with their operations. This is known as "Duty of Care."

Organisations need to look at all the risks throughout their entire operation and incorporate risk management into all planning and decision-making. However, the specific focus of this section is risk management as it applies to HR activities.

The Risk Management Process

Risk management is a cycle. That means that it is not something that gets checked off a "to do" list but it is a continuous activity. Having a risk management process means that your organisation knows and understands the risks to which you are exposed. It also means that your organisation has deliberately evaluated the risks and has strategies in place to remove the risk altogether, reduce the likelihood of the risk happening or minimize harm in the event that something happens. At a very basic level, risk management focuses you on two fundamental questions:

1. What can go wrong?
2. What will we do to prevent the harm from occurring in the first place and in response to the harm or loss if it actually happens?

Identify the Risks

- The very first step is to identify the risks. Ask yourself what can go wrong. Every activity of an organisation poses a risk so brainstorm and document the risks.
- Consider both the general risks (that could happen to any organisation) and the risks specific to your organisation.
- Risks can be:
  - Abuse that is either one-time or ongoing (physical, emotional, psychosocial, sexual, financial)
  - Personal injury
  - Medical
  - Environmental
  - Property
  - Financial
  - Reputation/goodwill
  - Other

Assess the Risks

- If you have done a thorough job of identifying risks, you may end up with a long (and overwhelming) list.
- The next step is to assess each of the risks based on the (1) likelihood or frequency of the risk occurring and (2) the severity of the consequences.
- Using a risk map to plot the likelihood of occurrence and the severity of the consequences will help you prioritize your next steps.

Develop Strategies for Managing Risks

Consider the most appropriate risk management strategies for each identified risk:

- Avoidance - Stop providing the service or doing the activity because it is too risky.
- Acceptance - Some risky activities are central to the mission of an organisation and an organisation will choose to accept the risks.
- Modification - Change the activity to reduce the likelihood of the risk occurring or reduce the severity of the consequences. Policies and procedures are an important part of this risk management strategy because they communicate expectations and define boundaries. Learn more about writing policies and procedures.
- Transfer or sharing - Purchase insurance or transfer the risk to another organisation through signing a contractual agreement. with other organisations to share the risk (for example, having a contractual agreement with a bus company to transport clients rather than staff driving clients).

Implement

When you have decided which risk management strategies will be the most effective and affordable for your organisation, practically outline the steps and who is responsible for each step in the risk management plan.

Communicate the plan and ensure that there is buy-in from all who are involved in the organisation (staff, volunteers, clients, other relevant stakeholders). Provide training for all organisational staff and volunteers so they understand the rationale of the risk management plan as well as the expectations, procedures, forms, etc.

Monitor

Consider the following questions and document any changes to the plan:

- Is your plan working?
- Have your risks changed?
- Have you expanded or reduced your programmes and services?
- Are changes or updates required?
- Are staff and volunteers following the risk management plan?
- Do they need re-training on the details?
- Do we need to better communicate the plan?

The Board's Role in HR

The board of directors is the governing body of a non-profit organisation. It provides oversight of the organisation to ensure that it meets its mission and is operated effectively and in the best interests of the stakeholders: members, clients, funders, employees, and the community at large.

The board has overall responsibility for strategic planning, finances, organisational operations, community relations and human resources. This section focuses on the board's responsibilities for HR.

Governance and Board Structure

As the oversight body of a non-profit organisation, the board of directors is ultimately responsible for an organisation's HR management activities. However, the level of involvement in HR management practices will depend in part on how long the organisation has been in existence and the governance structure (model) used. In most established organisations, the board is charged with hiring and managing the performance of an executive director to which the responsibilities for operational HR management are typically delegated.

The Institute On Governance identifies three distinct roles in an organisation:

- Governance - The interface with stakeholders, the source of strategic decisions that shape the organisation and its work, and the ultimate accountability for the work and actions of the organisation.
- Management - The link between governance and work. The organisation of tasks, people, relationships and technology to get the job done.
- Work - Performing the tasks required to fulfill the mission.

Newly established organisations often have a working or administrative board where board members are directly involved in the day-to-day operations of the organisation. These organisations often have no staff or they may hire a small number of staff to do work; but the board volunteers take on the management role and some of the work as well.

As organisations grow, the board will eventually hire a person (executive director, administrator or coordinator) to manage the day-to-day operations of the organisation. Even with a manager in place, the board of directors is usually still involved in some aspects of management which is reflected in a Mixed Board Structure.

Mature organisation usually develop a governance structure where the board of directors provides oversight on human resources management issues and only has direct involvement in the human resources management activities required to hire, supervise, and evaluate the executive director. Usually, one of two models of governance is adopted by mature organisations: Traditional Policy Board or a Policy Governance Board (Carver model).

Role and Responsibilities for HR Management

In a mature organisation, there are three participants in HR management: the board, executive director and line managers who directly supervise the work of other staff. An organisation with good governance practices clearly establishes the division of authority and accountability among the board, executive director and line managers. The role of the board is governance and the role of the executive director is management. Sometimes the roles can get blurred. In clarifying whose job it is, the board and the executive director must always keep in mind the board's legal responsibilities and liabilities as the employer.

Fulfilling Your Obligations as a Board Member

How can directors of the board demonstrate good governance?

- Fulfill your director's duties of diligence, skill/competence, loyalty, and obedience
- Know your legal responsibilities and liabilities
- Educate yourself about HR management
- Regularly attend board meetings
- Read all documents in advance of the board meeting
- Ask questions
- Take care when voting
- Register your dissent if you believe the board is acting improperly and ask to have your dissent recorded in the minutes
- Review the minutes of each meeting
- If you were not in attendance at a meeting where a decision was made that you disagree with, ask to have your dissent recorded in the minutes at the next meeting
- Establish sound organisational human resources management policies and practices
- On a regular basis, ask the executive director to report on the organisation's compliance with all legislation
- Seek a legal opinion before important human resources management decisions are made
- Purchase director's and officer's liability insurance

Compensation and Benefits

Though usually not ranked the most important, compensation is an important factor in job quality. Non-profit organisations have some obvious challenges when it comes to providing competitive salary and benefits to attract and keep the best staff. Organisations can, and should, market their strengths because people are also looking for jobs that make a difference, offer interesting and varied challenges and have positive working relationships. However, we'll never be able to escape the fact that compensation is important - and a deciding factor for people when they consider a job. The HR Council is currently developing new content to add to this section of the HR Toolkit to help non-profit organisations manage their employee pay and benefits.

Employee and Retirement Benefits

We know that only about half of the people who work in non-profit organisations have access to employee benefit plans such as life or disability insurance, dental plans or supplementary medical plans. Less than half (about 45%) have access to employer pension plans. If we are to recruit and retain the most committed and knowledgeable people in the sector, we will have to find ways and means to improve access to employee benefit plans and retirement plans, especially as the competition for talent becomes more intense. There are few, if any, studies in Canada that have clearly identified the barriers to accessing these plans. The three reports below have been prepared to build a body of knowledge around non-profit organisations and employee benefits and retirement plans.

Salary Surveys

Surveys collecting information about employee compensation, including salary and benefits, are commonly called "salary surveys". Salary surveys, in conjunction with other tools, can provide useful information to attract, support and retain employees within the context of an overall human resources and organisational plan. When designed and used properly, salary surveys can provide useful benchmarking information for comparing salaries and benefits.

Many organisations want to use salary surveys to set the compensation levels for their organisations. Unfortunately, it's not always as easy as reading a survey and using the information. Below you'll find important information about how to assess salary surveys and get the most out of the information they present.

How to Assess a Salary Survey

Below you'll find information on what makes a salary survey useful for benchmarking. Salary surveys need to be readily comparable and scientifically credible to be useful for benchmarking. The following provides a summary of how to assess a salary survey.

Compare Apples to Apples

It's important, when reviewing salary surveys, to make sure that you are comparing information that is similar. Looking at salary and benefits levels in organisations vastly different from your own will not provide the information you need. Here's what to look for:

- Review job descriptions or position profiles in the survey report
- It is important to look at job duties and responsibilities not just job title when deciding if salary survey information is comparable. To be comparable the jobs must have a similar level of responsibility and range of duties.
- Note province and region
- Appropriate salary comparisons will come from agencies with a similar geographic focus: local, regional, provincial or national. At the local level, the best salary comparisons will come from other organisations in the same city or town. Good salary comparison may come from a different city or town with similar labour market characteristics and a similar cost of living.
- Note operating budgets of respondent organisations
- As a general rule larger the operating budgets mean higher salaries. Comparable salaries come from organisations of a comparable size. Size is usually estimated by using the operating budget or looking at the number of paid full-time staff.
- Note the type and description of respondent organisations
- Are the functions, services offered, clientele, and sources of funding of the organisations in the salary survey comparable to your organisation? For example, an organisation providing child care services through provincial funding may have very different salaries than an organisation providing a parent/child resources through its own fundraising.
- Note the education level and (full/part-time/union/contract) status of respondents
- The level of education required for a job and the type of employment arrangement can have an impact on salaries.
- Note the year of data collection and the date of the report
- Labour market forces can result in significant changes in salaries in a short period of time. More recent data will be more useful in establishing current salaries.

- Note if the survey is a one time event or if it's repeated
- Surveys that have been repeated provide an added advantage of showing trends in salaries over the years of the survey.

Is it scientific?

- Methodology and technical details are reported and discussed
- Study is objective, valid (does what it is supposed to do) and reliable (accuracy of measurements)
- Note sampling frame, sample size, and response rate
- What is the margin of error? Is it reported?

For information to be valid it has to come from a large enough sample size. For example, if you collected just three salaries for the same position and one salary is high, one is low, and one is in the middle, you wouldn't be able to conclude much because your sample is too small to provide valid and useful information.

You also want to be sure that the information is reliable. Reliability means that the survey gives consistent results. You should therefore carefully consider how the information is gathered and decide if it makes sense to you. For example, if the survey instrument is included in the report, assess if it would be easy for you to give accurate answers to the questions.

Easy to use and understand:

- Technical terms are explained; report is comprehensible to non-specialists

A good salary survey will define terms and provide the user with enough information to help him or her easily understand the data.

Look at all of the numbers

- Numbers include mean, range, median
- Breakdowns are provided for positions (with profiles provided), sub-sectors and regions

The actual salary paid to an individual will be influenced in part by the person's years of experience and qualifications. Therefore, the salary range for a position provides more useful information than the actual salary an individual is being paid. Other statistical information such as median - the value in the middle when all the values are arranged from lowest to highest - will also help make sense of the data.

Consider the total compensation - review the benefits

- Consider total compensation
- Make sure that all of the benefits are listed

Having information on the total compensation package - retirement plan (pension or RRSP), bonuses, benefits and salary - allows for better comparisons. Without this information you might make wrong assumptions about salary level and not have the full picture. For example, in a situation where no benefits are provided, many people (particularly those in higher positions) will negotiate for higher salaries. Without seeing the whole compensation package, you might not understand that the high salary compensates for no benefits.

Other considerations when setting salaries

- Use more than one source of salary information; this will help you avoid any bias found in a single source.
- Determine who your competitors are: what other organisations, agencies, institutions, businesses, quasi-governmental organisations or governments requires staff with the same knowledge and skill. Based on exit interviews, to whom are you losing employees who leave your organisation?
- Position your salaries relative to your competitors. Strategically determine if your organisation wants to pay at the going market rate, above market, or below market.

In conclusion, salary surveys do not replace judgment. From deciding if the salary survey provides useful comparisons for your organisation to finally deciding what to pay your staff, good judgment will be essential for any compensation decisions.

THE CONCEPT OF HUMAN RESOURCE DEVELOPMENT

Increasingly, more importance is being given to "people" in organisations. This is mainly because organisations are realising that human assets are the most important of all assets. This emphasis can also be partly attributed to the new emerging values of humanism and humanisation. Moreover, with the increased emphasis on creativity, and autonomy, which people are increasingly acquiring and enjoying in the society, the expectations of people are fast changing. People cannot be taken for granted any more. In the past, people working in organisations were given attention merely in administering the necessary conditions of work. The traditional concept of personnel management was based on a very narrow view of human motivation. The basic assumption underlying that view was that human beings are primarily motivated by comforts and salary, and necessary attention may be given to rationalise these, so that people do not get dissatisfied. Most of the attention, therefore, was on administration of salary and other benefits.

It is now being increasingly realised that people working in organisations are human beings. They have their own needs, motivation and expectations, and that their contribution to the organisation is much more than that of any other resource being used. The concept of Human Resource System (HRS) assumes that human beings are a great asset to an organisation. They are not merely necessary evils to be reckoned with; in fact they can contribute a great deal to the achievement of organisational goals.

This positive view of people working in the organisations as an asset with unlimited potential is the core of the concept of the human resource system. Another underlying concept of the system is that investment in human beings is necessary. Investment for increasing the resource is important, and the more an organisation invests in its human resources, the greater the return from the investment is likely to be. This realisation of the need for continuous investment, and the possibility of substantial return, is an important concept of the human resource system.

There is also one more reason why investment in human resource is necessary. It is also being realised that organisations have an obligation to the society, that they should also contribute to the development of people, and operate with the new values of treating people as human beings, as well as contribute to this value of creating traditions and culture of respecting people as human beings.

Human resource development in the organisation context is a process by which the employees of an organisation are helped, in a continuous and planned way to:

- Acquire or sharpen capabilities required to perform various functions associated with their present or expected future roles;
- Develop their general capabilities as individuals and discover and exploit their own inner potentials for their own and/or organisational development purposes; and
- Develop an organisational culture in which supervisor—subordinate relationships, teamwork and collaboration among sub-units are strong and contribute to the professional well-being, motivation and pride of employees.

This definition of HRD is limited to the organisational context. In the context of a state or nation it would differ. HRD is a process, not merely a set of mechanisms and techniques. The mechanisms and techniques such as performance appraisal, counselling, training, and organisation development interventions are used to initiate, facilitate, and promote this process in a continuous way. Because the process has no limit, the mechanisms may need to be examined periodically to see whether they are promoting or hindering the process. Organisations can facilitate this process of development by planning for it, by allocating organisational resources for the purpose, and by exemplifying an HRD philosophy that values human beings and promotes their development.

CHANGING BOUNDARIES OF HRD

Over time there have been many changes in the HR function. Slowly the term Personnel Function has been replaced with the term Human Resource or HR Function, and Personnel departments and Personnel Managers have been re-designated as Human Resource Departments or Human Resources Managers. The status of the HR function got very much uplifted across the world, and particularly in India.

Lifting up the HR function to the Director level in the corporations, and representation of HR Directors on the Board are two significant indicators of the recognition of people as a resource and partners in business.

This is what was envisaged in some ways when the first HRD department was designed in Larsen and Toubro in mid-seventies. The HR function also got expanded to include some new initiatives in a few organisations. Some of the new roles the HR functionaries started performing in the last decade include the following.

Most of these relate to human resource development:

- Reorganisation and restructuring, including downsizing, rightsizing, flattening the structure, outsourcing etc.;
- Managing mergers and acquisitions by changing HR policies, realigning and redrafting HR policies and practices;
- Initiating and managing quality initiatives, including quality circles, small group activities, ISO certification etc.;
- Conducting a variety of surveys, including climate surveys, employee satisfaction surveys, internal customer satisfaction surveys, and bench marking with competitors and others globally;
- Restructuring salary and reward systems through compensation surveys, introduction of stock options, performance-linked pay or pay-for-performance, compensation planning etc.;
- Enhanced emphasis on recruitment or placem-ent.With the recognition of the need for competent people, the new economy industries like the IT, Telecom, Financial services, Insurance, BPO organisations (call centres) have further increased their focus on recruitment and outsourcing of recruitment;

- Introducing new technologies of training, including e-learning, on-line education, distance learning, off campus learning, web based learning and use of other technologies for learning;
- Starting of Corporate Universities and in-house training institutions and academies to encourage continuous education programmes and competency building;
- Introduction of 360 Degree Feedback, including using it for leadership development, evolving leadership models that fit into the company culture and take care of the unique needs of the company, and exploring it as an individual as well as performance development tools, experimenting with 360 degree feedback by linking with reward systems;
- Use of Assessment Centres or Development centres for identifying, developing and promoting talented individuals, starting of fast track systems, identification of high potential employees and designing retention strategies;
- Increased emphasis on mentoring and coaching;
- Increased emphasis on training of all employees, particularly operators, workmen etc., through multi-skilling, etc.,
- Emphasis on leadership and leadership development at all levels; and Participation in strategic thinking, business planning, mergers, acquisitions etc.
- Improving quality of work life. This has been has been brought into focus by the IT industry where the environment becomes a critical factor in effective functioning of knowledge workers.

All these new developments of the last decade are in the direction of making HR, more specifically HRD, a strategic business partner. Recently HR team from one company in India suggested seven ways of making HR a business partner.

Exhibit: Making HR a Business Partner

- Train HR people in business to get a holistic business perspectives
- Get involved in larger organisational issues and handle coordination at that level
- Align HR strategies with business strategies
- Keep in mind business strategy while designing training programmes
- Convene business strategies forums, hold strategic discuss meetings, and prepare discussion paper
- Initiate process of discussion on strategy formulation from the front-line upward

- Help in searching state of the art practices to discuss with the business team.

These new functions fall into one or more of the categories of the HRD system. The classification suggested earlier is only indicative. Organisation can structure their function the way that suits their requirements.

The principles remain the same. The boundary gets extended to participation in strategy and business planning (including planning of mergers, acquisitions, expansions, consolidations etc.). The HRD systems model is broad enough to include the new roles of HR managers.

Researches have shown that effective firms adopt some of the following HR practices:

- Financial incentives for excellent performance
- Practices that motivate employee effort and capture the benefits of knowhow and skill
- Rigorous selection and selectivity in recruiting
- Higher than average wages
- Plans of employee share of ownership
- Extensive information sharing
- Decentralisation of decision-making and empowerment
- Self-managing teams
- High investment in training and skill development
- Having people do multiple jobs and job-rotation
- Elimination of status symbols
- A more compressed distribution of salaries across and within levels
- Promotion from within long-term perspective
- Measurement of HR practices and policy implementation

DECIDING ON COMPETENCY-BASED OR TRADITIONAL HR PLANNING

Before the leaders of an organization commit to competency-based HR planning, they must weigh a number of issues, but they do not have to make an all-or-nothing decision. They may decide to use a competency-based approach to HR planning in some parts or at some levels of the organization, while they may continue to use a traditional approach in other parts of the organization.

Competency-based HR planning is advisable when the organization's leaders are willing to experiment with innovative or new methods. This may be entirely appropriate when qualitative approaches would be particularly helpful in meeting the need for talent. For instance, in a research and development department, individual talents may be far more important than head count. In such a situation, the potential payoffs of competency-based HR planning may outweigh the sizable costs of installing it.

An organization that is competing in a rapidly changing environment may have the most need for competency-based HR planning. A high-tech firm such as Microsoft or Intel is highly dependent on first-rate talent that can be found and used quickly and appropriately. Qualitative responses to competitive challenges must be mobilized quickly to head off disaster. Indeed, a competency-based HR planning approach may be more appropriate than a traditional approach that focuses on head count and relies on superficial approximations of talent or other indicators of accomplishment that are not clearly linked to the past or potential work results of individuals.

Competency-based HR planning may be more appropriate in an organization with a large population of professional, technical, or managerial employees. In those work categories, the quantity of the work-force is far less important than the quality of its available talent. Qualitative differences in talents such as interpersonal skill, emotional intelligence, and other, less tangible associations with creative ability may be key to success.

In organizations or departments that must assemble special teams to work on ill-defined and extremely difficult problems, a competencybased HR planning approach may be far more suitable to long-term results. For instance, in a high-end consulting firm, success may depend on the organization's ability to field a dream team of consultants on short notice to meet a unique challenge. Locating a certain number of consultants is less important than finding the most effective team of consultants who can work together to help the client solve a problem.

Organizations that rely on matrix management may benefit from a competency-based HR planning approach. Matrix management encourages cross-functional sharing and is somewhat complex in nature. In effect, leadership is diffuse. One manager may be responsible for a project, while another is responsible for daily supervision. Selecting and maintaining the right mix of leadership talent is essential to nurturing future talent.

A competency-based approach may also be appropriate for organizations that rely heavily on abstract competencies, such as interpersonal skill or achievement motivation. In a sales organization, for example, work results may hinge on a salesperson's ability to consult with clients and achieve complex solutions to difficult problems. Making the sale may require substantial industry knowledge. In that case, a competency-based HR planning approach would be preferable to a traditional approach.

But not all organizations are appropriate environments for competency-based HR planning. The success of a competency-based approach requires leaders who are willing to add a qualitative aspect to their quantitative mind-sets and are open to rethinking what they mean by "performance", especially when the work to be accomplished is strategic to the organization's success. Decision makers also need to adopt an understanding of competencies. Those who believe that competencies pertain only to knowledge components would not be adequate advocates for a competency-based HR planning system.

Creating, implementing, and maintaining a competency-based HR planning system each requires resources, and leaders must be willing to make the necessary sustained commitment. Of course, leaders in some organizations may prefer to use a competency-based HR planning approach selectively. In departments that perform more routine or repetitive work that is not of strategic importance, a traditional approach may continue to be used. The circumstances in each organization will usually provide clues to how or if competency-based HR planning should be used.

MAKING HR PLANNING COMPETENCY BASED

Transforming HR planning to a competency basis requires a major paradigm shift in the way HR planners think about organizations and people. They must rethink what they are doing, why they are doing it, and how they should do it. Putting a competency-based HR planning system in place begins with building the awareness of the organization's decision makers. Since they control the organization's resources, they must be convinced that the benefits of competency-based HR planning will outweigh the costs associated with the change. Often, that requires a simple leap of faith. After all, if Edison had waited to see a lightbulb before he invented one, we would all still be in the dark. If decision makers demand solid costbenefit projections or evidence that other organizations achieved competitive success by moving to competency-based HR planning, then the effort may be dead. There are few published case studies of organizations that achieved this switchover for all aspects of HR. (And those who have them would have a valuable secret weapon they would not be willing to share.)

As a part of the larger ACA research study on competency-based human resource management practices, 60 organizations with and in the process of developing staffing applications that were competency based provided details related to their practices on a separate questionnaire. Asked if they had a formal workforce planning process directed toward organizational needs, assessing, forecasting, and deploying the workforce, 59% indicated that such a planning process was in place. Of those who used formal planning processes, 69% responded that competencies were used in making decisions associated with the planning (Raising the Bar, 1996).

In a study conducted by Schoonover, Schoonover, Nemerov, and Ehly (2000), 29% of the 300 respondents rated the use of competencies in their strategic HR planning as either "effective" or "very effective"; however, there was a correlation between the level of sophistication of the implementers and the level of perceived effectiveness.

Competency-based HR planning requires, as a first step, that decision makers articulate the organization's strategic goals or business objectives. Every organization exists for at least one purpose. For instance, a business exists to make a profit; a government agency exists to meet a social need; and a charitable organization exists to offer services that other organizations do not offer. The organization's goals or objectives must be translated into desired organizational outputs or results. Workers support the achievement of their organization's strategic goals or business objectives. Competency-based HR planning requires practitioners to determine the quantity and quality of work that must be performed to support achievement of their organization's strategic goals or business objectives, the conditions and methods of work performance, who should perform it, and what worker characteristics will result in successful performance.

To move to a competency-driven HR planning process, planners must establish and maintain a human resource management system in which to store, update, and, most important, instantaneously access information about workers' competencies. An information management system must display clearly the expertise available in the organization.

It should go beyond the old-style "skill inventory" and become a "competency inventory" that catalogs and enables easy access to what people can do and the results they can achieve, not, for example, as in many skill inventories, their educational credentials. After all, educational credentials may not be directly related to organizational results.

Companies are developing methods of tracking competencies and then using the information and models created with software programs and human capital development applications, spreadsheets, and even paper when making important business decisions involving HR functions such as recruiting, training, and succession planning. Virtual Inc., a small integrated management-marketing firm based in Wakefield, Massachusetts, developed a matrix of skills and competencies to assist in hiring and training to meet the specific and continuously changing needs of the organization (Greengard, 2001).

After decision makers determine the organization's required competencies, they must compare their needs to the current workforce and develop a plan to acquire the competencies that are lacking (Gendron, 1996). PepsiCo India uses a model that tracks the competencies for each position through a period of 3 years, so that individuals who are hired have the needed competencies at the time of hiring, but also have the ability to acquire the competencies that will likely define their positions in the future (Chowdhury, 1999).

ELEMENTS OF PLANNING STRATEGIES OF HRD

Planning is a primary function in the management of any organization or system. In simple terms, planning involves setting the direction for the system and determining how to guide the system in that direction. Planning activities can be highly complex or simple, and can involve an individual or an entire multinational organization. The act of planning usually takes place at every level and within every function of a system and is crucial to the survival and success of the system. This section deals with the more specific application of planning in the realm of Human Resource Development. The authors deal with different yet complementary topics about HRD planning: the process of analyzing the work systems that HRD should address, the formulation of HRD objectives, the resources required to accomplish HRD goals, the types of activities associated with HRD, the levels at which HRD planning should occur, and the essential elements that make up strategic plans in HRD. As a part of their discussion, the authors also provide important insights into the history, philosophy, and values of HRD as a discipline, the complex, global context in which HRD operates, and some of the trends likely to emerge in HRD in the future.

Role of HRD

As part of the broader view of HRD, several of the authors define HRD and its purpose and role within a broader systems framework. Over the years numerous scholars have attempted to define HRD, resulting in a variety of conceptualizations of HRD. Some of the common themes suggested by other scholars appear here, such as the observation that HRD is an interdisciplinary field that involves research, theory, and practice involving the learning and development of individuals, groups, organizations and other systems. Certainly, HRD employs a variety of interventions or developmental activities to enhance human potential and productivity of individuals, groups, and organizations. HRD is more, however, than a collection of tools and techniques; it is a process. Going beyond the traditional boundaries of HRD, the authors of this section expand the purpose of HRD to include the need to "contribute to sustainable development," and the role of HRD in both "competence and culture building" for the purpose of achieving the current and future goals of an organization.

We are also reminded of HRD's role in ensuring that an organization develops a learning culture and a learning strategy to achieve its mission and goals. As an additional clarification, HRD is said to be strategic "if it is aligned with organizational goals, objectives, problems and developments." All of these points add to a richer understanding of the purpose and role of HRD, and highlight the common agreement on HRD's focus on learning for the betterment of individuals, organizations, and societies.

Global Context

The authors of this section note that HRD does not exist in isolation; rather it is part of a much broader context that must be considered in order to understand the complexity and variability of HRD across organizations. At the global level, HRD, with its ability to adopt both a production-oriented and a people-oriented role, is faced with the need to play a leadership role in critical economic and social problems. Thus, in a general sense, HRD's role is both economic and social. The development of human resources is fundamental to improving economic productivity and quality of life. Global trends including technological advances, global interconnections and communications, shifting demographics, environmental concerns, economic cycles, and changing employee and customer expectations affect the role that HRD plays and will continue to play throughout the world. By enhancing organizations' capacity to learn and change more quickly, HRD facilitates individual and organizational adaptation and progress in a turbulent world. We have seen a widening gap between those that have and do not have economic security and prosperity, often coupled with a knowledge and skills gap. HRD has the opportunity "to pave the way for a level of thinking and code of practice that enhances performance and stimulates greater enlightenment and meaning in people's lives."

3

Training and Development

Definition of Training & Development: Improve performance "Training & Development is any attempt to improve current or future employee performance by increasing an employee's ability to perform through learning, usually by changing the employee's attitude or increasing his or her skills and knowledge."

METHODS OF TRAINING

On the Job Trainings: These methods are generally applied on the workplace while employees is actually working. Following are the on-the-job methods.

- Advantages of On-the-Job Training
  - It is directly in the context of job
  - It is often informal
  - It is most effective because it is learning by experience
  - It is least expensive
  - Trainees are highly motivated
  - It is free from artificial classroom situations
- Disadvantages of On-the-Job Training
  - Trainer may not be experienced enough to train
  - It is not systematically organized
  - Poorly conducted programmes may create safety hazards

On the Job Training Methods

- *Job Rotation*: In this method, usually employees are put on different jobs turn by turn where they learn all sorts of jobs of various departments. The objective is to give a comprehensive awareness about the jobs of different departments. Advantage - employee gets to know how his own and other departments also function.

Interdepartmental coordination can be improved, instills team spirit. Disadvantage - It may become too much for an employee to learn. It is not focused on employees own job respons-ibilities. Employees basic talents may remain under utilized.

- *Job Coaching*: An experienced employee can give a verbal presentation to explain the nitty-gritty's of the job.
- *Job Instruction*: It may consist an instruction or directions to perform a particular task or a function. It may be in the form of orders or steps to perform a task.
- *Apprenticeships*: Generally fresh graduates are put under the experienced employee to learn the functions of job.
- *Internships and Assistantships*: An intern or an assistants are recruited to perform a specific time-bound jobs or projects during their education. It may consist a part of their educational courses.
- *Off the Job Trainings*: These are used away from work places while employees are not working like classroom trainings, seminars etc. Following are the off-the-job methods;
- *Advantages of Off-the-Job Training*:
  - Trainers are usually experienced enough to train
  - It is systematically organized
  - Efficiently created programmes may add lot of value
- *Disadvantages of Off-the-Job Training*:
  - It is not directly in the context of job
  - It is often formal
  - It is not based on experience
  - It is least expensive
  - Trainees may not be highly motivated
  - It is more artificial in nature

Off the Job Training Methods

- *Classroom Lectures*: It is a verbal lecture presentation by an instructor to a large audience. Advantage - It can be used for large groups. Cost per trainee is low. Disadvantages - Low popularity. It is not learning by practice. It is One-way communication. No authentic feedback mechanism. Likely to boredom.
- *Audio-Visual*: It can be done using Films, Televisions, Video, and Presentations etc. Advantages - Wide range of realistic examples,

quality control possible. Disadvantages - One-way communication, No feedback mechanism. No flexibility for different audience.

- *Simulation*: creating a real life situation for decision-making and understanding the actual job conditions give it. Following are some of the simulation methods of trainings
  - *Case Studies*: It is a written description of an actual situation and trainer is supposed to analyse and give his conclusions in writing. The cases are generally based on actual organizational situations. It is an ideal method to promote decision-making abilities within the constraints of limited data. *Role Plays*: Here trainees assume the part of the specific personalities in a case study and enact it in front of the audience. It is more emotional orientation and improves interpersonal relationships. Attitudinal change is another result. These are generally used in MDP.
  - *Sensitivity Trainings*: This is more from the point of view of behavioural assessment, under different circumstances how an individual will behave himself and towards others. There is no preplanned agenda and it is instant. Advantages - increased ability to empathize, listening skills, openness, tolerance, and conflict resolution skills. Disadvantage - Participants may resort to their old habits after the training.
- *Programmed Instructions*: Provided in the form of blocks either in book or a teaching machine using questions and Feedbacks without the intervention of trainer. Advantages - Self paced, trainees can progress at their own speed, strong motivation for repeat learning, material is structured and self-contained. Disadvantages - Scope for learning is less; cost of books, manuals or machinery is expensive.
- *Computer Aided Instructions*: It is extension of PI method, by using computers. Advantages - Provides accountabilities, modifiable to technological innovations, flexible to time. Disadvantages - High cost.
- Laboratory Training

Barriers to Effective Training:

- Lack of Management commitment
- Inadequate Training budget
- Education degrees lack skills
- Large scale poaching of trained staff
- Non-coordination from workers due to downsizing trends
- Employers and B Schools operating distantly
- Unions influence

How To Make Training Effective?

- Management Commitment
- Training & Business Strategies Integration
- Comprehensive and Systematic Approach
- Continuous and Ongoing approach
- Promoting Learning as Fundamental Value
- Creations of effective training evaluation system.

CONCEPT, NEEDS, SYSTEMATIC APPROACH TO TRAINING

Concept of training

What is meant by training? Training is the process of teaching the new and/or present employees the basic skills they need to effectively perform their jobs. Alternatively speaking, training is the act of increasing the knowledge and skill of an employee for doing his/her job.

Thus, training refers to the teaching and learning activities carried on for the primary purpose of helping members of an organisation to acquire and also to apply the required knowledge, skill and attitudes to perform their jobs effec-tively.

According to Edwin B. Flippo, "training is the act of increasing the knowledge and skills of an employee for doing a particular job."

Michael Armstrong points "training is the systematic modification of behaviour through learning which occurs as a result of education, instruction, development and planned experi-ence".

In the opinion of Michael J. Jucious, "training is any process by which the attitudes, skills and abilities of employees to perform specific jobs are improved."

Thus, it can be concluded that training is a process that tries to improve skills, or add to the existing level of knowledge so that the employee is better equipped to do his present job, or to mould him to be fit for a higher job involving higher responsibilities. In other words, training is a learning experience that seeks a relatively permanent change in an individual that will improve his/her ability to perform his job.

Difference between training, development and education

Some people consider the three terms, namely, training, development and education as synony-mous, i.e., meaning the same thing. But, all the three terms mean different things as explained hereunder.

Training

The meaning of training has just been explained.

Development

Compared to the term 'training', the term 'development' has broader scope and aim to develop people in all respects. Accordingly, development covers not only activities/skills which improve job performance, but also those activities which bring about growth of the personality, help individuals progress toward maturity and actualization of their potential.

Thus, development enables individuals to become not only good employees but better men and women also. Clearly, development is an ongoing continuous process, while training is a one-shot deal.

In ultimate sense, development refers to behavioural modification of people through continuous learning practices. Development relates to non-technical organisational functions such as problem solving, decision-making and relating to people.

Education

Like the term 'development', the term 'education' is also wider in scope and broader in purpose when compared to training.

Education is the (life-long) process of increasing the general knowledge and understanding of people about the total environment. Thus, education is person and theory- based. Its main purpose is to improve the conceptual understanding of the people about a subject or theme or environment.

Education is imparted through schools or colleges or universities, through the contents of programmes aimed at improving the knowledge and understanding of the people about their environment. Having gone through the meanings of the three terms, education is not found much different from development. However, training is found quite different from development in four ways as stated below:

(i) What is learned?

(ii) Who learns?

(iii) Why such learning takes place; and

(iv) When learning occurs?

Need for training

Training is the act of improving one's knowledge and skill to improve his/her job performance. Training is job-oriented. It bridges the gap between what the employee has and what the job demands. For that matter, imparting training to employees working in all organised sectors of human activity is no longer a matter of debate.

As a matter of fact, of late, the need for training has been recognized as an essential activity not only in the business organisations, but also in academic institutions, profes-sional bodies and the government departments.

For example, attending one orientation and two refresher courses has been made compulsory for the University/College teachers with an objective to improve their knowledge and skill for improving their job (teaching) performance.

Several conditions have contributed to make the organisations realize and recognize the need for imparting training to their employees.

Venkata Ratnam and Srivastava have listed these conditions as follows:

(i) Sub-optimal performance of organisations in government, public and private sectors.

(ii) The ever widening gap between planning, implementation and completion of projects.

(iii) Technological change necessitating acquisition of new knowledge, ability and skills.

(iv) Increasing qualitative demand for managers and workmen.

(v) Increasing uncertainties and complexities in the total environment necessitating flexible and adaptive responses from organisations.

(vi) Need for both individuals and organisations to grow at rapid pace.

(vii) To meet challenges posed by the global competition.

(viii) To harness the human potential and give expression to their creative urges.

(ix) To enable employees to move from one job to another.

(x) To bridge the gap between what employees has in terms of knowledge and skill and what his/ her job actually demands.

In view of the above needs, employees need training to be imparted in the following areas:

Areas of Training

Knowledge

Training aimed at imparting knowledge to employees provides for facts, information and principles related to his/her job.

In general, training imparted in the knowledge area considers three aspects, namely, job context, job content and quality of work.

Technical Skills

The training in this area aims at teaching the employees the physical acts or actions like operating a machine, working with a computer, using mathematical tools to take decisions, etc. It is somewhat like induction training.

Social Skills

The training in this area is broader in scope embracing many aspects. This cat-egory of training aims at the development of individuals and team work. Accordingly, employees are imparted training to acquire and sharpen such behavioural and human relations skills that help improve inter-personal relationship, better team work and effective leadership.

Techniques

Training in this area involves teaching employees the manners how to apply knowl-edge and skills to dynamic situations.

Attitudes

This involves orientation or induction programmes that help change the employees' attitudes favourable toward the achievement of organisational goals. Through training programmes, employees' attitudes are moulded to render support for the effective completion of company activities and inculcate the spirit of better co-operation and greater loyalty among the employees.

Experience

It is not and cannot be taught or imparted in the classroom. It is gained by putting knowledge, skills, techniques and attitudes into use over a period of time in different work situations. Experience makes one perfect.

Importance of training

The following two Chinese proverbs highlight the importance of the employee training:

"Give a man a fish, and you have given him meal. Teach man to fish, and you have given him livelihood."

"If you wish to plan for a year sow seeds, if you wish to plan for ten years plant trees, if you plan for life-time develop men."

The importance of employee training can best be appreciated with the help of various advantages it offers to both employees and employers.

These are explained under the following heads:

1. Better Performance: Training improves employee's ability and skills and, in turn, improves employee's performance both in quantity and quality. Better or increased employee performance directly leads to increased operational productivity and increased organisational profits. Improve-ments in employee performance/productivity in developed countries' lend support to this statement.
2. Improved Quality: In formal training programmes, the best methods of performing jobs are standardised and then taught to employees. This offers two-fold benefits. Firstly, uniformity in work performance helps improve the quality of work or service. Secondly, better informed, or say, trained workers are less likely to make operational mistakes.
3. Less Supervision: A trained worker is self-reliant. He knows his work and way to perform it well. Therefore, his work requires less supervision. The supervisor can devote his time on more urgent works.
4. Less Learning Period: A well planned and systematically organised training programme reduces the time and cost involved in learning. Training enables to avoid waste of time and efforts in learning through trial and error method'.
5. High Morale: Training not only improves the ability and skill of employees, but also changes employee attitude toward positive. Higher performance, job satisfaction, job security and avenues for internal promotion lead to high morale among the employees. High morale, in turn, makes employees' lore loyal to the organisation.
6. Personal Growth: Training improves employee's ability, knowledge and skills and, thus, prevents employee's obsolescence. This makes employees growth-oriented.
7. Favourable organisational climate: The aforesaid advantages combined lead to an im-proved and favourable organisational climate characterised by better industrial relations and disci-plines, reduced resistance to change, reduced absenteeism and turnover of employees, and improved stability of organisation.

Thus, it may be observed that the importance of training can be imbued with multiplicity of justifications. In fact, a systematic and effective training is an invaluable investment in the human resources of an organisation. Therefore, no organisation can choose whether or not to train employ-ees.

Systematic Approach to Training

Utilizing a systematic approach to training is beneficial in that it prioritizes a company's objectives and goals prior to initiating phases of training. A systematic approach to training is a type of formal training designed to ensure training begins and ends with the company's needs. Through a methodical tactic, this approach equips personnel with the knowledge and tools to pursue the company's interest with competent job performance.

Analysis

The first phase includes determination of training needs through analysis of employee performance and behavior, and comparisons of organizational goals. Input from supervisory staff is critical to efforts to identify needs. It may sometimes be difficult to distinguish between training requirements and other issues that lead to problems. For example, an inaccurate or late report might be due to insufficient training, but it also might be the result of willful negligence. Once training needs are established, the next phase can be initiated.

Design

In the design stage, input gathered during the analysis stage is used to create learning objectives, stipulate instructional methods, identify training materials to be used and specify the location at which training will take place. It will produce end-of-course evaluations of course content and examine students' competency.

Development

The development phase is used primarily for producing or acquiring materials needed for the upcoming training. This stage can be compared to producing a recording of a song from a page of sheet music. Hand-outs, tests, and evaluations are printed, slides are assembled and the use of multimedia tools is arranged.

Implementation

The implementation phase can be considered the climax of a strategic approach to training. It is the culmination of all the previous steps. The actual training is conducted for your staff. This is the component that integrates the research and data from the analysis phase, and in which your employees use learning tools and materials that emerge from the design and development stages.

Evaluation

Evaluation is conducted throughout the process. The effectiveness of each step must be continually assessed. An overarching evaluation of the entire approach measures the value of the training program as it applies to company goals and employee performance and behavior. Evaluations can be completed by testing knowledge and skills immediately after completion of training or through consultation with employees and supervisors after work has resumed.

MEANING OF TRAINING AND DEVELOPMENT

The need for Training and Development is determined by the employee's performance deficiency, computed as follows.

Training & Development Need = Standard Performance - Actual Performance We can make a distinction among Training, Development and Education.

Distinction between Training and Education

Training	Education
Application oriented	Theoretical Orientation
Job experience	Classroom learning
Specific Task in mind	Covers general concepts
Narrow Perspective	Has Broad Perspective
Training is Job Specific	Education is no bar

Training: Training refers to the process of imparting specific skills. An employee undergoing training is presumed to have had some formal education. No training programme is complete without an element of education. Hence we can say that Training is offered to operatives.

Education: It is a theoretical learning in classrooms. The purpose of education is to teach theoretical concepts and develop a sense of reasoning and judgment. That any training and development programme must contain an element of education is well understood by HR Specialists. Any such programme has university professors as resource persons to enlighten participants about theoretical knowledge of the topics proposed to discuss. In fact organizations depute or encourage employees to do courses on part time basis.

CEOs are known to attend refresher courses conducted by business schools. The education is more important for managers and executives rather than low cadre workers. Anyways education is common to all employees, their grades notwithstanding.

Development: Development means those learning opportunities designed to help employees to grow. Development is not primarily skills oriented. Instead it provides the general knowledge and attitudes, which will be helpful to employers in higher positions. Efforts towards development often depend on personal drive and ambition. Development activities such as those supplied by management development programmes are generally voluntary in nature. Development provides knowledge about business environment, management principles and techniques, human relations, specific industry analysis and the like is useful for better management of a company.

EMPLOYEE TRAINING AND DEVELOPMENT

Approach to Employment in Economic Planning

Planning in India focused at realising a high rate of growth of output in the long term. A basic assumption was that shortage of capital goods in relation to employable persons constituted a fundamental constraint on growth in the economy. Therefore the planning process made no attempt to define an independent employment strategy; the focus on economic growth was viewed as essential for improving the employment situation. Initially, labour force expansion was not seen as a problem to be contended with. Thus, in the Five Year Plans, the generation of employment was viewed as part of the process of development and not as a goal in conflict with, or to be pursued independently of economic development

Employment Planning in India

The approach to tackling the task of unemployment has varied from time to time. In the initial years of planning reliance was placed primarily on the expectations of a rapid industrial development and control of population. These expectations did not materialise and it was observed that the rate of growth of employment was generally much lower than the growth rate of GDP of the economy. Moreover the classical study of Dandekar and Rath (1969) showed a continuously increasing trend of people falling below the poverty line (BPL). Seasons of severe draught and failure of monsoons exposed large parts of population to extensive deprivations. Successive plans, strategies, policies and programmes were, therefore, redesigned to bring about a special focus on employment generation as a specific objective.

The seventies and eighties saw the emergence of special schemes like NREP, RLEGP to provide wage employment through public works programmes and schemes to promote self employment and entrepreneurship through provision of assets, skills and other support to the unemployed and the poor. While employment levels expanded steadily during the seventies and eighties, the rate of growth of employment continued to lag behind that of the labour force.

Unemployment among the educated showed a rising trend. Another feature of the employment situation is the sizeable proportion of the employed working at low levels of the productivity and income. The eighties exposed the weakness in the then ongoing strategies of expanding public sector irrespective of competition.

Employment and Unemployment Scenario in India

In India, due to the agrarian sector with seasonal operations time disposition and availability for work have been the criteria for measuring employment. The accepted method of measuring employment is the usual status. Reliable estimates of employment/unemployment are generated through National Sample Surveys conducted once in five years by National Sample Survey Organisation (NSSO).

In order to capture the complexities of the employment situation in India, the estimates of employment and unemployment by NSSO are derived on three concepts, Usual Status (US), Current Weekly Status (CWS) and Current Daily Status (CDS) as per the recommendation of "Dantwala Committee" set up by the Planning Commission in 1968. The three concepts are based on three different reference periods for ascertaining the activity status of a person. Under the Usual Status concept, the reference period is one year and activity status of a person as employed, unemployed or out of labour force is determined on the basis of activity pursued by him during the year. On the CWS criterion, a person is considered as employed or unemployed if he has worked or has not worked though was available for work, respectively, even for one hour during the week.

Under the CDS approach, the unit of classification is half a day. In this approach the person days are distributed by activity category during an average week. Considering Principal as well as Subsidiary activities the concept of Usual Principal Status (UPS) and Usual Principal and Subsidiary Status (UPSS) within the Usual Status are worked out. All the concepts are on time utilisation only. Quality of work or income does not get reflected in these approaches. National Sample Survey Organisation (NSSO) on the basis of the carries out detailed quinquennial surveys on employment, unemployment and labour force. The last survey for which results have been published relates to the year 1999-2000. As per the results of the National Sample Survey conducted in 1999-2000, total work force as on 1.1.2000, as per Usual Status approach (considering both principal and subsidiary activities) was of the order of 401 million. About 7% of the total work force is employed in the formal or organised sector (all public sector establishments and all non-agricultural establishments in private sector with 10 or more workers) while remaining 93% work in the informal or unorganised sector.

Global Employment Scenario

The global employment and unemployment situation just as to the World Employment Report 1998-99, was as follows:

- Out of an estimated 6 billion population in the year 1997 around 3 billion was in the labour force.
- 160 million persons have been estimated to be fully unemployed.
- 25 to 30 per cent of the employed labour force were underemployed.
- A large number of young people in the age group of 15 and 24 (around 60 million in 1997) are continuously in search of work. *i.e.*, unemployed.

A few important ceases which emerge from the report are:

Limited demand for unskilled and less skilled labour.

- Increase in demand for skilled labour on account of technological development and upgradation and changes in the organisation of work
- Problems in maintaining the continued employability of labour force

Demand for Multi Skilling

Some of the important strategies recommended in the World Employment Report are:

- Timely Investment in skill development and training at enhanced level.
- Enhancement of education and skill level of workers

Employment in the Eighth Plan

Labour force was projected to increase by about 35 million during eighth five year's plan period (1992-97) and by another 36 million during 1997-2002. Considering the backlog of unemployment of 17 million at the beginning of Eighth Plan the total number of persons requiring employment was estimated at 54 million during 1992-97 and 94 million during 1992-

2002. Employment growth was seen to result primarily from the growth of the economy and restructuring of output composition of growth. A GDP growth rate of 5.6% per annum was envisaged. This was projected to result an employment growth rate of 2.6 to 2.8% per annum or an average of about 8 to 9 million additional employment opportunities per annum.

Employment in the Ninth Plan

Growth of labour force was projected to be more during the Ninth Plan Period in comparison to the preceding decade. This required a commensurate increase in the pace of creation of additional work opportunities in the Ninth Plan. The growth target for Ninth Plan fixed is about 6.5% per annum on an average. The sectoral structure of growth corresponding to the target of 6.5% GDP growth along with the sectoral elasticities projected generation of 50 million work opportunities in the Ninth Plan Period (1997-2002).

The projected growth rate of employment was 2.44% in the Ninth Plan. The Ninth Plan envisaged a reduction in the unemployment rate from an average unemployment rate of 1.87% in the Eighth Plan to an average unemployment rate of 1.66% in the Ninth Plan as per Usual Status. Ninth Plan accorded priority to agriculture and rural development with a view to generating adequate productive employment and eradication of poverty. Productive employment is an important dimension of the state policy that seeks to achieve growth with equity. Greater productive employment was aimed in the growth process itself by concentrating on sectors, sub-sectors and technologies which are labour intensive, in region characterised by higher rates of unemployment and under employment.

Achievements During 1994-2000.

As has already been indicated the assessment of employment and unemployment situation is made through the National Sample Survey conducted by the National Sample Survey Organization on quinquennial basis. Therefore, the survey results of 1993-94 and 1999-2000 can only be used for assessing the employment generation took place in the economy. During the period 1994-2000 the labour force which was of the order of 384.29 million had gone up to 410.39 million resulting an annual increase of 1.10% during this period. This increase is considerably less than what was projected during 8th & 9th Plan.

Similarly, the total employment which was of the order 376.99 million in 1994 had gone up to 401.35 million resulting an annual average growth of 1.05% during this period. The growth rate of employment actually achieved is also substantially less than what was projected during the 8th and 9th Five Year Plan. The slow growth rate of the labour force may be due to reduction in the growth rate of population and other reasons like the more number of children may be joining the educational institutions instead of joining to the labour force. The slow growth of employment may be primarily due to (i) the fact that the GDP growth rate actually achieved had fallen short of what was expected during 8th & 9th Plan and (ii) growth of employment did not take place as per the employment projected during the Plan.

Trends in Employment and Unemployment

The rate of growth of employment declined sharply from 2.37% per year in the period 1987-88 to 1993-94 to only 1.05% per year in the period 1993-94 to 1999-2000. There was sharp deceleration in the growth of labour force from 2.24% in the period 1987-88 to 1993-94 to only 1.10% in the period 1993-94 to 1999-2000. Growth rate of employment is less than the growth rate of the labour force indicating an increase in the unemployment rate. The open unemployment which is of the order of 9 million was not significant compared to the size of the population in the country.

Though, open unemployment was only 2.21% (9 million), the percentage of the population below the poverty line was as high as 26.1%. The fact of being employed is obviously no guarantee of escaping the poverty, which in our situation refers to a very basic level of subsistence.

Percentage of population below the poverty line which was of the order of 36% in 1993-94 has come down to 26.1% indicating that during the period 1994-2000 improvement in the income level of the employed had taken place. Organised sector employment is not growing and its share is only 7% of the total employment.

There was decline in self-employment whereas regular salaried and casual employment showed an increasing trend during 1993-94 to 1999-2000. There was substantial increase in the average daily wage earnings in the rural areas.

Poverty Alleviation and Employment Generation Programmes

Anti-poverty strategy comprises of a wide range of poverty alleviation and employment generation programmes, many of which have been in operation for several years and have been strengthened to generate more employment, create productive assets, impart technical and entrepreneurial skill and raise the income level of the poor.

Under these schemes, both wage employment and self-employment are provided to people below the poverty line. In 1998-99, various poverty alleviation and employment generation programmes are grouped under two broad categories of Self-Employment Schemes and Wage Employment Schemes. Funding and organisational patterns are also rationalised to achieve better impact. These programmes are primarily meant for poverty alleviation and have generally not been helpful in sustainable employment generation.

DEVELOPMENT PRACTICES OF MANAGEMENT

The background to the study described was rooted in policy initiatives designed to remedy deficiencies identified in successive reports on management education and training during the 1980s and 1990s. In 1987 two reports were produced as part of a review of management education and training, prompted by the recognition that the UK still lagged behind other industrialized nations in terms of its formal management education. A few years later, the Cannon and Taylor Working Party Reports, arising out of the 1992 Institute of Management review of management development, noted that the challenges of organizational changes, especially contracting out, de-layering and empowerment, made the need for management development particularly acute. The situation was exacerbated by persistent structural unemployment, competitive pressures from low-wage economies, rapid technological change and standards in education that were inappropriate to the needs of employers.

The Handy Report recommended that a group of top companies form a Charter Group and establish a charter of good practice for management development. From these origins, the Management Charter Initiative (MCI) was established in 1988 as the operating arm of the National Forum for Management Education and Development and by the end of 1991 had the support of over 800 companies. Following the adoption of a competence-based approach to vocational training in the UK, MCI was recognized as the lead body for management and developed a generic set of occupational standards relating to areas of activity in which managers need to be competent.

In 1994, with renewed concern over developing the UK managerial workforce, the Employment Department decided to appraise the use of the Management Standards developed by MCI. The subsequent study that we undertook for the Department investigated the business benefits that could be attributed to competence-based management development in a range of sixteen organizations.

The Growth, Competitiveness, Employment White Paper from the European Commission (1994) argued that skills must be raised at all levels if European enterprises were to compete in global markets. At the same time the Teaching and Learning White Paper stressed the need to provide opportunities for continuous development in order to achieve this. The arguments resurfaced in successive Competitiveness White Papers in the UK during the 1990s and, after the Labour victory of 1997, in the work of the Skills Task Force and the emerging framework for lifelong learning. For UK managers, the need to increase the volume and quality of development is particularly acute given the dramatic changes taking place in the external environment and in organizations.

The study was therefore stimulated both by the need to increase management development and to evaluate the effectiveness of development that was competence based, the approach promoted under the reform of vocational education and training in the UK. If performance improvements could be identified and attributed to management development, managers would be more likely both to engage in development themselves and to make opportunities available for their subordinates. Moreover, if tangible benefits to business could be identified from the competence-based approach, more managers might use the NVQ/SVQ route to accredit their competence, thereby raising the overall level of managerial qualification.

The conceptual and theoretical underpinning of the study is first considered in relation to the literature on the role of HRD in general, and management development in particular, in improving performance. The empirical context, explaining the logic of the research design and briefly describing the sixteen organizations involved. Elaborating the design of the case-study protocol and the fieldwork that was involved. The critical analysis that follows highlights the significance of the findings. Clear performance benefits were identified from management development, and these were more evident where management development was linked with organizational strategy and where HRD systems and processes adopted a coherent set of competence statements, such as the Management Standards.

Theoretical Context

There is an extensive literature supporting the crucial role of human resources in improving organizational performance and sustaining competitive advantage. Snell and Dean (1992) showed that effective management of human capital, especially in relation to building employee skills and commitment, was the key factor in releasing the productive potential of advanced manufacturing technology. Where organizational strategies have focused on replacing employees with physical capital, the effect of human activity on organizational performance is correspondingly minimized. However, investment in human resources as the ultimate source of competitive advantage is more plausible in the context of globalization, which weakens the advantages deriving from economies of scale and access to product markets and capital. Therefore, the optimum human resources policy, and the potential role of human capital, is contingent upon the relative importance of cost, quality and flexibility imperatives in the manufacturing strategy adopted.

Nevertheless, there is insufficient robust evidence concerning the effect of HRD on organizational performance, because relatively few organizations bother to evaluate the impact of training and development beyond the reaction level as defined in Kirkpatrick's (1967) typology. The paucity of evaluation of HRD initiatives is often explained by the difficulty of attributing causality: 'at best, management development and training must always be an act of faith'. Not only is it difficult to identify operational results that are amenable to improvement through training and development, causality is difficult to establish because often 'no single factor, including training, could by itself have brought about the change that has taken place'.

The problem is compounded by 'political' considerations which deter proper evaluation because of vested interests in demonstrating the effectiveness of MD opportunities for which individuals are responsible or to which they have committed time or money. Because of these practical difficulties in measuring the effects of developing people, reported benefits are often anecdotal and confined to a single aspect of performance.

Not only is the cumulative body of knowledge under-developed, it also lacks a coherent conceptual framework and an accepted structural model. In one of the pioneering contributions to the HRD and performance literature, Rummler and Brache distinguished three different levels of analysis: individual; process; and organisation. In the influential Analysis for Improving Performance, Swanson adopted the same framework of analysis, which was perpetuated in subsequent work. This division of individual, process and organizational levels of performance has created conceptual confusion because it neglects the team or group level in the structure and conflates structures with processes. Performance at the team level links individuals with the organisation and therefore plays a pivotal role in translating individual performance improvements into bottom line results. Team level activities are important in facilitating the transfer between individual learning and organizational learning through the development of shared mental models and the adoption of routines that improve existing practices to develop core competence. However, as Russ-Eft (1996) has argued: 'We need more research on defining and measuring team performance.'

Individuals, groups and the organisation as a whole represent different structural levels, whereas processes (along with capacities and accomplishments) exist at each of these levels, as Fisher and Sleezer (1999) recognized. In advance of commissioning the research described here, the Department established an expert group to identify an appropriate methodology for assessing the business benefits of the Management Standards.

From the outset, the study group drew a clear distinction between levels in the organisational structure and work processes at each of these levels in exploring appropriate methodologies for tracing and measuring the business impact of management development, particularly that which was competence-based. Given the causal ambiguity concerning the mechanisms by which human resource practices translate into improved business performance, the expert group recognized that rigorous methods of analysis would be required.

The literature provided the expert group with some indication of the nature of performance benefits to be anticipated from management development. At the individual level, the literature demonstrates above all else the difficulties of measurement and attribution associated with identifying performance improvements arising from management development. In relation to team performance, the key message is the importance of developing collective knowledge so that when individuals change jobs, organizational capacity is not adversely affected. With organizational performance, the literature links the achievement of critical success factors to the management capability of organizations.

Strategies that recognize core competence as a key resource for gaining competitive advantage are prevalent in the recent literature. Clearly, if the development of core competence, including managerial competence, is a crucial determinant of improved organizational performance (as represented by competitive success), then improved performance of individuals and teams ought to be intervening outcomes. The need to link management development with organizational strategy is also prominent in recent literature, as is the need to justify individual development in terms of benefits to the organisation.

There is evidence that organizational performance is enhanced when there is a good fit between organizational strategy and employees' competences, whether employees are developed in line with strategy or strategies are designed to match employees' competences. Finally, recent literature contains claims that management development is more effective where HRD systems and procedures have adopted the MCI Standards. Having considered the literature alongside the evaluation needs of the Employment Department, the expert group proposed five testable hypotheses:

- Management development improves individual performance.
- Management development improves team performance.
- Management development improves organizational performance.
- Improvements in individual, team and organizational performance are more likely if management development is linked to organizational strategy.
- Improvements in individual, team and organizational performance are more likely if HRD systems and processes are based on a common, coherent integrated set of competence statements.

The expert group recommended to the Department that these hypotheses could best be tested using a case-study approach in a range of organizations.

The group drafted a preliminary case-study protocol identifying the evidence to be assessed in relation to the processes and performance outcomes to be investigated at each level. The draft protocol was included as part of the specification for the project when the tender was awarded to us with colleagues at PriME Research and Development of Harrogate.

Empirical Context

In order adequately to test all five hypotheses, it was necessary to include 'counterfactual cases'. We needed organizations that did not use the Management Standards as well as users, and to include organizations in which management development was not linked with organizational strategy as well as those where there was a clear link.

For each of the four categories defined by these two variables, the objective was to identify five organizations suitable for case study. Information therefore had to be gathered from potential case organizations before any fieldwork took place in order tentatively to allocate them to one of the four categories. Contenders for study were identified from discussions with MCI, the Department Steering Group, and from previous research. The organizations were to be drawn from a range of different economic sectors, and it was intended that one third of the organizations studied would be SMEs.

The MCI supplied details of twenty-five organizations known to have adopted the Management Standards and a second tranche of eighteen organizations, known to practise competence-based management development but not thought to be users of the occupational standards, was also identified. Initially, a letter was sent to each organisation by the Department, which the researchers followed up by telephone to arrange a meeting with senior managers and negotiate access. Difficulties in achieving access, particularly with SMEs, made it necessary to approach further organizations and out of a total of 126 organizations approached sixteen cases were selected for detailed study from those that agreed to collaborate.

The sixteen cases were tentatively allocated to the four categories on the basis of preliminary discussions with the contact in each organisation, and the cases appeared to be weighted in favour of Standards users, and especially in favour of those claiming that management development was closely linked with organizational strategy. There were early indications that using the double dichotomy as a basis for categorizing cases were an over-simplification and would prove less useful than intended. Each dimension was really a spectrum, with cases located somewhere along each continuum. Differentiating cases according to whether management development was linked to organizational strategy was especially problematic, since most respondents believed that development was linked to strategy. Clearly management development could be integrated with organizational strategy in some respects and not in others and the difficulty in establishing the extent to which the two were integrated was reflected in the different perspectives of individuals in the same organisation.

It was feared that these problems would impose limitations on the extent to which the first conditional hypothesis (concerning the impact of linking management development with organizational strategy) could be tested. Differentiating cases according to whether the organizations had adopted the Standards appeared less problematic, and cases were provisionally labelled as users and non-users (of the occupational standards developed by MCI). However, the case studies demonstrated that some organizations that were ostensibly users of the Standards had not, in fact, adopted them comprehensively.

The case reports and written evidence were evaluated by independent consultants and validated against the criteria established by the expert group. The cases were re-classified on the basis of this evaluation, producing the achieved cases. In this final classification, only four cases were defined as type A, while five were viewed as type D, and the remainder type C. Type B, in which HRD systems were based on the Management Standards but management development was not linked to organizational strategy, proved to be an empty cell. This finding confirmed empirically, for the cases studied, what, with the benefit of hindsight, might have been assumed a priori: that an organisation is unlikely to adopt the Management Standards and not link its management development to organizational strategy.

The sector, size and final classifications of the sixteen cases that were involved in the study and detailed information is provided in the extended account of the case studies. In terms of sectors involved, the cases were drawn from:

Methodological Issues

The Employment Department study group considered a variety of methodologies and recommended an embedded, multiple case-study approach to investigate the impact of CBMD and the adoption of the Management Standards.

The case study offers a distinct advantage in examining 'a contemporary set of events, over which the investigator has little or no control'. Case studies, whether exploratory, descriptive or explanatory, are by definition empirical inquiries that investigate a contemporary phenomenon within its real-life context, when the boundaries between phenomenon and context are not clearly evident, and in which multiple sources of evidence are used. Given appropriate research design, a series of case studies may be generalized to theoretical propositions, not to a universal population, as is the goal with statistical generalization from a sample. In recommending a case-study approach, the expert group recognized that observation would play a minor role in data collection and that case-study reports should be kept concise and focused on the issues relating to the hypotheses outlined above.

A multiple case-study approach was identified as most appropriate for this research. Multiple case studies offer the advantages associated with replication when cases are selected to offer either literal or theoretical replication, the theoretical framework establishing the conditions under which a phenomenon should be, and should not be, found. It was recognized that the research design for the case studies would have to embody the theoretical and conceptual underpinnings of what was being studied. As the elements of the design were developed, so the theory was more clearly articulated. In formulating the research design, five areas were addressed:

- The research question to be explored: how does management development or the adoption of the Management Standards developed by MCI improve performance?

- Propositions or hypotheses: such as the hypotheses that management development improves both individual and team performance.
- Unit of analysis: the primary unit of analysis was the organisation, but within this sub-units such as functional areas and individuals were defined.
- Logic linking data to propositions: such as evidence of improved performance following the adoption of the Management Standards.
- Criteria for interpreting a study's findings: it was necessary to establish criteria to assess what constitutes a significant improvement in performance.

After the initial theory development stage, the cases for study were selected and the hypotheses operationalized by defining appropriate measures and identifying methods of data collection. An embedded design (involving more than one unit of analysis) was most appropriate for this research since each case involved a consideration of different functional areas and different levels of analysis. Each case was a self-contained study, and each case report sought to establish conclusions concerning the propositions to be tested. The cross-case analysis aimed to explain convergence and divergence between cases in terms of a priori predictions made as part of the replication logic at the design stage.

The expert group offered a tentative case-study design including the data collection protocol that specified the written evidence required and recommended detailed interviews with key respondents in each organisation. This initial case-study protocol was operationalized, piloted and refined by the authors once the research was commissioned. The protocol defined the written evidence to be examined in relation to each hypothesis and the range of measures of performance to be considered. It also comprised interview schedules that were to be used for in-depth, semi-structured interviews with senior strategic managers (chief executive, finance director and head of human resources), line managers and junior managers. The full case-study protocol is contained in the official report of the study.

As a minimum in each case, face-to-face interviews were conducted with the three senior strategic managers, four line managers and four team members. Multiple sources of evidence were collected to increase the reliability of data through triangulation and interlocking questions in the interview schedules were designed to test for consistency between the views of managers at different levels.

Details of improvements in performance and of HRD systems and processes were collected through an extensive range of written evidence.

Managers' job specifications gave an indication of the extent to which responsibility for management development was a feature of their role, while company accounts were examined as evidence of improvements in organizational performance.

A dossier was compiled of written evidence and interviews for each organisation studied, and a case report was written in accordance with the protocol. The case reports provided background details of the organisation, details of the organizational strategy, the HRD systems and processes, and the evidence of improvements in individual, team and organizational performance attributed to management development by respondents. Each case report was validated with two senior managers in the organisation and revised before being evaluated and used in the cross-case analysis.

TRAINING AND DEVELOPMENT OF HUMAN RESOURCES MANAGEMENT

In the field of human resource management, training and development is the field concerned with organizational activity aimed at bettering the performance of individuals and groups in organizational settings. It has been known by several names, including employee development, human resource development, and learning and development. Harrison observes that the name was endlessly debated by the Chartered Institute of Personnel and Development during its review of professional standards in 1999/2000. "Employee Development" was seen as too evocative of the master-slave relationship between employer and employee for those who refer to their employees as "partners" or "associates" to be comfortable with. "Human Resource Development" was rejected by academics, who objected to the idea that people were "resources" — an idea that they felt to be demeaning to the individual. Eventually, the CIPD settled upon "Learning and Development", although that was itself not free from problems, "learning" being an overgeneral and ambiguous name. Moreover, the field is still widely known by the other names.

Training and Development Encompasses Three Main Activities: training, education, and development. Garavan, Costine, and Heraty, of the Irish Institute of Training and Development, note that these ideas are often considered to be synonymous. However, to practitioners, they encompass three separate, although interrelated, activities:

Training: This activity is both focused upon, and evaluated against, the job that an individual currently holds.

Education: This activity focuses upon the jobs that an individual may potentially hold in the future, and is evaluated against those jobs.

Development: This activity focuses upon the activities that the organization employing the individual, or that the individual is part of, may partake in the future, and is almost impossible to evaluate. The "stakeholders" in training and development are categorized into several classes. The sponsors of training and development are senior managers. The clients of training and development are business planners. Line managers are responsible for coaching, resources, and performance.

The participants are those who actually undergo the processes. The facilitators are Human Resource Management staff. And the providers are specialists in the field. Each of these groups has its own agenda and motivations, which sometimes conflict with the agendas and motivations of the others.

The conflicts are the best part of career consequences are those that take place between employees and their bosses. The number one reason people leave their jobs is conflict with their bosses. And yet, as author, workplace relationship authority, and executive coach, Dr. John Hoover points out, "Tempting as it is, nobody ever enhanced his or her career by making the boss look stupid."

Training an employee to get along well with authority and with people who entertain diverse points of view is one of the best guarantees of long-term success. Talent, knowledge, and skill alone won't compensate for a sour relationship with a superior, peer, or customer.

Employee benefits and (especially in British English) benefits in kind (also called fringe benefits, perquisites, perqs or perks) are various non-wage compensations provided to employees in addition to their normal wages or salaries. Where an employee exchanges (cash) wages for some other form of benefit, this is generally referred to as a 'salary sacrifice' arrangement. In most countries, most kinds of employee benefits are taxable to at least some degree.

Some of these benefits are: housing (employer-provided or employer-paid), group insurance (health, dental, life etc.), disability income protection, retirement benefits, daycare, tuition reimbursement, sick leave, vacation (paid and non-paid), social security, profit sharing, funding of education, and other specialized benefits. The purpose of the benefits is to increase the economic security of employees.

The term perqs or perks is often used colloquially to refer to those benefits of a more discretionary nature. Often, perks are given to employees who are doing notably well and/or have seniority. Common perks are take-home vehicles, hotel stays, free refreshments, leisure activities on work time (golf, etc.), stationery, allowances for lunch, and—when multiple choices exist—first choice of such things as job assignments and vacation scheduling. They may also be given first chance at job promotions when vacancies exist.

Employee benefits in Canada might include additional health coverage that are not included in the provincial plan such as (medical, prescription, vision and dental plans); health and dependent care; retirement benefit plans (in addition to Canada Pension Plan (CPP); group-term life and long term care insurance plans; legal assistance plans; transportation benefits; and possibly other miscellaneous employee discounts wellness programs, discounted shopping, hotels and resorts, and so on.

Employee benefits in the United States might include relocation assistance; medical, prescription, vision and dental plans; health and dependent care flexible spending accounts; retirement benefit plans (pension, 401(k), 403(b)); group-term life and long term care insurance plans; legal assistance plans; adoption assistance; child care benefits; transportation benefits; and possibly other miscellaneous employee discounts (e.g., movies and theme park tickets, wellness programs, discounted shopping, hotels and resorts, and so on).

Some fringe benefits (for example, accident and health plans, and group-term life insurance coverage up to US$50,000) may be excluded from the employee's gross income and, therefore, are not subject to federal income tax in the United States. Some function as tax shelters (for example, flexible spending accounts, 401(k)'s, 403(b)'s).

Fringe benefits are also thought of as the costs of keeping employees other than salary. These benefit rates are typically calculated using fixed percentages that vary depending on the employee's classification and often change from year to year. Normally, employer provided benefits are tax-deductible to the employer and non-taxable to the employee. The exception to the general rule includes certain executive benefits (e.g. golden handshake and golden parachute plans).

American corporations may also offer cafeteria plans to their employees. These plans would offer a menu and level of benefits for employees to choose from. In most instances, these plans are funded by both the employees and by the employer(s). The portion paid by the employees are deducted from their gross pay before federal and state taxes are applied. Some benefits would still be subject to the FICA tax, such as 401(k) and 403(b) contributions; however, health premiums, some life premiums, and contributions to flexible spending accounts are exempt from FICA. If certain conditions are met, employer provided meals and lodging may be excluded from an employee's gross income. If meals are furnished (1) by the employer; (2) for the employer's convenience; and (3) provided on the business premises of the employer they may be excluded from the employee's gross income per Section 119(a). In addition, lodging furnished by the employer for its convenience on the business premise of the employer (which the employee is required to accept as a condition of employment) is also excluded from gross income. Importantly, section 119(a) only applies to meals or lodging furnished "in kind." Therefore, cash allowances for meals or lodging received by an employee are included in gross income.

The term "fringe benefits" was coined by the War Labour Board during World War II to describe the various indirect benefits which industry had devised to attract and retain labour when direct wage increases were prohibited.

Employee benefits provided through ERISA are not subject to state-level insurance regulation like most insurance contracts, but employee benefit products provided through insurance contracts are regulated at the state level.

In the UK, Employee Benefits are categorised by three terms: Flexible Benefits (Flex) and Flexible Benefits Packages, Voluntary Benefits and Core Benefits.

Flexible Benefits, usually called a "Flex Scheme", is where employees are allowed to choose how a proportion of their remuneration is paid. Currently around a quarter of UK employers operate such a scheme.. This is normally delivered by allowing employees to sacrifice part of their pre-tax pay in exchange for a car, additional holiday, a shorter working week or other similar benefits, or give up benefits for additional cash remuneration. A number of external consultancies exist that enable organizations to manage Flex packages and they centre around the provision of an Internet or Extranet website where employees can view their current flexible benefit status and make changes to their package. Adoption of flexible benefits has grown considerably over the five years to 2008, with The Chartered Institute of Personnel and Development additionally anticipating a further 12% rise in adoption within 2008/9.. This has coincided with increased employee access to the internet and studies suggesting that employee engagement can be boosted by their successful adoption..

Voluntary Benefits is the name given to a collection of benefits that employees choose to opt-in for and pay for personally. These tend to be schemes such as the government-backed (and therefore tax-efficient) Bike to Work and Childcare Vouchers (Accor Services, Busybees, Sodexho, Fideliti, Kiddi Vouchers, Imagine, Early Years Vouchers Ltd) and also specially arranged discount schemes for employees such as group ISAs. Employee Discount schemes are often setup by employers as a perk of working at the organization. They can be run in house or arranged by an external employee benefits consultant.

Core Benefits is the term given to benefits which all staff enjoy, such as holiday, sick pay and sometimes flexible hours.

In recent years many UK companies have used the tax and national insurance savings gained through the implementation of salary sacrifice benefits to fund the implementation of flexible benefits. In a salary sacrifice arrangement an employee gives up the right to part of the cash remuneration due under their contract of employment. Usually the sacrifice is made in return for the employer's agreement to provide them with some form of non-cash benefit. The most popular types of salary sacrifice benefits include childcare vouchers and pensions.

4

Job Analysis and Satisfaction

Job Analysis is a process of collecting information about a job. The process of job analysis results into two sets of data.

- Job Description
- Job Specification

As a result Job analysis involves the following steps in a logical order.

Steps of Job Analysis:

- Collecting and recording job information
- Checking the job information for accuracy
- Writing job description based on information collected to determine the skills, knowledge, abilities and activities required
- Updating and upgrading this information.

JOB DESIGN

Definition 1: Integration of work, rewards and qualification

"Job Design integrates work content (tasks, functions, relationships), the rewards and qualifications required including skills, knowledge and abilities for each job in a way that meets the needs of employees and the organization."

Steps in Job Design:

- Specification of Individual Tasks
- Specification of Methods of Tasks Performance
- Combination of Tasks into Specific Jobs to be assigned to individuals

Factors affecting Job Design

Organizational factors:

- Characteristics of Tasks (Planning, Execution and Controlling of Task)

- Work Flow (Process Sequences)
- Ergonomics (Time & Motion Study)
- Work Practices (Set of ways of performing tasks)

Environmental Factors:

- Employee Abilities and Availability
- Social and Cultural Expectations

Behavioural Elements:

- Feedback
- Autonomy
- Use of Abilities
- Variety.

JOB ANALYSIS - USES, METHODS

Job Analysis Methods

Though there are several methods of collecting job analysis information yet choosing the one or a combination of more than one method depends upon the needs and requirements of organization and the objectives of the job analysis process. Typically, all the methods focus on collecting the basic job-related information but when used in combination may bring out the hidden or overlooked information and prove to be great tools for creating a perfect job-candidate fit.

Selecting an appropriate job analysis method depends on the structure of the organization, hierarchical levels, nature of job and responsibilities and duties involved in it.

So, before executing any method, all advantages and disadvantages should be analyzed because the data collected through this process serves a great deal and helps organizations cope with current market trends, organizational changes, high attrition rate and many other day-to-day problems.

Let's discuss few of job analysis methods that are commonly used by the organizations to investigate the demands of a specific job.

Job Analysis Methods

Observation Method: A job analyst observes an employee and records all his performed and non-performed task, fulfilled and un-fulfilled responsibilities and duties, methods, ways and skills used by him or her to perform various duties and his or her mental or emotional ability to handle challenges and risks. However, it seems one of the easiest methods to analyze a specific job but truth is that it is the most difficult one. Why? Let's Discover.

It is due to the fact that every person has his own way of observing things. Different people think different and interpret the findings in different ways. Therefore, the process may involve personal biasness or likes and dislikes and may not produce genuine results. This error can be avoided by proper training of job analyst or whoever will be conducting the job analysis process.

This particular method includes three techniques: direct observation, Work Methods Analysis and Critical Incident Technique. The first method includes direct observation and recording of behaviour of an employee in different situations. The second involves the study of time and motion and is specially used for assembly-line or factory workers. The third one is about identifying the work behaviours that result in performance.

Interview Method: In this method, an employee is interviewed so that he or she comes up with their own working styles, problems faced by them, use of particular skills and techniques while performing their job and insecurities and fears about their careers.

This method helps interviewer know what exactly an employee thinks about his or her own job and responsibilities involved in it. It involves analysis of job by employee himself. In order to generate honest and true feedback or collect genuine data, questions asked during the interview should be carefully decided. And to avoid errors, it is always good to interview more than one individual to get a pool of responses. Then it can be generalized and used for the whole group.

Questionnaire Method: Another commonly used job analysis method is getting the questionnaires filled from employees, their superiors and managers. However, this method also suffers from personal biasness. A great care should be takes while framing questions for different grades of employees.

In order to get the true job-related info, management should effectively communicate it to the staff that data collected will be used for their own good. It is very important to ensure them that it won't be used against them in anyway.

If it is not done properly, it will be a sheer wastage of time, money and human resources. These are some of the most common methods of job analysis. However, there are several other specialized methods including task inventory, job element method, competency profiling, technical conference, threshold traits analysis system and a combination of these methods. While choosing a method, HR managers need to consider time, cost and human efforts included in conducting the process.

Why job analysis? (Uses):

Job analysis is useful for overall management of all personnel activities. The same is specified as follows:

1. Human Resource Planning: The estimates the quantity and quality of people will be required in future. How many and what type of people will be required depends on the jobs to be staffed. Job-related information available through job analysis is, therefore, necessary for human resource planning.
2. Recruitment and Selection: Recruitment succeeds job analysis. Basically, the goal of the human resource planning is to match the right people with the right job. This is possible only after having adequate information about the jobs that need to be staffed. It is job analysis that provides job information. Thus, job analysis serves as basis for recruitment and selection of employees in the organisation.
3. Training and Development: Job analysis by providing information about what a job entails i.e., knowledge and skills required to perform a job, enables the management to design the training and development programmes to acquire these job requirements. Employee development programmes like job enlargement, job enrichment, job rotation, etc.
4. Placement and Orientation: As job analysis provides information about what skills and qualities are required to do a job, the management can gear orientation programmes towards helping the employees learn the required skills and qualities. It, thus, helps management place an employee on the job best suited to him/her.
5. Job Evaluation: The job evaluation refers to determination of relative worth of different jobs. It, thus, helps in developing appropriate wage and salary structures. Relative worth is determined mainly on the basis of information provided by job analysis.
6. Performance Appraisal: Performance appraisal involves comparing the actual performance of an employee with the standard one, i.e., what is expected of him/her. Such appraisal or assessment serves as basis for awarding promotions, effecting transfers, or assessing training needs. Job analysis helps in establishing job standards which may be compared with the actual performance/contribution of each employee.

7. Personnel Information: Increasing number of organisations maintain computerised informa-tion about their employees. This is popularly known as Human Resource Information System (HRIS). HRIS is useful as it helps improve administrative efficiency and provides decision support^ Information relating to human resources working in the organisation is provided by job analysis only.
8. Health and Safety: Job analysis helps in identifying and uncovering hazardous conditions and unhealthy environmental factors such as heat, noise, fumes, dust, etc. and, thus, facilitates management to take corrective measures to minimise and avoid the possibility of accidents causing human injury

Process of job analysis

Job analysis is as useful is not so easy to make. In fact, it involves a process. Though there is no fool-proof process of making job analysis, following are the main steps involved in job analysis:

Organisational Job Analysis

Job analysis begins with obtaining pertinent information about a job'. This, according to Terry is required to know the makeup of a job, its relation to other jobs, and its contribution to performance of the organisation. Such information can be had by dividing back-ground information in various forms such as organisation charts i.e., how the particular job is related to other jobs; class specifications i.e., the general requirement of the job family; job description i.e., starting point to build the revised job description, and flow charts i.e., flow of activities involved in a particular job.

Selecting Representative Jobs for Analysis

Analysing all jobs of an organisation is both costly and time consuming. Therefore, only a representative sample of jobs is selected for the purpose of detailed analysis.

Collection of Data for Job Analysis

In this step, job data features of the job and required qualifications of the employee are collected. Data can be collected either through questionnaire, observation or interviews. However, due care should be taken to select and use the method of data collection that is the most reliable in the given situation of the job.

Preparing Job Description

The job information collected in the above ways is now used to prepare a job description. Job description is a written statement that describes the tasks, duties and responsibilities that need to be discharged for effective job performance.

Uses of Job Analysis

A job analysis programme is indispensable part of sound human resource management. The information, generated through job analysis, is used for taking right decisions, related to organization's human resources. It provides useful information for overall management of all the personnel activities. Some of the specific uses of job analysis are given below

1. Organizational Design - Job analysis identifies the job requirements and the interrelationship among jobs. It reveals the contents, tasks, duties and responsibilities at all levels, which help in minimizing duplication or overlapping. Job analysis also provides information for taking sound decisions, concerning hierarchical positions and functional differentiation. This helps in improving the efficiency of the organization.
2. Human Resource Planning- Human resource planning is a process of estimating the manpower needs and developing plans to meet these needs. The main aim of HR planning is to choose the right kind of people for the right job at the right time. For this, the information obtained through job analysis is very essential. Such information helps in accurate determination of the number and types of employees to be recruited or exited from the organization.
3. Recruitment and Selection- Job description and job specification serve as a realistic basis for the recruitment strategy and selection process. For example, job description statement helps in deciding whether the internal or external sources of recruitment are used for filling up a job. Similarly, job specification statement helps in assessing the candidates in the process of selection. Without job analysis, it is not possible to select a right person for a right job.
4. Training and Development- Job analysis provides essential data to an organization, required to assess the training needs of its employees. Job description and job specification provide clear idea of what is required for a job in terms of skills and knowledge. This information helps in determining the level of training that need to be provided to employees. The content, duration and method of training are also decided on the basis of the information procured through job analysis.
5. Performance Appraisal- Performance appraisal is the process of

comparing the actual performance of an employee against what is required. Such comparison serves as a basis for taking various decisions, like, promotion, transfer or training needs. Job analysis helps in setting standards for performance, criteria for evaluation, and the individual's output. On this basis, the actual performance of employees is compared and appraised accordingly.

6. Job Evaluation- Job analysis is useful in determining the relative worth of each job in the organization. A firm can use information, relating to tasks, duties, responsibilities, difficulty level, skill requirements, work environment etc., in developing a proper compensation package for each job.
7. Safety and Health- The process of job analysis reveals hazardous conditions and Unhealthy environmental factors i.e. heat, noise, dust, fumes etc., in various jobs. This information can be used for taking corrective measures to ensure the health and safety of the employees.
8. Industrial Relations- In an organization, grievances and disputes arise due to misunderstanding and disagreement among management and trade unions over job contents. Job analysis provides clear description about the job in terms of skills, knowledge, abilities, qualifications, degree of risk etc. that helps in resolving such disputes. Job analysis information can also be used by management and unions for collective bargaining.
9. Career Planning and Development- The process of job analysis reveals various opportunities in terms of career paths and the jobs available in the organization. With the help of this information, organization and the employees can make efforts for career planning and development.
10. Job Design- In an organization, work design and work methods can be improved with the help of information, provided by job analysis. This helps in improving productivity and enhancing job satisfaction among employees. When the job is redesigned to improve the efficiency and to reduce the cost, it is known as industrial engineering. On the other hand, if it is redesigned to match the efficiency level of employees with that of job, it is known as human engineering

TECHNIQUES OF JOB DESIGN

Work Simplification: Job is simplified or specialized. The job is broken down into small parts and each part is assigned to an individual. To be more specific, work simplification is mechanical pacing of work, repetitive work processes, working only on one part of a product, predetermining tools and techniques, restricting interaction amongst employees, few skills requirement. Work simplification is used when jobs are not specialized.

Job Rotation: When incumbents become bore of routine jobs, job rotation is an answer to it. Here jobs remain unchanged, but the incumbents shift from one job to another. On the positive side, it increases the intrinsic reward potential of a job because of different skills and abilities needed to perform it. Workers become more competent in several jobs, know variety of jobs and improve the self-image, personal growth. Further the worker becomes more valuable to the organization. Periodic job changes can improve interdepartmental cooperation.

On the negative side, it may not be much enthusiastic or efficiency may not be more. Besides jobs may not improve the relationships between task, while activities and objectives remain unchanged. Further training costs also rise and it can also de-motivate intelligent and ambitious trainees who seek specific responsibilities in their chosen specialties.

Job Enlargement: It means expanding the number of tasks, or duties assigned to a given job. Job enlargement is naturally opposite to work simplification. Adding more tasks or duties to a job does not mean that new skills and abilities are needed. There is only horizontal expansion. It is with same skills taking additional responsibilities like extending working hours etc. Job enlargement may involve breaking up of the existing work system and redesigning a new work system. For this employees also need to be trained to adjust to the new system. Job enlargement is said to contribute to employee motivation but the claim is not validated in practice.

Benefits of Job Enlargement:

- Task Variety
- Meaningful Work Modules
- Full Ability Utilization
- Worker Paced Control
- Meaningful Performance Feedback

Disadvantages of Job Enlargement:

- High Training Costs
- Redesigning existing work system required
- Productivity may not increase necessarily
- Workload increases
- Unions demand pay-hike

- Jobs may still remain boring and routine

Job Enrichment: Job enrichment is improvisation of both tasks efficiency and human satisfaction by building into people's jobs, quite specifically, greater scope for personal achievement and recognition, more challenging and responsible work and more opportunity for individual advancement and growth. An enriched job will have more responsibility, more autonomy (vertical enrichment), more variety of tasks (horizontal enrichment) and more growth opportunities. The employee does more planning and controlling with less supervision but more self-evaluation. In other words, transferring some of the supervisor's tasks to the employee and making his job enriched.

Benefits of Job Enrichment

- It benefits employee and organization in terms of increased motivation, performance, satisfaction, job involvement and reduced absenteeism.
- Additional features in job meet certain psychological needs of jobholders due to skill variety, identity, significance of job etc.
- It also adds to employee self-esteem and self-control.
- Job enrichment gives status to jobholder and acts as a strong satisfier in one's life.
- Job enrichment stimulates improvements in other areas of organization.
- Empowerment is a by-product of job enrichment. It means passing on more authority and responsibility.

Demerits of Job Enrichment

- Lazy employees may not be able to take additional responsibilities and power. It won't fetch the desired results for an employee who is not attentive towards his job.
- Unions resistance, increased cost of design and implementation and limited research on long term effect of job enrichment are some of the other demerits.
- Job enrichment itself might not be a great motivator since it is job-intrinsic factor. As per the two-factor motivation theory, job enrichment is not enough. It should be preceded by hygienic factors etc.
- Job enrichment assumes that workers want more responsibilities and those workers who are motivated by less responsibility, job enrichment surely de-motivates them

- Workers participation may affect the enrichment process itself.
- Change is difficult to implement and is always resisted as job enrichment brings in a changes the responsibility.

Autonomous of Self-Directed Teams: Empowerment results in self-directed work teams. A self -directed team is an intact group of employees responsible for whole work segment, they work together, handle day-to-day problems, plan and control, and are highly effective teams.

High Performance Work Design: Improving performance in an environment where positive and demanding goals are set leads to high performance work design. It starts from the principle of autonomous groups working and developing an approach, which enables group to work effectively together in situations where the rate of innovation is very high.

Operational flexibility is important and there is the need for employees to gain and apply new skills quickly with minimum supervision. However due to bureaucracy high performance work design does not work.

JOB EVALUATION

Job Evaluation involves determination of relative worth of each job for the purpose of establishing wage and salary differentials. Relative worth is determined mainly on the basis of job description and job specification only. Job Evaluation helps to determine wages and salary grades for all jobs. Employees need to be compensated depending on the grades of jobs which they occupy. Remuneration also involves fringe benefits, bonus and other benefits. Clearly remuneration must be based on the relative worth of each job. Ignoring this basic principle results in inequitable compensation. A perception of inequity is a sure way of de-motivating an employee. Job evaluation is a process of analyzing and assessing the various jobs systematically to ascertain their relative worth in an organization.

Jobs are evaluated on the basis of content, placed in order of importance. This establishes Job Hierarchies, which is a purpose of fixation of satisfactory wage differentials among various jobs.

SCOPE OF JOB EVALUATION

The job evaluation is done for the purpose of wage and salary differentials, demand for and supply of labour, ability to pay, industrial parity, collective bargaining and the like.

Process of Job Evaluation:

- Defining objectives of job evaluation
  - Identify jobs to be evaluated (Benchmark jobs or all jobs)

- Who should evaluate job?
- What training do the evaluators need?
- How much time involved?
- What are the criteria for evaluation?
- Methods of evaluation to be used

- Wage Survey
- Employee Classification
- Establishing wage and salary differentials.

METHODS OF JOB EVALUATION

Analytical Methods

- *Point Ranking Methods*: Different factors are selected for different jobs with accompanying differences in degrees and points. Factor Comparison Method: The important factors are selected which can be assumed to be common to all jobs. Each of these factors are then ranked with other jobs. The worth of the job is then taken by adding together all the point values.

Non-Analytical Methods

- *Ranking Method*: Jobs are ranked on the basis of its title or contents. Job is not broken down into factors etc.
- *Job Grading Method*: It is based on the job as a whole and the differentiation is made on the basis of job classes and grades. In this method it is important to form a grade description to cover discernible differences in skills, responsibilities and other characteristics.

Pitfalls of Job Evaluation:

- Encourages employees on how to advance in position when there may be limited opportunities for enhancement as a result of downsizing.
- It promotes internal focus instead of customer orientation
- Not suitable for forward looking organizations, which has trimmed multiple job titles into two or three broad jobs.

PURPOSE OF JOB ANALYSIS

- *Human Resource Planning (HRP)*: The numbers and types of personnel are determined by the jobs, which need to be staffed. Job related information in the form of Job Analysis serves this purpose or use.

- *Recruitment & Selection*: Recruitment precedes job analysis. It helps HR to locate places to obtain employees. It also helps in better continuity and planning in staffing in the organization. Also selecting a good candidate also requires detailed job information. Because the objective of hiring is to match the right candidate for right job
- *Training & Development*: Training and development programmes can be designed depending upon job requirement and analysis. Selection of trainees is also facilitated by job analysis.
- *Job Evaluation*: Job evaluation means determination of relative worth of each job for the purpose of establishing wage and salary credentials. This is possible with the help of job description and specifications; i.e. Job Analysis.
- *Remuneration*: Job analysis also helps in determining wage and salary for all jobs.
- *Performance Appraisal*: Performance appraisal, assessments, rewards, promotions, is facilitated by job analysis by way of fixing standards of job performance.
- *Personnel Information*: Job analysis is vital for building personnel information systems and processes for improving administrative efficiency and providing decision support.
- *Safety & Health*: Job Analysis helps to uncover hazardous conditions and unhealthy environmental factors so that corrective measures can be taken to minimize and avoid possibility of human injury.

JOB DESCRIPTION

"Job Description implies objective listing of the job title, tasks, and responsibilities involved in a job." Job description is a word picture in writing of the duties, responsibilities and organizational relationships that constitutes a given job or position.

It defines continuing work assignment and a scope of responsibility that are sufficiently different from those of the other jobs to warrant a specific title. Job description is a broad statement of purpose, scope, duties and responsibilities of a particular job.

Contents of Job Description:

- Job Identification
- Job Summary
- Job Duties and Responsibilities
- Supervision specification
- Machines, tools and materials

- Work conditions
- Work hazards
- Definition of unusual terms

Format of Job Description:

- Job Title
- Region/Location
- Department
- Reporting to (Operational and Managerial)
- Objective
- Principal duties and responsibilities

Features of Good Job Description:

- Up to date
- Proper Job Title
- Comprehensive Job Summary
- Clear duties and responsibilities
- Easily understandable
- State job requirements
- Specify reporting relationships
- Showcase degrees of difficulties
- Indicates opportunities for career development
- Offer bird's-eye-view of primary responsibilities

Job Specifications

"Job Specification involves listing of employee qualifications, skills and abilities required to meet the job description. These specifications are needed to do job satisfactorily." In other words it is a statement of minimum and acceptable human qualities necessary to perform job properly. Job specifications seeks to indicate what kind of persons may be expected to most closely approximate the role requirements and thus it is basically concerned with matters of selection, screening and placement and is intended to serve as a guide in hiring.

Contents of Job Specifications:

- Physical Characteristics
- Psychological characteristics
- Personal characteristics
- Responsibilities
- Demographic features

Further the job specifications can be divided into three broad categories:

1. Essential Attributes
2. Desirable Attributes
3. Contra-Indicators - indicators hampering the success of job

PROCESS OF JOB ANALYSIS

- *Process 1*: Strategic Choices
- *Process 2*: Collecting Information
- *Process 3*: Processing Information
- *Process 4*: Job Description
- *Process 5*: Job Specification
- *Strategic Choices*:

Extent of involvement of employees: Extent of employee involvement is a debatable point. Too much involvement may result in bias in favor of a job in terms of inflating duties and responsibilities. Too less involvement leads to suspicion about the motives behind the job. Besides it may also lead to inaccurate information. Hence extent of involvement depends on the needs of the organization and employee.

Level of details of job analysis: The nature of jobs being analysed determines the level of details in job analysis. If the purpose were for training programmes or assessing the worth of job, levels of details required would be great. If the purpose is just clarification the details required would be less.

Timing and frequency of Job Analysis: When do you do Job Analysis?

- Initial stage, for new organization
- New Job is created
- Changes in Job, Technology and Processes
- Deficiencies and Disparities in Job
- New compensation plan is introduced
- Updating and upgrading is required.

Past-oriented and future-oriented Job Analysis: For rapidly changing organization more future oriented approach would be desired. For traditional organizations past oriented analysis would be required. However more future oriented analysis may be derived based on past data.

Types of Data for Job Analysis:

- Work Activities (Tasks details)
- Interface with other jobs and equipments (Procedures, Behaviours, Movements)

- Machines, Tools, Equipments and Work Aids (List, Materials, Products, Services)
- Job Context (Physical, Social, Organizational, Work schedule)
- Personal Requirement (Skills, Education, Training, Experience)

Methods of Data Collection:

- Observation
- Interview
- Questionnaires
- Checklists
- Technical Conference
- Diary Methods

Who to Collect Data?

- Trained Job Analysts
- Supervisors
- Job Incumbents

Processing Information: Once the job information is collected it needs to be processed, so that it would be useful in various personnel functions. Specifically job related data would be useful to prepare job description and specifications, which form the next two processes of job analysis.

JOB SATISFACTION

Job satisfaction is the result of various attitudes possessed by an employee towards his job, related factors and life in general. The attitudes related to job may be wages, supervision, steadiness, working conditions, advancement opportunities, recognitions, fair evaluation of work, social relations on job, prompt settlement of grievances etc. In short job satisfaction is a general attitude, which is the result of many specific attitudes in three areas namely, job factors, individual characteristics and group relationships outside the job.

Components of Job Satisfaction

Personal factors: Sex, Dependents, Age, Timings, Intelligence, Education and Personality.

Job inherent factors: Type of work, Skills, Occupational status, Geography, Size of plant.

Management controlled factors: Security, Payment, Fringe benefits, Advancement opportunities and Working conditions, Co-workers, Responsibilities, Supervision Job Satisfaction & Behaviour relationship is described through following examples.

- Satisfaction & Turnover
- Satisfaction & Absenteeism
- Satisfaction & Accidents
- Satisfaction & Job Performance

Work Sampling

Definition 1: Measuring and quantifying activities"A measurement technique for the quantitative analysis of non-repetitive or irregularly occurring activity."

Meaning of Work Sampling Work sampling is based on the theory that the percentage of the number of observations on a particular activity is a reliable measure of the percentage of the total actual time spent on that activity.Work sampling operates by an observer taking a series of random observations on a particular "thing" of interest (machine, operating room, dock, etc.) to observe its "state" (working, idle, sleeping, empty, etc.). When enough samples are taken, an analysis of the observations yields a statistically valid indication of the states for each thing analysed. Assume, for example, that you wish to determine the proportion of time a factory operator is working or idle. Also assume that 200 random observations were made of the operator and during 24 of these he or she was observed to be idle. Therefore, you find that the individual is working 176/200 = 88% of the time.Advantages of Work SamplingIt is relatively inexpensive to use and extremely helpful in providing a deeper understanding of all types of operations. When properly used, it can help pinpoint those areas, which should be analysed in, further detail and can serve as a measure of the progress being made in improving operations

Questions of work sampling study

- What is our equipment/asset utilization?
- When we are not adding value to the product, how are we spending our time?
- How are our inter-dependent systems performing?
- Where should we focus our continuous improvement activities?

Distinction between Work sampling and "Time Studies"

- Work sampling is lower cost because it uses random samples instead of continuous observations.
- Many operators or machines can be studied by a single observer
- Work sampling can span several days or weeks, thus minimizing the effects of day to day load or equipment variations

- Work Sampling tends to minimize operator behaviour modification during observation.
- Work Sampling, in general, does not require a trained time-study analyst to take the observations. Also, stopwatches or other timing devices are not required. Many studies make use of off-shift technicians or operators to take the observations. Work sampling Methodology

An analyst RANDOMLY observes an activity (equipment, operating room, production line) and notes the particular states of the activity at each observation.

The ratio of the number of observations of a given state of the activity to the total number of observations taken will approximate the percentage of time that the activity is in that given state.

Note that random observations are very critical for a work sampling study. A brief example might be that 77 of 100 observations showed a machine to be running. We might then conclude, within certain statistical limits, that the equipment is operational 77% of the time.

JOB DESCRIPTION & JOB SPECIFICATIONS

Job Specification

A brief description of these follows:

Job Description

Job description is prepared on the basis of data collected through job analysis. Job description is a functional description of the contents what the job entails. It is a narration of the contents of a job. It is a description of the activities and duties to be performed in a job, the relationship of the job with other jobs, the equipment and tools involved, the nature of supervision, working conditions and hazards of the job and so on.

All major categories of jobs need to be spelled out in clear and compre-hensive manner to determine the qualifications and skills required to perform a job. Thus, job descrip-tion differentiates one job from the other. In sum, job description is a written statement of what a job holder does, how it is done, and why it is done.

Purposes of Job Description

Job description is done for fulfilling the following purposes:

1. Grading and classification of jobs

2. Placement and Orientation of new employees
3. Promotions and transfers
4. Outlining for career path
5. Developing work standards
6. Counselling of employees
7. Delimitation of authority.

Job Specification

While job description focuses on the job, job specification focuses on the person i.e, the job holder. Job specification is a statement of the minimum levels of qualifications, skills, physical and other abilities, experience, judgment and attributes required for performing job effectively. In other words, it is a statement of the minimum acceptable qualifications that an incumbent must possess to perform a given job. It sets forth the knowledge, skills and abilities required to do the job effectively.

Usages of Job Specification: The usages of job specification include:

1. Personnel planning
2. Performance appraisal
3. Hiring
4. Training and development
5. Job evaluation and compensation
6. Health and safety
7. Employee discipline
8. Work scheduling
9. Career planning.

5

Performance and Appraisal

HUMAN RESOURCE PROFESSIONALS

Human resource professionals in all areas of human resource management — training and development, recruiting and hiring, wage and salary administration, and so on — are in a unique position in most organizations. They are concerned specifically with making the personnel resource more productive. Consequently, human resource professionals should play a role in bringing about productivity improvement by challenging the existing way of doing things. They need to get both line managers and operational employees to think about their effectiveness and productivity. Human resource professionals should be the catalysts that challenge the status quo.

One of your authors once worked with a large electrical utility, which was striving to adjust and become more competitive under deregulation. Regulated utilities tend to prefer the status quo and established routines. When deregulation hits regulated industries, it is very difficult to get people to change behaviour. They are comfortable with the old behaviour, yet it soon becomes evident that new forms of behaviour are required to survival in a newly competitive environment. These companies face this critical question: How can we get our managers and employees to re-examine their present work routines, question those that need to be changed, and establish new more effective and productive behaviors?

In this electrical utility the personnel manager and training and development director established a series of workshops that examined the essential management skills of planning, problem-solving, communication, and leadership. In a seminar format, groups of managers were asked to review and evaluate their performance of these skills. Imagery exercises were used to help with the evaluation and with establishing new work routines using these skills. As a result of this nine-month programme, a new strategic planning and a new performance appraisal process were adopted.

The significant aspect about this example is that the questioning or unfreezing of behaviour was initiated by the two key human resource professionals in the company. Of course they had to sell the president on the idea of change. Once the CEO was sold, however, other managers accepted the need for the examination and change. Catalytic involvement of human resource professionals in the change and productivity enhancement process puts a new slant on an old technique known as organizational development.

Integrating human resource professionals into the productivity enhancement efforts of companies by using imagery ties both imagery and organisation change and development efforts to the bottom line of productivity enhancement. Since the practice of imagery is skill-specific, emphasis is placed on improving various work routines so that new (and more productive) skills can be practiced. In basketball a free-throw shooter who hits nine out of ten throws is more efficient and productive than one who hits six out of ten. By the same token, a manager who conducts an effective, worthwhile performance appraisal interview contributes more to organizational productivity than one who bumbles through such an interview. Imagery enhances managerial skill in conducting such an interview, and human resource professionals enhance the use of imagery.

Productivity Catalysts

The first step is achieving and maintaining credibility. Human resource professionals will not be listened to unless they are viewed as a credible source of ideas. This is not the place to go into methods to enhance credibility. However, by properly using techniques that work — such as imagery — credibility can be enhanced. The second step is appropriateness. Imagery should be suggested only for areas where appropriate. These are areas of management that are skill-specific and exist where skill enhancement will improve productivity. Imagery, like any management technique, is not a panacea.

The third step is articulateness. Imagery, as a technique to enhance productivity, must be presented in a clear, straightforward manner. Enhancing productivity and the bottom line, rather than making people feel good, must be stressed; backup documentation illustrating such productivity successfully enhancing sports, counseling, and business should be presented.

The fourth step is patience. To many people, imagery sounds like a far-out method. Of course it is not, but patience is required when explaining the technique over and over again. Fifth, follow up is necessary from two standpoints. First, in selling the idea, and second, in evaluating its results. It may be necessary to offer the suggestion several times when selling the idea before the organisation decides to buy it because the initial reaction is often one of unfamiliarity and skepticism. After imagery sessions are conducted, follow-up evaluation as to its effectiveness must be conducted. This includes participant evaluations immediately at the conclusion of a session as well as evaluations several weeks later to see if the technique is being used and if it is enhancing productivity. Success breeds success so it is especially important that the initial sessions go well. This means careful planning and script writing as well as rehearsal on the facilitator's part. Finally, and perhaps most important, the CEO and corporate officers must eventually be sold on the idea and become visible role models. Noel Tichy et al. point out that no fundamental change in a corporation's approach to business will likely occur until these individuals become involved. He describes how training has been used successfully at General Electric to bring about changes in leadership styles. Tichy et al. reason that most corporations support benign management development activities out of fear that truly effective programmes will create leaders who will rock the boat. Corporations encourage survivalist cultures. Any radical change could result in the people in power losing their jobs. Consequently, getting the people in charge to support any new programme is essential. By being credible, articulate, using appropriate imagery applications, and by practicing patience and follow-up, human resource professionals can win this support.

Holistic Management

Since World War II, managers of organizations have been drilled in the hard, quantitative issues of managing. Subjects such as finance, economics, operations research, simulation, and so on have dominated business school curricula both at the credit and non-credit levels. The soft issues of values, culture, vision, and human relations have not received so much rigorous attention. These soft areas are harder to teach and learn. They are difficult to quantify and research in a systematic way compared to the hard areas. This overemphasis on the hard issues has highly rationalized business decision making and management.

The overemphasis on quantification of variables ignores those elements that do not lend themselves to easy quantification. Yet it is precisely these elements of vision and values that a true leader exemplifies. Achieving this holistic management approach is necessary to improve productivity. Emphasizing the quantitative measures at the expense of the soft measures is a left-sided approach. A holistic approach that uses the whole brain is needed instead. Imagery is a systematic way to engage the right side of the brain to achieve this holism. The argument is not to replace the hard with the soft, but to use both. Imagery supplements but does not supplant rigorous, logical analysis.

Let's look at some examples. First, consider a plant location decision. This decision lends itself to a high level of quantification. Land costs and taxes, prevailing wage rates, transportation costs, road configurations, construction and leasing costs, delivery times, port and rail capacities, cost-of-living indexes all can be quantified. Yet some of the most important factors cannot. These include quality of schools and neighborhoods, the cultural environment, the quality of the work force, and other issues such as restaurants, shopping, community spirit, traffic congestion, climate, and so on. Yet these so called soft factors have as much to do with a plant location decision as do the hard factors. So the dilemma involves how to systematically consider these factors.

To some extent they can be quantified. Funding spent on education, mean high and low temperatures, and the number of restaurants and malls in the community all help to give a picture of many of the soft variables. But the use of imagery can add to the understanding of these variables. For example, people who will be asked to move to the new plant can be asked to imagine what it would be like to live in different cities under consideration. A script of living a typical day in Atlanta could be compared with that of Denver, Tallahassee, Little Rock, or Minneapolis if those are the cities under consideration for the new facility. This will enable the people to vicariously experience a typical day in the new city helping them to better understand what it would be like to live there. (Of course this should be a realistic presentation of a typical day, rather than a chamber of commerce city promotion.)

Another example where imagery can be useful in helping to understand an event from a more holistic view is in employment recruiting and selection. Much has been written about realistic job previews where job applicants are given a more balanced picture of working in a particular job. Typically, the employer only presents positive aspects of employment to job candidates while ignoring the negative. In a realistic job preview both are presented. Of course there are many quantitative factors that are presented to a job applicant: wage or salary, vacation days, holidays, sick leave, insurance benefits, seniority rights, production or sales standards, and so on. But many important factors in weighing a job decision cannot be quantified.

This is where imagery applies. It can be used to highlight such important but non-quantitative issues as job pressure, potential job satisfaction, corporate culture, job morale factors, job duties, and other important hard to quantify factors. This will help the candidate decide if the job is right for him or her. Here is an example of how imagery can be used to provide a realistic job preview for a cook in a restaurant:

You will be working under the supervision of Chef Vito along with three other cooks. Your job will be to cook all of the sautéed dishes on a gas stove. All of our dinners are prepared fresh to order so this means you will sauté items freshly prepared, not frozen. The pace of your work will depend on the pace at which the prep cook can prepare the items. His work is determined by the number of sautéed items turned in by the waiters with their orders.

The kitchen is hot and crowded. Six of you will be working in a ten-by-twenty-five-foot space. There is much movement as all the cooks work very quickly to fill and put up orders, From 7 P.M. to 9:30 P.M. the pace is especially hectic. People yell for items, grab items, rub shoulders. The floor becomes wet and slightly slippery. Steam rises off the water bottles. Even with adequate ventilation, the temperature will rise to 90 degrees in the winter and to 105 degrees in the summer. The humidity usually runs at 90 percent. Under these circumstances Chef Vito will yell at you to perform various duties. He may even call you names.

You are expected to clean up the kitchen once the restaurant closes. This means washing large pots and pans, wiping down counters, mopping the floor, and emptying garbage. Even though you will work five evenings per week, you may be expected to come in on an off night at very short notice if one of the other cooks takes ill or is otherwise unable to come in. Sometimes you will need to work when we are short-handed with help in the kitchen and will need to double up with your duties so as to help others. This means, for example, that from time to time you will need to do your own prep.

The above script gives a potential job applicant a pretty clear idea of what the job is like. Some people disagree with using a realistic job preview such as this by arguing that it makes the job more difficult to fill. Yet it is better to fill the job with someone who has clear expectations and knows what to expect than to fill it with someone who does not know what to expect and cannot work under the job conditions. It is better to hire someone who will stay at the job and perform the duties than to hire someone who quits or has to be fired. Both a disgruntled employee and the turnover rate are very expensive for any organisation.

Let's look at one final example where mental imagery can be used to supplement quantitative analytical techniques in order to achieve a holistic approach. One area of significant research for most companies is consumer or market behaviour. Systematic research of market and consumer behaviour is a must today for any company that wishes to remain competitive. Even governmental agencies, such as the city of Tallahassee, annually conduct resident opinion surveys both to assess citizen evaluation of government services and to obtain input on future services.

Market and consumer research is highly quantitative and well it should be. A host of demographic factors for a market or potential market can readily be obtained today from the U.S. Census Bureau, private demographic companies, or original survey research conducted by the company or consultant.

These demographics include such easily qualified factors as age, gender breakdown, median family income, family size, occupational breakdown, educational level, neighborhood location, and so on. Even such factors as number of automobiles owned, number of bathrooms, ownership of particular appliances such as televisions or VCRs can be obtained. But what is more difficult to quantify are the psychological and social reasons why people buy or don't buy a product. These often are as important if not more so than the easily measurable demographics.

While is true that demographics are often used to represent psychological factors (*e.g.*, families with teenagers have a need for saving for a college education), actual measurement of psychological factors can be difficult. How do you measure a person's need for luxury or status in making an automobile purchase decision? Self-report measures are used (*e.g.*, "rank your need for status on a one-to-five scale"), but these have many inherent biases and inaccuracies. Indirect measurements are also sometimes used (*e.g.*, "rank the factors in order of importance that most people consider in buying a new car"), but these may not apply to the motivation of the particular respondent. Therefore, imagery can be used to help get a better picture of market and consumer behaviour. We have used imagery in two different ways to help better understand consumer behaviour. First, we have asked representative sample groups of present or potential consumers of a certain product to experience an imagery session. Second, we have asked key decision makers to experience an imagery script from the point of view of the customer. Let's look at each of these scripts. First, let's consider the script that we used with key decision makers of a mail order catalogue house. The objective of this script was an attempt to get them to see their product and service from the eyes of the customer. Go through the script after a relaxation excercise.

Company Key Decision Makers

Now imagine that you are a woman who has just arrived home from work at about 5:30 P.M.. You pull the mail out of your mail box. As you glance through it, you notice a couple of bills, a letter from an old friend and two catalogues. One of the catalogues is from ___. You casually look at the cover of each catalogue and place them along with the rest of the mail on the kitchen counter. As you hang up your coat, put away your purse, and change into something more comfortable, you think about fixing dinner. But first you read the letter from the old friend and place the other mail, including the catalogues, on an end table.

You fix and eat dinner, and later that evening pick up the catalogues. (As a regular catalogue shopper, you receive an average of two or three catalogues a week and usually look through them.) As you glance at the pictures of the fashions in the ______ catalogue, you admire how nice the clothes look on the models. You casually wonder about price, ordering information, refund policy, etc.

The phone rings and you answer it after placing the catalogue down on the sofa. Soon after the telephone call, one of your favourite TV shows comes on, so you watch it. While watching it you glance again at the catalogue. You see something you might want to order but your attention is distracted by the television. At that point your husband arrives home from work late and wants to talk with you about his day. You close the catalogue and place it in the magazine rack with about a dozen other catalogues.

Okay, come back to the present. take a few minutes to jot down the observations you have that would help your company better make a sale to that particular person.

The above script experience attempts to place the executives of the company in the actual position of the customers, including the context of the situation in which the customer considers the product. Too often key decision makers of a company lose sight of what it feels like to be a customer. Imagery can help them to live that experience vicariously. In the example above, as a result of the imagery experience, the catalogue company decided to do the following:

- Make a brightly covered catalogue;
- Place ordering information and a toll free number on the front and back of the catalogue;
- Follow up with a post card mailing one week after mailing the catalogue to remind the customer to relook at the catalogue.

Now, let's look at how imagery can be used to achieve a more holistic approach in understanding the consumer, only this time using a customer focus group. In this case we used a representative cross-sample of eighteen customers of a major bank. After explaining the purposes of our research and putting them through a relaxation exercise, we used the following imagery script:

Focus Group Script

Imagine that you are driving in your car on your way home from work when you realise that you still have several checks in your wallet that you have forgotten to deposit this week. You wish to deposit these checks and keep a portion in the form of cash. Immediately you think of the location of the bank you usually patronize as well as both close by branches and Automatic Teller Machines (ATMs). As you decide to drive to your normal banking location, what do you think about?

Once you arrive at the bank, you notice long lines at the drivethrough bays so you pull into the lot and park. You then leave your car and walk into the lobby. What do you think about now? While standing in line you notice a sign advertising a home equity line of credit (second mortgage) account. Does this interest you? Why or why not?

Finally, you have your turn at the teller window. What comes into your mind as the teller greets you? You finish your transaction and turn to walk out of the lobby. How do you feel? Do you decide to investigate the home equity account now? At a later time? Never? You notice the ATM as you leave the bank and think about using it next time. You also hope the drive-through lines are not so long. You also consider banking by mail.

As you get into your car, start it, and begin to leave the parking area, what are your thoughts about your banking experience? Please jot down all ideas that come to mind.

This script resulted in several findings for the bank.

- ATMs were not conveniently located.
- Customers were afraid the ATM would make a mistake.
- Customers dreaded the crowded traffic and parking in and around the bank.
- Customers disliked the long lines at teller windows and had difficulty choosing the right line.
- Customers did not want to take the time to learn more about home equity accounts when they made a routine visit to the bank.

As a result of these findings, the bank made several changes in its ATM locations, parking configuration, hours of operation, and teller line queuing.

Both of these examples on how imagery can better help a company understand the customer show that imagery can do much to supplement the hard data gathered about a firm's customers or clients.

GOALS OF PERFORMANCE ASSESSMENT

Conducting performance assessments on employee's performance should be more than a simple checklist of Do's and Don'ts. Performance evaluation should serve as a vital component, one that is of interest to both the organization and the employee. From the organizational perspective, sound performance assessments can ensure that correct work is being done, work that assists in meeting department goals simply put.

Each employee's work should support the activities needed to action his or her supervisor's performance objectives. This should ultimately continue up the hierarchy, with all efforts supporting corporate strategic goals. From the employee perspective, properly operating performance assessment systems provide a clear communication of work expectations. Knowing what is expected is a first step in helping one to cope better with the stress usually associated with a lack of clear direction. Secondly, properly designed performance assessments should also serve as a means of assisting an employee's personal development. To make effective performance assessments a reality, four criteria need to be present.

These are:

- Employees should be actively involved in the evaluation and development process.
- Supervisors need to enter performance assessments with a constructive and helpful attitude.
- Realistic goals must be mutually set.
- Supervisors must be aware, and have knowledge of the employee's job and performance.

OBJECTIVES OF PERFORMANCE ASSESSMENT

Performance assessment has a number of specific objectives:

- To review past performance;
- To assess training needs;
- To help develop individuals;
- To audit the skills within an organizations;
- To set targets for future performance;

- To identify potential for promotion.

Some employees may believe that performance assessment is simply used by the organization to apportion blame and to provide a basis for disciplinary action. They see it as a stick that management has introduced with which to beat people. Under such situations a well thought out performance assessment is doomed to failure. Even if the more positive objectives are built into the system, problems may still arise because they may not all be achievable and they may cause conflict. For example, an appraise is less likely to be open about any shortcomings in past performance during a process that affects pay or promotion prospects, or which might be perceived as leading to disciplinary action. It is therefore important that performance assessment should have specific objective.

Not only should the objectives be clear but also they should form part of the organization's whole strategy. Thus incorporating objectives into the assessment system may highlight areas for improvement, new directions and opportunities.

CONCEPT OF PERFORMANCE ASSESSMENT

What is Performance?

What does the term performance actually mean? Employees are performing well when they are productive. Productivity implies both concern for effectiveness and efficiency, effectiveness refers to goal accomplishment. However it does not speak of the costs incurred in reaching the goal.

That is where efficiency comes in. Efficiency evaluates the ratio of inputs consumed to outputs achieved. The greater the output for a given input, the greater the efficiency. It is not desirable to have objective measures of productivity such as hard data on effectiveness, number of parts produced, or per cent of crimes solved etc. and hard data on efficiency (average cost per part or ratio of sales volume to number of calls made etc.). In addition to productivity as measured in terms of effectiveness and efficiency, performance also includes personnel data such as measures of accidents, turnover, absences, and tardiness. That is a good employee is one who not only performs well in terms of productivity but also minimizes problems for the organisation by being to work on time, by not missing days, and by minimizing the number of work-related accidents.

What is Assessment?

Assessments are judgments of the characteristics, traits and performance of others. On the basis of these judgments we assess the worth or value of others and identify what is good or bad. In industry performance assessment is a systematic evaluation of employees by supervisors. Employees also wish to know their position in the organization.

Assessments are essential for making many administrative decisions: selection, training, promotion, transfer, wage and salary administration etc. Besides they aid in personnel research. Performance Assessment thus is a systematic and objective way of judging the relative worth of ability of an employee in performing his task. Performance assessment helps to identify those who are performing their assigned tasks well and those who are not and the reasons for such performance.

PERFORMANCE ASSESSMENT METHODS

This part looks at how management can actually establish performance standards and devise instruments that can be used to measure and appraise an employee's performance. A number of methods are now available to assess the performance of the employees.

Critical Incident Method

Critical incident assessment focuses the rater's attention on those critical or key behaviours that make the difference between doing a job effectively and doing it ineffectively. What the appraiser does is write down little anecdotes that describe what the employee did that was especially effective or ineffective. In this approach to assessment, specific behaviours are cited, not vaguely defined personality traits. A behaviourally based assessment such as this should be more valid than trait-based assessments because it is clearly more job related.

It is one thing to say that an employee is "aggressive" or "imaginative" or "relaxed," but that does not tell anything about how well the job is being done. Critical incidents, with their focus on behaviours, judge performance rather than personalities. Additionally, a list of critical incidents on a given employees provides a rich set of examples from which the employee can be shown which of his or her behaviours are desirable and which ones call for improvement.

This method suffers from following two drawbacks:

1. Supervisors are reluctant to write these reports on a daily or even weekly basis for all of their subordinates as it is time consuming and burdensome for them
2. Critical incidents do not lend themselves to quantification. Therefore the comparison and ranking of subordinates is difficult.

Checklist

In the checklist, the evaluator uses a bit of behavioural descriptions and checks of those behaviours that apply to the employee. The evaluator merely goes down the list and gives "yes" or "no" responses. Once the checklist is complete, it is usually evaluated by the staff of personnel department, not the rater himself.

Therefore the rater does not actually evaluate the employee's performance; he/she merely records it. An analyst in the personnel department then scores the checklist, often weighting the factors in relationship to their importance. The final evaluation can then be returned to the rating manager for discussion with the subordinate, or someone from the personnel department can provide the feedback to the subordinate.

Graphic Rating Scale

One of the oldest and most popular methods of assessment is the graphic rating scale. They are used to assess factors such as quantity and quality of work, job knowledge, cooperation, loyalty, dependability, attendance, honesty, integrity, attitudes, and initiative etc.

However, this method is most valid when abstract traits like loyalty or integrity are avoided unless they can be defined in more specific behavioural terms. The assessor goes down the list of factors and notes that point along the scale or continuum that list of factors and notes that point along the scale or continuum that best describes the employee. There are typically five to ten points on the continuum. In the design of the graphic scale, the challenge is to ensure that both the factors evaluated and the scale pints are clearly understood and unambiguous to the rater. Should ambiguity occur, bias is introduced.

Following are some of the advantages of this method:

- They are less time-consuming to develop and administer.
- They permit quantitative analysis.
- There is greater standardization of items so comparability with other individuals in diverse job categories is possible.

Forced Choice Method

The forced choice assessment is a special type of checklist, but the rater has to choose between two or more statements, all of which may be favourable or unfavourable. The appraiser's job is to identify which statement is most (or in some cases least) descriptive of the individual being evaluated. To reduce bias, the right answers are not known to the rater. Someone in the personnel department scores the answers based on the key. This key should be validated so management is in a position to say that individuals with higher scores are better-performing employees.

The major advantages of the forced choice method are:

- Since the appraiser does not know the "right" answers, it reduces bias.
- It looks at over all performance.
- It is based on the behaviour of the employees.

Behaviourally Anchored Rating Scales

These scales combine major elements from the critical incident and graphic rating scale approaches. The appraiser rates the employees based on items along continuum, but the points are examples of actual behaviour on the given job rather than general descriptions or traits. Behaviourally anchored rating scales specify definite, observable, and measurable job behaviour. Examples of job-related behaviour and performance dimensions are generated by asking participants to give specific illustrations on effective and ineffective behaviour regarding each performance dimension. These behavioural examples are then retranslated into appropriate performance dimensions. Those that are sorted into the dimension for which they were generated are retained. The final group of behaviour incidents are then numerically scaled to a level of performance that each is perceived to represent.

The incidents that are retranslated and have high rater agreement on performance effectiveness are retained for use as anchors on the performance dimension. The results of the processes are behavioural descriptions, such as anticipates, plans, executes, solves immediate problems, carries out orders, and handles emergency situations.

This method has following advantages:

- It does tend to reduce rating errors.
- It assesses behaviour over traits.
- It clarifies to both the employee and rater which behaviours connote good performance and which connote bad.

Group Order Ranking

The group order ranking requires the evaluator to place employees into a particular classification, such as "top one-fifth" or "second one-fifth".

Evaluators are asked to rank the employees in the top 5 per cent, the next 5 per cent, the next 15 per cent.

So if a rater has twenty subordinates, only four can be in the top fifth and, of course, four must also be relegated to the bottom fifth.

The advantage of this method is that it prevent raters from inflating their evaluations so everyone looks good or from homogenizing the evaluations for everyone is rated near the average outcome that are usual with the graphic rating scale.

It has following disadvantages:

- It is not good if the number of employee being compared is small. At the extreme, if the evaluator is looking at only four employees, it is very possible that they may all be excellent, yet the evaluator may be forced to rank them into top quarter, second quarter, third quarter, and low quarter!
- Another disadvantage, which plagues all relative measures, is the "zero-sum game": consideration. This means, any change must add up to zero. For example, if there are twelve employees in a department performing at different levels of effectiveness, by definition, three are in the top quarter, three in the second quarter, and so forth. The sixth-best employee, for instance, would be in the second quartile. Ironically, if two of the workers in the third or fourth quartiles leave the department and are not replaced, then our sixth best employee now fit into the third quarter.
- Because comparison are relative, an employee who is mediocre may score high only because he or she is the "best of the worst". Similarly, an excellent performer who is matched against "stiff" competition may be evaluated poorly, when in absolute terms his or her performance is outstanding.

Individual Ranking

The individual ranking method requires the evaluator merely to list all the employees in an order from highest to lowest. Only one can be the "best". If the evaluator is required to appraise thirty individuals ranking method carries the same pluses and minuses as group order ranking.

Paired Comparison

The paired comparison method is calculated by taking the total of [n (n-1)]/2 comparisons. A score is obtained for each employee by simply counting the number of pairs in which the individual is the preferred member. It ranks each individual in relationship to all others on a one-on-one basis. If ten people are being evaluated, the first person is compared, with each of the other nine, and the number of items this person is preferred in any of the nine pairs is tabulated. Each of the remaining nine persons, in turn, is compared in the same way, and a ranking is evolved by the greatest number of preferred "victories". This method ensures that each employee is compared against every other, but the method can become unwieldy when large numbers of employees are being compared.

Management by Objectives

Management by objectives (MBO) is a process that converts organizational objectives into individual objectives. It can be thought of as consisting of four steps: goal setting, action planning, self-control, and periodic reviews:

1. In *goal setting*, the organization's overall objectives are used as guidelines from which departmental and individual objectives are set. At the individual level, the manager and subordinate jointly identify those goals that are critical for the subordinate to achieve in order to fulfill the requirements of the job as determined in job analysis. These goals are agreed upon and then become the standards by which the employee's results will be evaluated.
2. In *action planning,* the means are determined for achieving the ends established in goals setting. That is, realistic plans are developed to attain the objectives. This step includes identifying the activities necessary to accomplish the objective, establishing the critical relationships between these activities, estimating the time requirement for each activity, and determining the resources required to complete each activity.
3. *Self control* refers to the systematic monitoring and measuring of performance. Ideally, by having the individual review his or her own performance. The MBO philosophy is built on the assumptions that individuals can be responsible, can exercise self-direction, and do not require external controls and threats of punishment.
4. Finally, with *periodic progress reviews*, corrective action is initiated when behaviour deviates from the standards established in the goal-setting phase. Again, consistent with MBO philosophy, these manager-subordinate reviews are conducted in a constructive rather than punitive manner. Reviews are not meant to degrade the individual but to aid in future performance. These reviews should take place at least two or three times a year.

Following are the advantages of MBO:

- It is result-oriented. It assists the planning and control functions and provides motivation.

- Employees know exactly what is expected of them and how they will be evaluated.
- Employees have a greater commitment to objectives that they have participated in developing than to those unilaterally set by their bosses.

360 Degree Assessment

The 360 degree feedback process involves collecting perceptions about a person's behaviour and the impact of that behaviour from the person's boss or bosses, direct reports, colleagues, fellow members of project teams, internal ad external customers, and suppliers.

Other names for 360 degree feedback are multi-rater feedback, multisource feedback, full-circle assessment, and group performance review. 360 degree feedback is a method and a tool that provides each employee the opportunity to receive performance feedback from his or her supervisor and four to eight peers, subordinates and customers. 360 degree feedback allows each individual to understand how his effectiveness as an employee, co-worker, or staff member is viewed by others. The most effective processes provide feedback that is based on behaviours that other employees can see. The feedback provides insight about the skills and behaviours desired in the organization to accomplish the mission, vision, goals and values. The feedback is firmly planted in behaviours needed to exceed customer expectations. People whoe are chosen as raters are usually those that interact routinely with the person receiving feedback.

The purpose of the feedback is to:

- Assist each individual to understand his or her strengths and weaknesses.
- Contribute insights into aspects of his or her work needing professional development.

Following are some of the major considerations in using 360 degree feedback.

These are basically concerned with how to:

- Select the feedback tool and process;
- Select the raters;
- Use the feedback
- Review the feedback; and
- Manage and integrate the process into a larger performance management system.

Features of 360 Degree Assessment

Organizations that are using with the 360 degree component of their performance management systems identify following positive features of the process.

These features will manifest themselves in well-managed, well-integrated 360 degree processes:

- *Improved Feedback from more springs*: Provides well-rounded feedback from peers, reporting staff, co-workers, and supervisors. This can be a definite improvement over feedback from a single individual. 360 feedback can also save managers' time in that they can spend less energy providing feedback as more people participate in the process. Co-worker perception is important and the process helps people understand how other employees view their work.
- *Team Development*: Helps team members learn to work more effectively together. Team members know more about how other members are performing than their supervisor. Multirater feedback makes team members more accountable to each other as they share the knowledge that they will provide input on each member's performance. A well-planned process can improve communication and team development.
- *Personal and Organizational Performance Development*: 360 degree feedback is one of the best methods for under-standing personal and organizational developmental needs.
- *Responsibility for Career Development*: For many reasons, organizations *per se* are no longer responsible for developing the careers of thei employees. Multirater feedback can provide excellent information to individuals about what they need to do to enhance their career. Additionally, many employees feel 360 degree feedback is more accurate, more reflective of their performance, and more validating than feedback from the supervisor along. This makes the information more useful for both career and personal development.
- *Reduced Discrimination Risk*: When feedback comes from a number of individuals in various job functions, biases because of varying reasons are reduced. The judgemental errors of the supervisors are eliminated as the feedback comes from various springs.
- *Improved Customer Services*: Feedback process involves the internal or external customer. Each person receives valuable feedback about the quality of his product or services. This feedback should enable the individual to improve the quality, reliability, promptness, and comprehesiveness of these products and services to his/her customers.

- *Training Needs Assessment*: Multirater feedback provides comprehensive information about organization training needs and thus helps in mounting relevant training programmes. Such programmes add value to the contribution made by the individual employee.

Benefits of 360 Degree Assessment

Following benefits of 360 degree Assessment accrue to the individual, team and organization:

To the individual:

- This process helps individuals to understand how others perceive them.
- It uncovers blind spots.
- It provides feedback that is essential for learning.
- Individuals can better manage their own performance and careers.
- Quantifiable data on soft skills is made available.

To the team:

- It increases communication between team members.
- It generates higher levels of trust ad better communication as individuals identify the causes of breakdowns.
- It creates better team environment as people discover how to treat others and how they want to be treated.
- It supports teamwork by involving team members in the development process.
- It increased team effectiveness.

To the organization:

- It reinforces corporate culture and openness and trust.
- It provides better opportunities for career development for employees.
- Employees get growth and promotional opportunities.
- It improves customer service by having customers contribute to evaluation.
- It facilitates the conduct of relevant training programmes.

PERFORMANCE MANAGEMENT SYSTEMS

Many of our actions that involve the imagery part of our brain are undertaken with little conscious forethought. We daydream, perform a routine skill (like tying shoes), or hold a routine conversation without necessarily forming a mental image of what we are doing. Whereas at one time we may have used imagery to learn or perfect a skill, now we often carry out an action without thinking about it. We act on the basis of habit, routine, and convenience. We automatically perform many functions without thinking because they are so familiar to us that we feel entirely comfortable with them. These actions are second nature to us.

This unthinking routinizing behaviour occurs because it simplifies our life. We do not need to think about performing countless everyday actions. Yet there is a great danger here. Precisely because we do not think about these actions we cease to learn. We no longer look for ways to change and improve these actions. We take the status quo for granted.

One of the most interesting aspects about Frank and Lillian Gilbreth, two early time study engineers, is that they applied time and motion study principles to everyday, routine actions. Invariably, they would develop a faster more efficient way to do such everyday chores as clearing the table, washing the dishes, or mopping a floor. Though the Gilbreths made a conscious effort to examine existing methods in order to improve efficiency, most of us do not make such concerted effort in any daily lives unless a major change occurs. It often takes the birth of our first child, a divorce, the death of a loved one, or a serious illness to cause us to re-examine our daily routine. Then we may undertake action to improve or change the mental scripts and templates we unthinkingly follow.

The scripts and templates in our minds, which we follow every day at work, also provide us with a work routine based largely on a set of habits. Most of us do not systematically question these routines to see if they can be improved or if they are even necessary. Again, just as in our personal lives, this does not happen unless we face a serious crisis or major problem that is disruptive. Important deadlines are missed, a key employee quits, we are promoted, or we get a new boss. These situations usually will cause a rethinking of our normal work routine. We will question our present scripts and templates and devise new ones if necessary. Sometimes we try to change or interpret events to make them fit our existing templates. The key for productivity improvement, however, lies in making improvement changes before the crisis hits. That is where imagery can have its greatest impact.

PERFORMANCE APPRAISALS

Systematic Evaluation

"It is a systematic evaluation of an individual with respect to performance on the job and individual's potential for development."

Formal System, Reasons and Measures of future performance

"It is formal, structured system of measuring, evaluating job related behaviours and outcomes to discover reasons of performance and how to perform effectively in future so that employee, organization and society all benefits."

Past Oriented Methods

- *Rating Scales*: Rating scales consists of several numerical scales representing job related performance criterions such as dependability, initiative, output, attendance, attitude etc. Each scales ranges from excellent to poor. The total numerical scores are computed and final conclusions are derived. Advantages - Adaptability, easy to use, low cost, every type of job can be evaluated, large number of employees covered, no formal training required. Disadvantages - Rater's biases
- *Checklist*: Under this method, checklist of statements of traits of employee in the form of Yes or No based questions is prepared. Here the rater only does the reporting or checking and HR department does the actual evaluation. Advantages - economy, ease of administration, limited training required, standardization. Disadvantages - Raters biases, use of improper weighs by HR, does not allow rater to give relative ratings
- *Forced Choice Method*: The series of statements arranged in the blocks of two or more are given and the rater indicates which statement is true or false. The rater is forced to make a choice. HR department does actual assessment. Advantages - Absence of personal biases because of forced choice. Disadvantages - Statements may be wrongly framed.
- *Forced Distribution Method*: here employees are clustered around a high point on a rating scale. Rater is compelled to distribute the employees on all points on the scale. It is assumed that the performance is conformed to normal distribution. Advantages - Eliminates Disadvantages - Assumption of normal distribution, unrealistic, errors of central tendency.
- *Critical Incidents Method*: The approach is focused on certain critical behaviours of employee that makes all the difference in the performance. Supervisors as and when they occur record such incidents. Advantages - Evaluations are based on actual job behaviours, ratings are supported by descriptions, feedback is easy, reduces recency biases, chances of subordinate improvement are

high. Disadvantages - Negative incidents can be prioritized, forgetting incidents, overly close supervision; feedback may be too much and may appear to be punishment.

- *Behaviourally Anchored Rating Scales*: statements of effective and ineffective behaviours determine the points. They are said to be behaviourally anchored. The rater is supposed to say, which behaviour describes the employee performance. Advantages - helps overcome rating errors. Disadvantages - Suffers from distortions inherent in most rating techniques.
- *Field Review Method*: This is an appraisal done by someone outside employees' own department usually from corporate or HR department. Advantages - Useful for managerial level promotions, when comparable information is needed, Disadvantages - Outsider is generally not familiar with employees work environment, Observation of actual behaviours not possible.
- *Performance Tests & Observations*: This is based on the test of knowledge or skills. The tests may be written or an actual presentation of skills. Tests must be reliable and validated to be useful. Advantage - Tests may be apt to measure potential more than actual performance. Disadvantages - Tests may suffer if costs of test development or administration are high.
- *Confidential Records*: Mostly used by government departments, however its application in industry is not ruled out. Here the report is given in the form of Annual Confidentiality Report (ACR) and may record ratings with respect to following items; attendance, self expression, team work, leadership, initiative, technical ability, reasoning ability, originality and resourcefulness etc. The system is highly secretive and confidential. Feedback to the assessee is given only in case of an adverse entry. Disadvantage is that it is highly subjective and ratings can be manipulated because the evaluations are linked to HR actions like promotions etc.
- *Essay Method*: In this method the rater writes down the employee description in detail within a number of broad categories like, overall impression of performance, promoteability of employee, existing capabilities and qualifications of performing jobs, strengths and weaknesses and training needs of the employee. Advantage - It is extremely useful in filing information gaps about the employees that often occur in a better-structured checklist. Disadvantages - It its highly dependent upon the writing skills of rater and most of them are not good writers. They may get confused success depends on the memory power of raters.

- *Cost Accounting Method*: Here performance is evaluated from the monetary returns yields to his or her organization. Cost to keep employee, and benefit the organization derives is ascertained. Hence it is more dependent upon cost and benefit analysis.
- *Comparative Evaluation Method (Ranking & Paired Comparisons)*: These are collection of different methods that compare performance with that of other co-workers. The usual techniques used may be ranking methods and paired comparison method.
  - *Ranking Methods*: Superior ranks his worker based on merit, from best to worst. However how best and why best are not elaborated in this method. It is easy to administer and explanation.
  - *Paired Comparison Methods*: In this method each employee is rated with another employee in the form of pairs. The number of comparisons may be calculated with the help of a formula as under.

$$N \times (N-1)/\ 2$$

Future Oriented Methods

- *Management By Objectives*: It means management by objectives and the performance is rated against the achievement of objectives stated by the management. MBO process goes as under.
  - Establish goals and desired outcomes for each subordinate
  - Setting performance standards
  - Comparison of actual goals with goals attained by the employee
  - Establish new goals and new strategies for goals not achieved in previous year.

Advantage: It is more useful for managerial positions.

Disadvantages: Not applicable to all jobs, allocation of merit pay may result in setting short-term goals rather than important and long-term goals etc.

- *Psychological Appraisals*: These appraisals are more directed to assess employees potential for future performance rather than the past one. It is done in the form of in-depth interviews, psychological tests, and discussion with supervisors and review of other evaluations. It is more focused on employees emotional, intellectual, and motivational and other personal characteristics affecting his performance. This approach is slow and costly and may be useful for bright young members who may have considerable potential. However quality of these appraisals largely depend upon the skills of psychologists who perform the evaluation.

- *Assessment Centres*: This technique was first developed in USA and UK in 1943. An assessment centre is a central location where managers may come together to have their participation in job related exercises evaluated by trained observers. It is more focused on observation of behaviours across a series of select exercises or work samples. Assessees are requested to participate in in-basket exercises, work groups, computer simulations, role playing and other similar activities which require same attributes for successful performance in actual job. The characteristics assessed in assessment centre can be assertiveness, persuasive ability, communicating ability, planning and organizational ability, self confidence, resistance to stress, energy level, decision making, sensitivity to feelings, administrative ability, creativity and mental alertness etc. Disadvantages - Costs of employees traveling and lodging, psychologists, ratings strongly influenced by assessee's inter-personal skills. Solid performers may feel suffocated in simulated situations. Those who are not selected for this also may get affected.

Advantages: well-conducted assessment centre can achieve better forecasts of future performance and progress than other methods of appraisals. Also reliability, content validity and predictive ability are said to be high in assessment centres.

The tests also make sure that the wrong people are not hired or promoted. Finally it clearly defines the criteria for selection and promotion.

- *360-Degree Feedback*: It is a technique which is systematic collection of performance data on an individual group, derived from a number of stakeholders like immediate supervisors, team members, customers, peers and self. In fact anyone who has useful information on how an employee does a job may be one of the appraisers. This technique is highly useful in terms of broader perspective, greater self-development and multi-source feedback is useful. 360-degree appraisals are useful to measure inter-personal skills, customer satisfaction and team building skills. However on the negative side, receiving feedback from multiple sources can be intimidating, threatening etc. Multiple raters may be less adept at providing balanced and objective feedback.

Ethics of Performance Appraisals/ Legally defensible Performance Appraisals

- *Ethics of Procedures*:
  - Formal Standardized Performance Appraisal Systems

- Uniform to all employees, no illegal differentiations based on cast, religion etc.
- Standards formally communicated to all employees
- Freedom to review performance appraisal results
- Formal appeal process about ratings and judgments
- Written instructions and training to raters
- All personal decision makers should be aware of anti-discrimination laws.

• *Ethics of Contents*:
  - Content based on job analysis
  - Traits based appraisals should be avoided
  - Objectively verifiable data should be used
  - Constraints on performance beyond control should be prevented
  - Specific job related dimensions to be used rather than single or global dimensions.
  - Dimensions must be assigned weight to reflect relative importance in performance score

• *Ethics of Documentation of Results*:
  - A thoroughly written record of evidence leading to termination should be maintained
  - Written documentation of extreme ratings should be maintained
  - Documentation should be consistent among the raters.

• *Ethics of Raters*:
  - The raters should be trained in how to use an appraisal system
  - The rater must have opportunity to observe ratees first hand and review important ratee performance products.
  - Use of more than one rater is desirable to reduce biases.

PERFORMANCE MANAGEMENT AND APPRAISAL

The hardest task in respect to HRM of small businesses is to convince owners and managers that there is much to be gained in the long term if financial and time investments are made in the short term. Of all the functional aspects of HRM, it is most difficult to convince small business managers of the need for taking a strategic approach to developing formal performance appraisal systems. Partly, the choice is cost related but it also results from the over-confidence of small business managers that employees are prepared to trade-off extrinsic benefits that are seen to exist in large businesses for the intrinsic benefits they perceive as characteristic of small businesses.

Performance management involves a series of processes focused on managing employee performance. It includes work and job design, reward structures, the selection of people for work, the training of these employees, assessment of work performance and policies associated with rewarding and improving performance. Thus, like other HR functions, performance management is in no small way related to all other HR functions. It is but one part of a performance management system.

Performance Appraisal

Performance appraisal is the HRM activity by which organisations assess the extent to which employees are performing their jobs effectively. The purposes of performance appraisals are to improve performance; identify potential candidates for promotion; provide feedback to employees; communicate between supervisor and subordinate; assist HR planning; and develop management.

A formal performance appraisal system encompasses a method for gathering appraisal data, identification of standards of criteria for analysing data, knowledge of the validity and reliability of the method being utilised for appraisal, understanding of the characteristic of the rater and ratee, a defined process for utilising the information acquired, and an evaluation of the appraisal and its stated objectives. While small businesses may recognise the value of performance appraisals, very few utilise formal appraisal systems. Most small businesses communicate with employees in a personalistic style that places little emphasis on formal and standardised methods and techniques. Assessments of performance are usually made on the basis of employee conversations with the owner, family and co-workers, although the process may be more explicit in the larger 'small' companies that have a hired manager with prior HRM experience.

There are six usual methods used in performance appraisals including comparative standards; absolute standards; objectives based; direct or objective indices; accomplishment records; and means based. The form that is used is determined by what is being measured; what people are, what people do, or what people achieve. Whichever method is used, it is important that it has been tested for validity and reliability and standards are measurable. Interviews are the most commonly used form of undertaking a performance appraisal and may utilise four styles: tell and sell (directive); tell and listen; problem-solving; or mixed. Appraisal interviews should include a review of job responsibilities; a review of performance standards;

a review of the employee's performance; a discussion of strengths and weaknesses; setting of goals and targets; a discussion of career plans; and development of an action plan. The major advantage of such formalised approaches is that they allow employees to actively engage in their own setting of goals and objectives and to work with a supervisor to improve their performance.

Performance Appraisal in Small Businesses

As most small businesses do not engage in formal appraisal systems, they open themselves up to accusations of being subjective in their assessment of employees' performance and bias in their appraisal. It should be noted, however, that in small businesses in the professional service areas and high technology sector, there might be greater job autonomy and more formal appraisal. This does not reflect management strategy per se but rather the nature of the work in this particular market environment. Further, informal conversations with employees and cursory summaries of their performance do not provide much scope for development of career plans and management potential from within an existing workforce. Divergence in management abilities across small businesses also means divergence in potential to develop employees as the role of the supervisor is key to small business performance.

This is supported by Jennings and Beaver's (1997) finding that emphasises that small business success or failure hinges on managerial skills and decision-making. As they argue, the role of small business managers being, in general, more multifaceted than their large company counterparts, makes them a key factor at both the strategic and operational level.

The other difficulty that small businesses face in not implementing formal performance appraisal systems is that employees' understanding of the psychological contract and the conditions they have been offered (rewards and promotion prospects) are a matter of perception and what is offered may be changed by management at any time. This has consequences for employee satisfaction and performance as well as turnover.

Though there are certainly costs to a small business of implementing a formal performance appraisal system, the short-term costs may be counteracted by long-term reductions in turnover, absenteeism, poor job performance, job dissatisfaction and hostile attitudes towards management by employees. So, in developing formal performance appraisal systems, small businesses not only are able to ensure that performance management may become strategically aligned with organisational goals, but also increase accountability, decrease underutilisation of human resources, address concerns of productivity, and decrease employees' concerns about fairness and accuracy.

Reward Management

It has been consistently argued that the rewards offered in small businesses differ markedly from those in larger businesses. Ram (1998) argued that pay determination is usually an individualistic affair in small businesses and rarely pursued in a systematic manner. Further, pay is not usually regularly reviewed, pay increases are normally a product of individual bargains and most small businesses have no recognised pay structure. In sum, issues associated with pay are opaque at best.

Yet while small businesses may not have taken a strategic approach to developing monetary rewards, it is also often argued that many individuals join small businesses for non-monetary rewards such as the sense of organisational loyalty and commitment they find and that the work itself may be viewed as a means of self-expression and self-development. While it is recognised that small businesses may not viably compete with large organisations in terms of extrinsic compensatory rewards, Golhar and Deshpande (1997) maintain that the ability to adequately provide competitive compensation (at least internal pay equity) and employee participation initiatives are crucial factors associated with the effective and efficient operations of small businesses.

Defining Rewards

An organisation's reward system may be defined as the need to attract, retain and motivate employees. A total reward package includes base pay (possibly award-set or minimum standards) + performance-based pay (if applicable) + compulsory employer-provided benefits (such as superannuation) + discretionary employer-provided benefits (such as bonuses). While the ability to attract, retain and motivate individuals is partly explained by the value that money has for individuals, people are often willing to perform work for non-monetary gains such as status and prestige, job security, responsibility and variety, power, affiliation, or softer rewards such as travel or camaraderie. These non-monetary rewards often explain an individual's choice to take one job over another, or to choose one organisation over another when the monetary gains may be higher elsewhere. Rewards may be defined as extrinsic and intrinsic. Extrinsic rewards are those that receive external recognition, such as pay, bonuses and promotion. Intrinsic rewards are those that may not be recognised by others but hold considerable worth to the individual, such as job variety, and autonomy.

Some forms of rewards are useful in attracting employees, yet it is acknowledged that other forms of rewards are required to retain and motivate employees. Ting (1997) suggests that factors of non-monetary motivation decrease in effectiveness when implemented without consideration to pay satisfaction. Yet, it is also argued that pay satisfaction is not sufficient in itself and that pay equity within an organisation is often more important a linkage between compensation and employee loyalty/ retention and compensation. It is suggested that rewards such as hiring bonuses, paid holidays, and benefits will induce applicant attraction while promotion possibilities and new employee training were significantly related to retention rates. While motivational factors such as organisational culture, customer focus, teamwork and problem-solving are cited as having a positive relationship in the context of implementing quality improvements, job enrichment is viewed as the best way of increasing employee motivation and productivity.

Though small businesses in the professional service and high technology sectors offer high rates of pay, reflecting the market power of such individuals (Ram 1998:22), most small businesses offer more to their employees in terms of intrinsic rewards, though these may not include the job enrichment cited as the key factor in motivation (Grensing 1996). Small businesses often use non-traditional benefits to give employees a feeling of greater control over the destiny of their work lives. Benefits may include more responsibility and autonomy, latitude in direction of product marketing, flexibility in handling personal matters, leave and leisure-time activities. Other rewards offered can include liberal dress codes, personnel counseling, assistance with tax preparation, subsidised childcare and welfare programmes.

In many industrialised nations, a key determiner of pay rates and benefits is the award systems that set minimum rates of pay for particular jobs, occupational, industries and sectors. Moreover, legislation also establishes minimum conditions that organisations need to provide.

These conditions usually include workers' compensation, superannuation schemes, sick leave, holidays and holiday pay, and long service leave. In some nations, organisations are also required by law to provide paid maternity leave and carers' leave. However, it should be noted that a small number of organisations fail to provide the minimum standards legislated by government to their employees. While small businesses are noted for offering non-traditional benefits, unfortunately they are also overly represented among those businesses that do not provide minimum legal standards.

While small businesses should be providing their employees with minimum conditions, they are not as open to litigation as large corporations. Essentially, the onus falls to employees (where unionisation does not exist in the workplace) to make themselves aware of their entitlements under the law and to seek redress where these standards are not being met. However, where those employees are very young, uneducated, illegal immigrants or immigrants with poor language skills, employers can usually count on the employees remaining uninformed of their rights.

Managing Diversity and Thinking Globally

From the late 1970s most industrialised nations began to implement employment policies targeted at removing discrimination in workplaces on grounds of gender, marital and pregnancy status, race, age, disability, religious belief or political persuasion. These policies were designed to ensure that all individuals had equal employment opportunity in respect to recruitment and selection, training and development, pay and other rewards, and promotion opportunities.

Legislation was also enacted to ensure that individuals would not be subjected to sexual or other harassment in the workplace and could take legal action against perpetrators of such harassment. By the mid-1980s most industrialised nations had also brought in affirmative action policies that suggested or mandated organisations to employ techniques and methods to create equal employment opportunity. While it may be argued by some that small businesses are not as concerned with implementing such policies due to their nepotistic hiring practices, close proximity to their employees, their size, and lesser unionisation, legislatively they are just as obligated to comply as are large corporations. Beyond just the legislative compliance to which organisations must adhere, there is a moral and economic imperative to manage diversity and think globally.

Managing Diversity

The effects of internationalisation and the changing nature of the labour market (partially because of increased international migration) mean that business owners can no longer be assured of the culturally and ethnically homogenous workforces that characterised businesses in the past. This means that there is now an onus on employers and supervisors to manage increasingly diverse workforces that much of the popular press has argued is intrinsically good for organisations. Managing diversity refers to valuing differences between stakeholders and developing and implementing policies to manage those differences. Managing diversity can be argued to be a moral issue, but it is also an economic imperative for organisations in the sense that managing the needs of a diverse workforce can contribute to an organisation's ongoing survival.

Diversity issues confronting organisations include the obvious legislative requirements of equal employment opportunity and anti-discrimination as well as concerns for tolerance of individual difference, communicating with and motivating ethnically diverse populations, managing workers with family responsibilities, conflict resolution among diverse workforces, managing older workers, managing career paths diversely, managing diverse teams, and meeting the needs of those with disabilities. Further, being effective at managing diversity can contribute to an organisation's competitive advantage through the arguments of costs, resource acquisition, marketing, creativity, problem-solving and system flexibility.

Though small businesses may not be confronted with the same demands to manage diversity as larger organisations that have much greater numbers of employees and consequently the likelihood of more diversity, it is also in the interests of small businesses to develop an appreciation of diversity and to engender an organisational culture that supports diversity. Benefits to organisations of thinking diversely include breadth of perspectives in decision making; larger talent pools in acquisition; and greater marketing to ethnically diverse communities domestically and internationally. Potential disadvantages include: difficulties in recruiting, training and managing a diverse workforce; and increased potential for organisational conflict.

Despite the disadvantages, the ever-increasing diversity of modern industrialised nations suggests that there are on-going strategic advantages in employing a diverse workforce. While many small employers may argue that it is cost prohibitive to provide special conditions or facilities for employees with 'divergent' needs, there is no increased financial cost in simply showing respect for difference within their workplaces. Moreover, it may make those organisations more competitive (as employers and businesses) in the future.

Thinking Globally

Increasing numbers of organisations are recognising that effectively managing their human resources also necessitates recognition and incorporation of the global context. While we would not suggest that the vast majority of small businesses would ever be in a position, or indeed have the desire to, take their businesses offshore, it is almost impossible in an age of internationalisation to conceive of any business as being purely domestic in its focus. Though most small businesses may never sell their products internationally or establish subsidiaries in other nations, they are affected by global fiscal and monetary trends, fluctuations in stock markets and swings in economic conditions. Small businesses will also increasingly find that some, if not most of, the products or services they buy and sell, or the components from which they make their products, are produced overseas. Further, the increasing international mobility and cultural diversity of workforces will mean that thinking globally will be essential to business survival, and to this end, there is much that small businesses may learn from the disciplines of international human resource management and cross-cultural management.

The essence of international human resource management (IHRM) is knowledge of conditions in a variety of nations and knowledge of how to manage both within and across them. Strategic international human resource management (SIHRM) is thecollective of HRM issues, functions and practices that result from the strategic activities of multinational organisations and that impact the international concerns and goals of those enterprises.

SIHRM includes issues associated with people management through acquisitions and mergers, expatriate selection and preparation, creation of global thinking managers, managing, motivating, leading and negotiating in other nations, and corporate social responsibility. While management of expatriates and the human resource aspects of mergers and acquisitions will never be necessary for most small businesses, the cross-cultural management aspects of SIHRM do have application to domestic small businesses and all managers may benefit from cross-cultural competence.

In essence, cross-cultural differences arise from culturally divergent attitudes and behaviour and differences in understanding, interpretation and application.

Culture may impact on the values people have in the workplace, the manner in which decisions are made, negotiations are conducted, jobs are designed and disputes resolved. As such being able to appreciate and work with differences is essential to achieving organisational harmony and is dependent upon undertaking a comprehensive analysis of the culture of an organisation and its HRM practices. In so doing, Cox and Blake (1991) argue that it will be possible to uncover sources of potential bias unfavourable to some, and to identify ways that corporate culture may place some members at a disadvantage.

In recognising possible sources of disadvantage either in an existing business or one that is in its start-up phase, it then becomes possible for the organisation, its employees and its supervisors to move forward to an appreciation of diversity consistent with global consciousness. While these more proactive aspects of SIHRM are usually characteristic of large organisations (and primarily those in the public sector) it is not beyond the means of small businesses to also implement such thinking and to benefit strategically and economically from doing so.

Performance and Pay

Reward planning and management requires organisations to consider four key issues: determing the value of jobs; establishing a pay structure; building a link with performance; and communication and administration. One of the most neglected aspects of this process in small businesses is determining the value of jobs and relates to the lack of initial HR planning and job analysis characteristics of small businesses. Determining the value of jobs entails evaluating a job from job analysis, considering compensable factors, designing a system for evaluation and determining who will do the evaluation *e.g.* management or peers. From this initial analysis it is then possible to rank and classify jobs, and tie this to the development of selection criteria and other HRM functions.

Employees need some acknowledgement of their accomplishments and validation of task accomplishment is a strong predictor of employee satisfaction. Hence, performance appraisal also has an important link to rewards, particularly where performance-related pay and promotion are offered within an organisation. Without a valid and accepted performance appraisal system, diminished motivation and lowered performance may result.

Again it should be noted that the performance appraisal system should also take account of the value of non-monetary or intrinsic rewards such as prestige, job recognition and job enrichment and variety. Building a link between pay and performance needs to involve the development of outcomes to be sought and may entail performance-based pay systems, merit pay plans, individual incentive plans, and managerial incentive plans (that focus on the workgroup rather than specific individuals).

Communicating Rewards

The management and administration of a reward system also has the potential to be a significant form of employee communication. The rewards are clear indications of human resource values, goals and priorities of the organisation. There are three primary reasons why it is important: it ensures the organisation is aware of business trends; it ensures links with overall business objectives of the organisation; and it ensures that employees are aware of how their pay and benefits are determined and how the organisation fits relative to its competitors. There are four important aspects raised by this. First, whether employees should be involved in their own pay determination, *e.g.* a flexible approach. Second, whether there should be pay secrecy or whether pay rates for particular grades of work as they are in the public sector (market loadings not negated). Third, whether pay equity has an impact on absenteeism and turnover. Fourth, whether all employees should receive annual salaries or whether organisations should have a mix of salaried and performance-based pay employees.

There are non-monetary approaches that may be used to gain firm attractiveness in obtaining and keeping valuable human assets. Appelbaum and Kamal argue that job enrichment, employee recognition, pay equity and managerial skill affect job satisfaction in small business. It is acknowledged that small businesses do not have the financial resources available to offer monetary rewards competitive with larger organisations. However, we suggest that there are practices that small businesses can employ that will ensure that they meet some non-monetary rewards for their employees and are responsive communicators and are of minimal financial cost to the business.

Small businesses can improve their practices in respect to how they communicate benefits and rewards to their employees. They have been known to rely on informal techniques to assist employees to understand the psychological contract. Uncertainty and ambiguity about remuneration need to be removed. While in small businesses the promises made to employees may not be made explicit through formal HRM procedures as they are in large organisations, promises can be made explicit by being actioned.

For instance, promises made may satisfy an employee's extrinsic needs by pay and bonuses and benefits being tied to performance, and promises made may satisfy an employee's intrinsic needs in the form of increased responsibilities and opportunities for personal growth that may lead to promotion. Doing so would ensure that small businesses can minimise negative feelings and attitudes of employees towards the business, increase levels of commitment and minimise absenteeism and turnover. Employees who feel that their organisation gives them challenges and opportunities or more responsibility, freedom to develop new skills, and autonomy and control, are likely to demonstrate more loyalty towards their employer and hence contribute to the growth of the business. Thus, for small businesses to communicate better with their employees and action opportunities for their employees are critical factors in building a committed and quality workforce and organisation.

In addition to removing ambiguity about rewards, small businesses can also ensure that they provide feedback to their employees, both constructive criticism at the time of errors being made and praise when a job is well done. If a manager has no time to give praise, then it should be delegated to someone else. Given the value stowed on independence and autonomy of owner-managers and the concern for loss of control through delegation this may take some time to infiltrate the organisational culture. Moreover, Appelbaum and Kamal suggest that small businesses should hire managers that have the skill to implement incentive programmes and ensure that existing managers understand the value of incentives so that they show commitment to accomplishing tasks. Despite the investment involved, the savings realised through lower employee turnover and anticipated benefit to revenues through more efficient functioning should more than compensate. Further, instituting communication mechanisms that inform employees about how decisions are made and implementing procedures that allow employees to challenge or appeal decisions made by the business also contributes to employees' intrinsic self-worth.

Kickul suggests that small businesses can openly communicate to employees what they can reasonably expect in terms of organisational inducements and practices through open-book management. By sharing an array of organisational information (promises and obligations as well as financial and marketing practices), Kickul argues that small businesses help their employees recognise their contribution and significance to the success of the business. Effective communication between employees and management also must entail information from employees being acted upon by management and efforts made to bring employees on board to implement required changes.

ORGANIZATIONAL SUPPORT FACTORS FOR PERFORMANCE APPRAISAL SYSTEMS

Performance appraisal serves many organizational objectives and goals. Besides encouraging high level of performance, the evaluation system is useful in identifying employees with potential, rewarding them equitably, and determining employee needs for development. All these activities are instrumental in achieving corporate plans and long-term growth, typical appraisal system in most organizations have been focused on short-term goals only.

From the strategic management point of views, organizations can be grouped under 3 different categories as defenders, prospectors and analysers.

Defenders: They have narrow and stable product market domain. They don't need to make any adjustment in technology, structure or methods of operations etc. They devote entire attention on improving existing operations. Because of emphasis on skill building successful defenders use appraisals as means for identifying training needs. It is more behaviour oriented.

Prospectors: They continuously search for new products and opportunities. They experiment regularly to new and emerging trends. They more focus on skills identification and acquisition of human resources from external sources prospectors often use appraisals for identifying staffing needs. The focus is on results.

Analysers: They operate in two type of product domain markets. One is stable and other is changing. They watch their competitors closely and rapidly adopt the ideas that are promising.

They use cost effective technologies for stable products and matrix technologies for new products. Analysers tend to emphasize on skills building and skills acquisitions and employ extensive training programmes. Hence they use appraisal more for training and staffing purposes.

However performance appraisal systems has strategic importance in three different ways.

Feedback Mechanism: Performance evaluation is the central mechanism that not only provides feedback to individuals but also aids in the assessment of the progress of organization as a whole. Without appraisals managers of any firm can only guess as to whether or not employees are working towards realization of the organization goals.

Consistency between strategy and job behaviour: Performance appraisal not only is a means of knowing if the employee behaviour is consistent with the overall strategies focus but also a way of bringing to the fore any negative consequence of the strategy - behaviour fit. Thus the performance appraisal system is an important mechanism to elicit feedback on the consistency of the strategy - behaviour link.

Consistency between Values and Job Behaviour link: Performance evaluation is a mechanism to reinforce values and culture of the organization. Another importance is to align appraisal with organizational culture. Thus the purpose of performance evaluation is to make sure that employee's goals, employees behaviour and feedback of information about performance are all linked to the corporate strategy.

Essentials of a Good Performance Appraisal System:

- Standardized Performance Appraisal System
- Uniformity of appraisals
- Defined performance standards
- Trained Raters
- Use of relevant rating tools or methods
- Should be based on job analysis
- Use of objectively verifiable data
- Avoid rating problems like halo effect, central tendency, leniency, severity etc.
- Consistent Documentations maintained
- No room for discrimination based on cast, creed, race, religion, region etc.

Problems of Rating:

- Leniency & Severity
- Central Tendency
- Halo Error
- Rater Effect
- Primacy & Recency Effect
- Perceptual Sets
- Performance Dimensions Order
- Spillover Effects
- Status Effect

Incentives Based Compensation

Incentives are monetary benefits paid to workmen in recognition of their outstanding performance. They are defined as variable rewards granted according to variations in the achievement of specific results.

- *Advantages of Incentive based compensations*:
- Incentives are important for inducement and motivation of workers for higher efficiency and greater output.
  - Employee earnings go up
  - Enhanced standard of livings of employees
  - Reduction in total unit cost of production,

  - Productivity increases.
  - Production capacity is also likely to increase
  - Reduced supervision
- *Disadvantages of Incentive based compensation*:
  - Tendency of quality of products deteriorated due to increased output and low cost
  - Employees may oppose introduction of new machines
  - Workers demand for minimum wage limit may go up due to high incentive earnings
  - Sometimes employees may disregard security regulations due to payment by results approach adopted for higher incentive figures
  - Overworking may affect employee health
  - Employee jealousies with respect to high and low performers

6

Strategic Human Resource Management

The human resource management that aims to improve the productive contribution of individuals while simultaneously attempting to attain other societal and individual employee objectives has undergone drastic change with the passing of years. We all know that HRM is concerned with the "people" & keeping the fact in mind that HRM helps in acquiring, developing, stimulating & retaining the outstanding employees as it gives both effectiveness & efficiency to the working of the organisation, it has been started being used strategically & is now termed as Strategic human resource management.

THE CHANGING ROLE OF HRM

The role of human resource management is changing & is changing very fast, to help companies achieve their goals. HRM has gone through many phases – from hiring & firing to relationship building, from there to legislation role, & now its role is shifting from protector & screener to strategic partner & as a change agent.

Defining SHRM

- Organisational use of employees to gain or keep a competitive advantage against competitors.
- Involves aligning initiatives involving how people are managed with organisational mission and objectives.

In today's flattened, downsized & high-performing organisations, highly trained & committed employees – not machines – are often the firm's competitive key.

Perhaps the most drastic change in HR's role today is its growing involvement in developing & implementing the company's strategy.

In order to understand the modern aspect of HR i.e. SHRM, lets discuss the terms which would help us in understanding the concept:

- Core Competency can be defined as - A unique capability in the organisation that creates high value and that differentiates the organisation from its competition.
- Mission Statement explains purpose and reason for existence; it is usually very broad, but not more than a couple of sentences & it serves as foundation for everything organisation does.
- Strategy: the company's plan of how it will balance its internal strengths & weaknesses with external opportunities & threats in order to maintain a competitive advantage, earlier this role was performed by the line managers, but now it is carried by the HR manager.

Strategies increasingly depend on strengthening organisational competitiveness & on building committed work teams, & these put HR in a central role. In the fast changing, globally competitive & quality oriented industrial environment, it's often the firm's employees – its human resources – who provide the competitive key. And so now it is a demand of the time to involve HR in the earlier stages of development & implementing the firm's strategic plan, rather than to let HR react to it. That means now the role of HR is not just to implement the things out but also to plan out in such a manner that the employees can be strategically used to get edge over the competitors, keeping in mind the fact that this is the only resource (HUMANS), which cannot be duplicated by the competitors.

Approaches of the SHRM

- attempts to link Human Resource activities with competency based performance measures;
- attempts to link Human Resource activities with business surpluses or profit.

These to approaches indicate two factors in an organisational setting. The first one is the human factor, their performance and competency and the later is the business surplus. An approach of people concern is based on the belief that human resources are uniquely important in sustained business success. An organisation gains competitive advantage by using its people effectively, drawing on their expertise and ingenuity to meet clearly defined objectives. Integration of the business surplus to the human competency and performance required adequate strategies. Here the role of strategy comes into picture. The way in which people are managed, motivated and deployed, and the availability of skills and knowledge will all shape the business strategy. The strategic orinetation of the business then requires the effective orinetation of human resource to competency and performance excellance.

The Strategic Management Process Includes

- Determining what needs to be done to achieve corporate objectives, often over 3 - 5 years
- Examining organisation and competitive environment
- Establishing optimal fit between organisation and its environment
- Reviewing and revising strategic plan

The Stage in the Process of Strategic Management

Mission statement- Business definition and future plan for success.

Environmental analysis- OT analysis and preparing to meet environmental pressures.

Organisational self-assessment- SW analysis and chalking road map for attaining goals.

Establishing goals and objectives- Laying concrete figures that will help in benchmarking the performance. These benchmarks will lead to the development of strategy that will decide how the company intends to meets its environmental challenges with given environmental and resource constraints in the time to come.

Benefits of a Strategic Approach to HR

- Facilitates development of high-quality workforce through focus on types of people and skills needed
- Facilitates cost-effective utilization of labor, particularly in service industries where labor is generally greatest cost
- Facilitates planning and assessment of environmental uncertainty, and adaptation of organisation to external forces
- Successful SHRM efforts begin with identification of strategic needs
- Employee participation is critical to linking strategy and HR practices
- Strategic HR depends on systematic and analytical mindset
- Corporate HR departments can have impact on organisation's efforts to launch strategic initiatives

Factor Linkages of HR Plans and Strategies

Given diagram presents various factors that have an impact on HR plans and Strategy and how are they interlinked with each other. Their interactions and impact on each element and the resulting change in HR Plan and policy is also indicated clearly. The table given above takes into consideration two of the generic strategies and the strategic focus required to generate each of these competitive advantages along with HR strategy and activities needed to be done by HR Department to help the organisation in generating these strategic advantages and to move successfully towards desired goals and objectives.

To understand these linkages we can look at them as tasks and steps needed to be taken in order to complete the tasks. The selected strategic focus should be very clear and well integrated into organisational policy and clearly communicated to HR Department to help in drafting suitable HR strategy and last in carrying out all activities.

Benefits of SHRM

1. Identifying and analyzing external opportunities and threats that may be crucial to the company's success.
2. Provides a clear business strategy and vision for the future.
3. To supply competitive intelligence that may be useful in the strategic planning process.
4. To recruit, retain and motivate people.
5. To develop and retain of highly competent people.
6. To ensure that people development issues are addressed systematically.
7. To supply information regarding the company's internal strengths and weaknesses.
8. To meet the expectations of the customers effectively.
9. To ensure high productivity.
10. To ensure business surplus thorough comopetency.

Barriers of SHRM

Barriers to successful SHRM implementation are complex. The main reason is a lack of growth strategy or failure to implement one. Other major barriers are summarized as follows:

1. Inducing the vision and mission of the change effort.
2. High resistance due to lack of cooperation from the bottom line.
3. Interdepartmental conflict.
4. The commitment of the entire senior management team.
5. Plans that integrate internal resource with external requirements.

6. Limited time, money and the resources.
7. The statusquo approach of employees.
8. Fear of incomopetency of senior level managers to take up strategic steps.
9. Diverse work-force with competitive skill sets.
10. Fear towards victimisation in the wake of failtures.
11. Improper strategic assignments and leadership conflict over authority.
12. Ramifications for power relations.
13. Vulnerability to legislative changes.
14. Resistance that comes through the legitimate labour institutions.
15. Presence of an active labour union.
16. Rapid structural changes.
17. Economic and market pressures influenced the adoption of strategic HRM.
18. More diverse, outward looking approach.

HR Practitioners Role

The HR managers have keen role in the effective planning and implementation of the policies and decisions that in tune with the business changes. They should act as strategic partners and be proactive in their role than mere reactive, passive spectators. The HT managers should understand how far their decisions contribute to business surplus incorporating human competency and performance to the organisation. Strategic HR managers need a change in their outlook from seeing themselves as relationship managers to strategic resource managers. Kossekargues that major HRM innovations occur when senior management takes the lead and adoption of innovative SHRM practices is dependent on the nature of relationship of the HR Department with the CEO and the line managers. Legge commenting on the actions of the personnel practitioner in the innovation process suggests that adoption of an innovation by an organisation depends largely on HR practitioners' credibility with information and resource providers. HR Department and HR managers in these innovative organisations play a strategic role (Ulrich, 1997) linking the HR strategy with the business strategy of the organisation. A crucial aspect concerning SHRM is the concepts of fit and flexibility. The degree of fit determines the human resource system's integration with organisation strategy. It is the role of HR Managers to ensure this fit in between Human Resource System with the Organisation Strategy.

Conceptual Design

Organisations and companies succeed, or fail, based on the quality and effectiveness of their employees. Today's successful firms recognize that to compete in global markets, they must have world class Human Resource managers who are active participants in strategic and operational decision. Whether they are reengineering the pay and benefits of the company or implementing Total Quality Management (TQM) programmes, Human Resources Managers play a central role. Most importantly, the practice of Human Resource Management is undergoing a technological revolution. We speak now of managing not only human resources and capital, but also information and information systems. HR functions, from employee selection to benefits planning, are being redesigned to take advantage of advanced information technology.

Basic Concepts

Business organisations exist in a competitive environment with scarce resources.

Controlling these resources (physical, organisational, information and human) that gives the company the competitive advantage.

The goal of strategic management in an organisation is to deploy and allocate resources in order to provide the management with a competitive advantage.

It goes without saying that two out of three classes of resources (organisational and human) correlated with the human resource functions. Towards maximum effect, the HRM functions must be integrally involved in the company's strategic management process. Strategic management process first analyzes a company's competitive situation, develops its strategic goals and mission, it's external opportunities and threats, and its internal strength and weaknesses to generate alternatives. In his second phase, strategic management process determines a plan of actions and deployment of resources to achieve the pre-specified goals. This kind of strategic approach should be emphasized in human resources management.

Strategic human resources management (SHRM) is the pattern of planned human resources deployments and activities intended to enable an organisation to achieve its goals. Then we are addressing the question of the instruments that will make the odds of the competition in our favour.

Four levels of integration exist between the HR functions and the strategic management function:

- Administrative linkage: HR function's attention is focused on day-to-day activities.
- One-way linkage: the firm develops the strategic plan and then informs the HR.
- Two-way linkage: strategic planing team informs HR of the various strategies, HR analyze them and present the results to the team. After deciding, the strategic plan is passed to HR to implement.
- Integrative linkage: it is a dynamic process, based on continuing rather than sequential interaction, done by the HR executive who is a member of the senior management team.

Strategy formulation consists of five major components:

- Mission is a statement of the organisation's reason for being, customers served and their needs, and the technology used. Also presents the company's vision and values.
- Goals are what the firm hopes to achieve in the medium-to-long term future.
- External analysis examines the firm's operating environment to identify the strategic opportunities and threats.
- Internal analysis identifies the firm's strengths and weaknesses, focuses on the quantity and quality of resources available.
- Strategic choice is done after the Strengths Weaknesses Opportunities Threats (SWOT) analysis to define strategic alternatives, then the choice is made among these alternatives.

Mechanisms for integration the HR function into strategy formulation may help the strategic planning team to make the most effective strategic choice, since HR will implement it.

Strategy Implementation

It is now time to execute the strategy formulated, indicating certain HR needs.

HR function can be viewed as having six menus of HR practices from which companies can choose the ones that are most appropriate to implementing the strategy.

While, all of the strategy types require competent people in a generic sense, each of the strategies also requires different types of employees with types of behaviours and attitudes. The emerging strategic role of the HR function requires that HR professionals in the future develop business, professional-technical, change management, and integration competencies.

THE STRATEGY HIERARCHY

In most (large) corporations there are several levels of management. Strategic management is the highest of these levels in the sense that it is the broadest - applying to all parts of the firm - while also incorporating the longest time horizon. It gives direction to corporate values, corporate culture, corporate goals, and corporate missions. Under this broad corporate strategy there are typically business-level competitive strategies and functional unit strategies. Corporate strategy refers to the overarching strategy of the diversified firm. Such a corporate strategy answers the questions of "in which businesses should we compete?" and "how does being in these business create synergy and/or add to the competitive advantage of the corporation as a whole?"

Business strategy refers to the aggregated strategies of single business firm or a strategic business unit (SBU) in a diversified corporation. According to Michael Porter, a firm must formulate a business strategy that incorporates either cost leadership, differentiation or focus in order to achieve a sustainable competitive advantage and long-term success in its chosen arenas or industries. Functional strategies include marketing strategies, new product development strategies, human resource strategies, financial strategies, legal strategies, supply-chain strategies, and information technology management strategies. The emphasis is on short and medium term plans and is limited to the domain of each department's functional responsibility. Each functional department attempts to do its part in meeting overall corporate objectives, and hence to some extent their strategies are derived from broader corporate strategies. Many companies feel that a functional organisational structure is not an efficient way to organize activities so they have reengineered according to processes or SBUs. A strategic business unit is a semi-autonomous unit that is usually responsible for its own budgeting, new product decisions, hiring decisions, and price setting. An SBU is treated as an internal profit centre by corporate headquarters. An additional level of strategy called operational strategy was encouraged by Peter Drucker in his theory of management by objectives (MBO). It is very narrow in focus and deals with day-to-day operational activities such as scheduling criteria. It must operate within a budget but is not at liberty to adjust or create that budget. Operational level strategies are informed by business level strategies which, in turn, are informed by corporate level strategies.

Since the turn of the millennium, some firms have reverted to a simpler strategic structure driven by advances in information technology. It is felt that knowledge management systems should be used to share information and create common goals. Strategic divisions are thought to hamper this process. This notion of strategy has been captured under the rubric of dynamic strategy, popularized by Carpenter and Sanders's textbook. This work builds on that of Brown and Eisenhart as well as Christensen and portrays firm strategy, both business and corporate, as necessarily embracing ongoing strategic change, and the seamless integration of strategy formulation and implementation. Such change and implementation are usually built into the strategy through the staging and pacing facets.

Strategic Human Resource Planning

A comprehensive Human Resource Strategy plays a vital role in the achievement of an organisation's overall strategic objectives and visibly illustrates that the human resources function fully understands and supports the direction in which the organisation is moving.

A comprehensive HR Strategy will also support other specific strategic objectives undertaken by the marketing, financial, operational and technology departments.

In essence, an HR strategy should aim to capture "the people element" of what an organisation is hoping to achieve in the medium to long term, ensuring that:-

- it has the right people in place;
- it has the right mix of skills;
- employees display the right attitudes and behaviours, and
- employees are developed in the right way.

If, as is sometimes the case, organisation strategies and plans have been developed without any human resource input, the justification for the HR strategy may be more about teasing out the implicit people factors which are inherent in the plans, rather than simply summarising their explicit "people" content.

An HR strategy will add value to the organisation if it:

- articulates more clearly some of the common themes which lie behind the achievement of other plans and strategies, which have not been fully identified before; and
- identifies fundamental underlying issues which must be addressed by any organisation or business if its people are to be motivated, committed and operate effectively.

The first of these areas will entail a careful consideration of existing or developing plans and strategies to identify and draw attention to common themes and implications, which have not been made explicit previously.

The second area should be about identifying which of these plans and strategies are so fundamental that there must be clear plans to address them before the organisation can achieve on any of its goals. These are likely to include:

- workforce planning issues;
- succession planning;
- workforce skills plans;
- employment equity plans;
- black economic empowerment initiatives;
- motivation and fair treatment issues;
- pay levels designed to recruit, retain and motivate people;
- the co-ordination of approaches to pay and grading across the organisation to create alignment and potential unequal pay claims;
- a grading and remuneration system which is seen as fair and giving proper reward for contributions made;
- wider employment issues which impact on staff recruitment, retention, motivation etc.;
- a consistent performance management framework which is designed to meet the needs of all sectors of the organisation including its people;
- career development frameworks which look at development within the organisation at equipping employees with "employability" so that they can cope with increasingly frequent changes in employer and employment patterns;
- policies and frameworks to ensure that people development issues are addressed systematically : competence frameworks, self-managed learning etc.

The HR strategy will need to show that careful planning of the people issues will make it substantially easier for the organisation to achieve its wider strategic and operational goals.

In addition, the HR strategy can add value is by ensuring that, in all its other plans, the organisation takes account of and plans for changes in the wider environment, which are likely to have a major impact on the organisation, such as:

- changes in the overall employment market - demographic or remuneration levels;
- cultural changes which will impact on future employment patterns;
- changes in the employee relations climate;

- changes in the legal framework surrounding employment;
- HR and employment practice being developed in other organisations, such as new flexible work practices.

Finding the right opportunity to present a case for developing an HR Strategy is critical to ensuring that there will be support for the initiative, and that its initial value will be recognised by the organisation.

Giving a strong practical slant to the proposed strategy may help gain acceptance for the idea, such as focusing on good management practice. It is also important to build "early or quick wins" into any new strategy.

Other opportunities may present the ideal moment to encourage the development of an HR Strategy:-

- A major new internal initiative could present the right opportunity to push for an accompanying HR strategy, such as a restructuring exercise, a corporate acquisition, joint venture or merger exercise.
- A new externally generated initiative could similarly generate the right climate for a new HR strategy - e.g. Black economic empowerment initiatives.
- In some instances, even negative news may provide the "right moment", for example, recent industrial action or employee dissatisfaction expressed through a climate survey.

Making the HR Strategy Integral to the Organisation

The human resources practitioner should ensure that the HR Strategy is integrated with broader organisational objectives. Above all, it should ensure that the rest of the organisation accepts the Strategy. To achieve this objective, practitioners should:-

- consult all stakeholders on the nature of the strategy;
- cultivate and develop allies and supporters of the strategy through the consultation process;
- focus on the benefits which are being derived from the strategy through talking to and persuading others, and by marketing the benefits of the strategy with concrete examples of how it has helped;
- check that there is real commitment to the strategy at all levels of the organisation;
- give regular feedback on the implementation of the plan through employee newsletters, exhibitions etc;
- where possible, build into the strategy quantifiable outcomes which can be easily monitored and evaluated, so that it is possible to show the effect;

- make the strategy part of the induction process - especially for senior managers.

A Strategic Human Resource Planning Model

There is no single approach to developing a Human Resources Strategy. The specific approach will vary from one organisation to another. Even so, an excellent approach towards an HR Strategic Management System is evident in the model presented below. This approach identifies six specific steps in developing an HR Strategy:-

1. Setting the strategic direction
2. Designing the Human Resource Management System
3. Planning the total workforce
4. Generating the required human resources
5. Investing in human resource development and performance
6. Assessing and sustaining organisational competence and performance

The six broad interconnected components of this system consist of three planning steps and three execution steps.

The top three components represent the need for planning. Organisations must determine their strategic direction and the outcomes they seek. This is usually accomplished with some form of strategic planning. Classic strategic planning is a formal, top-down, staff-driven process. When done well, it is workable at a time when external change occurs at a more measured pace.

However as the pace and magnitude of change increases, the approach to strategic planning changes substantially:

- First, the planning process is more agile; changes in plans are much more frequent and are often driven by events rather than made on a predetermined time schedule.
- Second, the planning process is more proactive. Successful organisations no longer simply respond to changes in their environment, they proactively shape their environment to maximize their own effectiveness.
- Third, the planning process is no longer exclusively top-down; input into the process comes from many different organisational levels and segments. This creates more employee ownership of the plan and capitalises on the fact that often the most valuable business intelligence can come from employees who are at the bottom of the organisational hierarchy.

- Lastly, the strategic planning process less reactive and more driven by line leadership.

Once strategic planning is under way, a process must be undertaken by the organisation to design and align its HRM policies and practices to provide for organisational success. The remaining step in planning is to determine the quality and quantity of human resources the organisation needs for its total force.

The rest of the HR strategic system exists for and is guided by these plans, policies, and practices. These execution components contain mechanisms that generate the correct skill sets, invest in staff development and performance, and productively employ them in the organisation. The last component provides a means to assess and sustain the competence and performance of the organisation and the people in it with regard to outcomes that the organisation seeks.

Analysis

Using the process model discussed earlier, the specific components of the HR Strategic Plan are discussed in greater detail below.

Setting the Strategic Direction

This process focuses on aligning human resource policies to support the accomplishment of the Company's mission, vision, goals and strategies. The business' goals sit at the heart of any HR strategy and in order to align business and HR you need to answer one key question, "Can your organisation's internal capability deliver the organisation's business goals?"

Many organisations cite their people as their primary source of competitive advantage. Successful companies continuously identify and adopt innovative human resource management policies and practices to sustain that advantage. More importantly, they structure work and design training, performance management, pay, and reward policies to help members of the organisation succeed in achieving desired organisational outcomes. In other words, they integrate and align HRM policies and practices to reinforce employee behaviours that can best realize the leaders' strategic intent. In the most successful companies, the set of policies and practices that collectively make up a company's HRM system is the critical management tool for communicating and reinforcing the leaders' strategic intent.

Recommended actions:-

- Conduct an external environmental scan and evaluate its impact on the organisation;

- Identify the organisation's vision, mission and guiding principles;
- Identify the mission's outcomes and strategic goals;
- Consult all relevant stakeholders;
- Evaluate the impact of legislation on the organisation;

This stage focuses on the selection, design and alignment of HRM plans, policies and practices. Various options may be open to the organisation such as drawing on industry best practices.

Emerging HRM policies and practices range from outsourcing certain non-core functions, adopting flexible work practices (telework, work from home) and the increased use of information technology. Not every industry trend may be appropriate for a specific organisation. In addition, it is essential that a cost-benefit analysis of implementing new HRM policies and practices be undertaken. For example, the costs (monetary and in allocation of resources) of implementing a new job grading system may outweigh the benefit of such an undertaking. There may be more cost-effective alternatives available to the organisation at this point in time. Particular HRM policies and practices may be necessary to support strategic organisational objectives, such as improving the retention of women in the organisation or promoting diversity, especially the representation of designated groups amongst senior management.

A good approach in selecting the appropriate HRM policies, procedures and practices is to identify the appropriate HRM practices which support the organisation's strategic intent as it relates to recruitment, training, career planning and reward management.

Recommended actions:-

- Identify appropriate human resource plans, policies and practices needed to support organisational objectives
- Identify relevant human resource best practices
- Conduct an employment systems review.

Planning the Total Workforce

Determining future business requirements, especially those relating to manpower requirements, represents one of the most challenging tasks facing human resource practitioners.

The development of a workforce plan is a critical component of any human resource strategy and one of the expected outcomes of human resource practitioners activities. Despite this, manpower or workforce planning, as well as succession planning, has only recently enjoyed a resurgence in popularity. To some extent this has been prompted by the need to develop employment equity and workplace skills plans and set numerical employment equity targets. The failure of many organisations to develop and implement workforce planning is rather indicative of the lack of strategic planning itself.

Workforce planning is a systematic process of identifying the workforce competencies required to meet the company's strategic goals and for developing the strategies to meet these requirements. It is a methodical process that provides managers with a framework for making human resource decisions based on the organisation's mission, strategic plan, budgetary resources, and a set of desired workforce competencies. Workforce planning is a *systematic process* that is integrated, methodical, and ongoing. It identifies *the human capital required to meet organisational goals*, which consists of determining the number and skills of the workers required and where and when they will be needed. Finally workforce planning entails d*eveloping the strategies to meet these requirements*, which involves identifying actions that must be taken to attract (and retain) the number and types of workers the organisation needs.

A workforce plan can be as simple or as complex as the organisational requires. Workforce planning can be conducted for a department, division or for the organisation as a whole. Whatever the level or approach being adopted, it must nevertheless be integrated with broad-based management strategies.

In addition to workforce planning, ensure that organisational structure and jobs ensure the efficient delivery of services and effective management of the organisation as a whole.

Recommended actions:-

- Determine the appropriate organisational structure to support the strategic objectives
- Structure jobs (competencies, tasks and activities) around key activities
- Develop a workforce plan designed to support the organisations strategic objectives
- Compile workforce profiles, identifying designated groups, an inventory of current workforce competencies, competencies required in the future and identified gaps in competencies

Generating the Required Human Resources

This process focuses on recruiting, hiring, classifying, training and assigning employees based on the strategic imperatives of the organisation's workforce plan. A comprehensive workplace skills plan will identify appropriate training priorities based on the organisations workforce needs now and in the future. New recruitment practices may need to be adopted to increase the representation of designated groups, or securing essential skills in the organisation. A comprehensive "learnership strategy" may assist in developing future workforce needs, identified either in terms of the organisations workforce plan or required in terms of industry black economic empowerment charters.

Recommended actions:-

- Evaluate recruitment and selection practices in light of the organisation's strategic objectives
- Develop and implement a comprehensive workplace skills plan (with a thorough training needs analysis)
- Implement a learnership strategy
- Adopt or clarify occupational levels and category classifications.

Investing in Human Resource Development and Performance

Traditional approaches to career planning, performance appraisals, reward management and employee development must be re-appraised in light of the vision, characteristics and mission outcomes as reflected in the HRM plans, policies, and practices.

Development responses will aim to increase business skills, the application of business skills (sometimes called competencies) and the behavioural elements - all of which contribute to an organisation's effective performance. In many ways, the Skills Development legislation have required organisations to re-engineer their developmental methods and practices. New concepts such as lifelong learning and recognising prior learning should form an integral component of the process of investing in employees.

Clearly, where a workforce planning exercise reveals that there is little projected growth in the workforce or that promotional or career development opportunities are limited, strategies aimed at employee retention will be very different from organisations which are experiencing considerable growth and expansion.

Investment initiatives for the individual, team and organisation are all geared to achieve high levels of organisational performance. It is important that at an individual level, particularly for senior staff, that they feel their development needs are agreed and that they are provided with the skills to do their jobs. At a team level, it defines the individuals' ability to work flexibly with others and align individual and team skills and activities to business goals - all of which ensures that the organisation is equipped to achieve its goals.

Reward strategies aim to align the performance of the organisation with the way it rewards its people, providing the necessary incentives and motivation to staff. Its components can be a combination of base pay, bonuses, profit sharing, share options, and a range of appropriate benefits, usually based on market or competitor norms and the organisation's ability to pay.

Recommended actions:- Identify appropriate policies, procedures and practices in respect of

- Career pathing;
- Performance appraisals;
- Employee development and learning;
- Reward Management (compensation and benefits);
- Promotions and job assignments;
- Separation.

Assessing and Sustaining Organisational Competence and Performance

Finally, few organisations effectively measure how well their different inputs affect performance. In particular, no measures may be in place for quantifying the contribution people make to organisational outcomes or, more important, for estimating how changes in policies and practices, systems, or processes will affect that contribution. Implementing clear quantifiable measures, identifying milestones in the achievement of specific organisational goals, and using concepts such as a "balanced scorecard" will articulate the results of the HR Strategic Plan in measurable terms. Regular evaluation of the plan will also assist in fine-tuning the HR strategic plan itself.

STRATEGIC APPLICATIONS OF HR BUSINESS FUNCTIONS

Human resources functions refer to " those tasks and duties performed in both large and small organisations to provide for the coordinate human resources. The Society of Human Resources Management identified six main functions:

1. HR planning, recruitment, and selection
2. HR development & training
3. Compensation and benefits

4. Safety and health
5. Employee and labor relations
6. HR research.

Activities of the HR Planning, Recruitment and Selection Function

Performing job analysis that is " the process of determining and reporting pertinent information relating to the nature of a specific job". This can be done using a motion study, a time study or a statistical sample to draw inference about the demands of the job. Questionnaires, interviews and observation are tools to analysis jobs. This analysis produces job description and job specifications. The following step is the job design that is " the process of structuring work and designating the specific work activities of an individual or a group to achieve certain organisational objectives" (Byars, (1)).

HR planning that is " the process of determining the human resource needs of an organisation and ensuring that the organisation has the right number of qualified people in the right jobs at the right time ". (Ivancwich, (3)) First of all be familiar with the business strategy, define the impact of this strategy over the specific units of the organisation. Define the skills needed and the additional human resources required and develop action plans to meet the needs.

Methods for forecasting and planning the HR needs:

1. Judgmental methods such as managerial estimates, and Delphi technique. Finally, Scenario analysis using work force environmental scanning data to develop alternative work force scenarios. Brainstorming between managers and HR managers to forecast the future, then the managers will go back to define changing points.
2. Statistical and modeling techniques using historical data to predict the future. Time series analysis, personnel ratios, productivity ratios and regression analysis
3. Benchmarking is to carefully examine internal practice and procedures and measure them against the ways other successful organisations operate. Forecast methods will be compared to other successful organisations.
4. Determining the additional need using both skill inventory and management inventory to specify all available data about the current employees.

Depending on a single method of forecasting is not always accurate, in fact a mixture of different types of these methods may be very helpful according to the activity of the organisation and type of data.

- Developing and implementing an action plan to meet the requirements.
- Recruiting the HR needed to fulfill the organisation's goals.
- Selecting and hiring HR to specific jobs needed.

Activities of the HR Development and Training Function are:

- Orienting and training employees. Orientation is to introduce a new employee to the organisation, unit and job. Training involves the acquisition of new skills, concepts, attitude that improves the employee performance.
- Designing and implementing management and organisational development programmes that develops the experience, attitudes and skills of actual or soon to become managers.
- Building effective teams within the organisation to face any emergency possible
- Assisting employees in developing career plans. Career development is an ongoing effort done by the organisation to enrich its human resource to meet both the organisation and the employ's needs.
- Designing performance appraisal systems for the employees that is " a process of determining and communicating to an employee on the job and, establishing a plan of improvement".(Dessler, (2)) Performance appraisal can focus on individual or the process. Three different approaches exist for doing appraisals: employees can be appraised against absolute standards, relative standards or objectives, no one approach is always best:
    a. Management By Objectives (MBO): used with professional and managerial employee. Involves setting specific measurable goals with each employee and then periodically reviewing the progress made, take corrective action if necessary and set new objectives.
    b. Absolute standards: means comparing the employee to a standard, and their evaluation is independent of any other employee in a work group. Theses standard may be driven from time studies work sampling, average production, expert's opinion. This group includes the following methods:
        - Essay appraisal in which the rater prepares a written statement describing the employee's performance, quantity and quality of work, knowledge...etc.
        - Critical-incident appraisal, the rater keeps a record of positive and negative incidents of the employee, this considered as a basis to evaluate his performance.

- Graphical rating scale, evaluating factors like quantity of work, accuracy, attendance and others using an ordinal scale.
- Checklist is a yes/no questionnaire about an employee
- Forced-choice appraisal is a special type of checklist, the rater has two choose between two or more statements, the most descriptive. Each may be favourable or unfavourable.
- Behaviourally anchored rating scales (BARS), the performance done based on whether or not certain specially described job behaviours are present.

3-Relative standards: means comparing the employee against other individuals. The most popular relative methods are:

- Group order ranking requires the rater to place employees into a particular classification, such as " top 20 per cent".
- Individual ranking, rater lists the employees in order from highest to lowest.
- Paired comparison ranking is calculated by taking the total of [N(N-1)]/2. The employee score is the number of pairs in which this employee was preferred. Applying this method is difficult in large numbers.
- Forced distribution, the rater compares the performance of employees and places a certain percentage of employees at various performance levels.

Several common errors have been identified in performance appraisals such as:

- Leniency when the manager's rating are grouped in the positive end and not spread through the scale
- Central tendency when the manager tend to rate his employees near the middle of the performance scale
- Recency when the manager rates his employee on work recently done only
- Hallo effect when the rater is influenced by a single prominent characteristic of the employee, which effects his judgment resulting in giving this employee the same rating every time.

The usage of a single method is not recommended, actually a mixture is more appropriate.

Activities of the Compensation and Benefits Function are:

- Designing and implementing compensation and benefits systems.

The HR managers have to assist in this design and administer the system to minimize reward inequities. Payroll and HR applications should always be logically integrated - but not necessarily physically - because they have a lot of data in common and because they both support the same conpensation process. Wage and salary curves show the relationship between the relative worth of jobs and their wages or salary rates.

- Ensuring that compensation and benefits are fair and consistent.

Activities of the Safety and Health Function are:

- Designing and implementing programmes to ensure health and safety. Improving safety of the working conditions can be done using the following approaches:
  - — Safety design and preventive approaches of the workplace through safety engineering.
  - — Inspection, reporting and accident research. The safety specialist is looking for: application of the safety rules, availability of safety guards and equipment, potential hazards and potential health hazards. Accident research involves computation of organisational accident rates and compares them with industrial and national figures to determine the organisation's relative safety performance. Several statistics are computed. The organisation's statistics should be compared with the industry's statistics and government statistics. Also the trend of these ratios over time must be observed.
  - — Safety training and motivation programmes. Safety training is part of the orientation programme.
- Providing assistance to employee with personnel problems influencing their work performance.

Activities of the Employee and Labor Relations Function are:

- Serving as intermediary between the organisation and the unions
- Designing discipline grievance handling system.

STRATEGIC MANAGEMENT

Strategic management is the art, science and craft of formulating, implementing and evaluating cross-functional decisions that will enable an organisation to achieve its long-term objectives. It is the process of specifying the organisation's mission, vision and objectives, developing policies and plans, often in terms of projects and programmes, which are designed to achieve these objectives, and then allocating resources to implement the policies and plans, projects and programmes. Strategic management seeks to coordinate and integrate the activities of the various functional areas of a business in order to achieve long-term organisational objectives. A balanced scorecard is often used to evaluate the overall performance of the business and its progress towards objectives.

Strategic management is the highest level of managerial activity. Strategies are typically planned, crafted or guided by the Chief Executive Officer, approved or authorized by the Board of directors, and then implemented under the supervision of the organisation's top management team or senior executives. Strategic management provides overall direction to the enterprise and is closely related to the field of Organisation Studies. In the field of business administration it is useful to talk about "strategic alignment" between the organisation and its environment or "strategic consistency". According to Arieu, "there is strategic consistency when the actions of an organisation are consistent with the expectations of management, and these in turn are with the market and the context."

"Strategic management is an ongoing process that evaluates and controls the business and the industries in which the company is involved; assesses its competitors and sets goals and strategies to meet all existing and potential competitors; and then reassesses each strategy annually or quarterly [i.e. regularly] to determine how it has been implemented and whether it has succeeded or needs replacement by a new strategy to meet changed circumstances, new technology, new competitors, a new economic environment., or a new social, financial, or political environment."

Processes

Strategic management is a combination of three main processes which are as follows (as documented by Lemon Consulting).

Strategy Formulation

- Performing a situation analysis, self-evaluation and competitor analysis: both internal and external; both micro-environmental and macro-environmental.
- Concurrent with this assessment, objectives are set. These objectives should be parallel to a timeline; some are in the short-term and others on the long-term. This involves crafting vision statements (long term view of a possible future), mission statements (the role that the organisation gives itself in society), overall corporate objectives (both financial and strategic), strategic business unit objectives (both financial and strategic), and tactical objectives.

- These objectives should, in the light of the situation analysis, suggest a strategic plan. The plan provides the details of how to achieve these objectives.

This three-step strategy formulation process is sometimes referred to as determining where you are now, determining where you want to go, and then determining how to get there. These three questions are the essence of strategic planning. I/O Economics for the external factors and RBV for the internal factors.

Strategy Implementation

- Allocation and management of sufficient resources (financial, personnel, time, technology support).
- Establishing a chain of command or some alternative structure (such as cross functional teams).
- Assigning responsibility of specific tasks or processes to specific individuals or groups.
- It also involves managing the process. This includes monitoring results, comparing to benchmarks and best practices, evaluating the efficacy and efficiency of the process, controlling for variances, and making adjustments to the process as necessary.
- When implementing specific programmes, this involves acquiring the requisite resources, developing the process, training, process testing, documentation, and integration with (and/or conversion from) legacy processes.

Thus this type of problem can occur in strategy.

In order for a policy to work, there must be a level of consistency from every person in an organisation, including from the management. This is what needs to occur on the tactical level of management as well as strategic.

Strategy Evaluation

- Measuring the effectiveness of the organisational strategy. It's extremely important to conduct a SWOT analysis to figure out the strengths, weaknesses, opportunities and threats (both internal and external) of the entity in question. This may require to take certain precautionary measures or even to change the entire strategy. In corporate strategy, Johnson and Scholes present a model in which strategic options are evaluated against three key success criteria:
- Suitability (would it work?)

- Feasibility (can it be made to work?)
- Acceptability (will they work it?)

Suitability

Suitability deals with the overall rationale of the strategy. The key point to consider is whether the strategy would address the key strategic issues underlined by the organisation's strategic position.

- Does it make economic sense?
- Would the organisation obtain economies of scale, economies of scope or experience economy?
- Would it be suitable in terms of environment and capabilities?

Tools that can be used to evaluate suitability include:

- Ranking strategic options
- Decision trees
- What-if analysis.

Feasibility

Feasibility is concerned with the resources required to implement the strategy are available, can be developed or obtained. Resources include funding, people, time and information.

Tools that can be used to evaluate feasibility include:

- cash flow analysis and forecasting;
- break-even analysis;
- resource deployment analysis.

Acceptability

Acceptability is concerned with the expectations of the identified stakeholders (mainly shareholders, employees and customers) with the expected performance outcomes, which can be return, risk and stakeholder reactions.

- Return deals with the benefits expected by the stakeholders (financial and non-financial). For example, shareholders would expect the increase of their wealth, employees would expect improvement in their careers and customers would expect better value for money.
- Risk deals with the probability and consequences of failure of a strategy (financial and non-financial).
- Stakeholder reactions deals with anticipating the likely reaction of stakeholders. Shareholders could oppose the issuing of new shares, employees and unions could oppose outsourcing for fear of losing

their jobs, customers could have concerns over a merger with regards to quality and support.

Tools that can be used to evaluate acceptability include:

- what-if analysis;
- stakeholder mapping.

General Approaches

In general terms, there are two main approaches, which are opposite but complement each other in some ways, to strategic management:

- The Industrial Organisational Approach
  - — based on economic theory — deals with issues like competitive rivalry, resource allocation, economies of scale;
  - — assumptions — rationality, self discipline behaviour, profit maximization.
- The Sociological Approach
  - — deals primarily with human interactions;
  - — assumptions — bounded rationality, satisfying behaviour, profit sub-optimality. An example of a company that currently operates this way is Google.

Strategic management techniques can be viewed as bottom-up, top-down, or collaborative processes. In the bottom-up approach, employees submit proposals to their managers who, in turn, funnel the best ideas further up the organisation. This is often accomplished by a capital budgeting process. Proposals are assessed using financial criteria such as return on investment or cost-benefit analysis. Cost underestimation and benefit overestimation are major sources of error. The proposals that are approved form the substance of a new strategy, all of which is done without a grand strategic design or a strategic architect. The top-down approach is the most common by far. In it, the CEO, possibly with the assistance of a strategic planning team, decides on the overall direction the company should take. Some organisations are starting to experiment with collaborative strategic planning techniques that recognize the emergent nature of strategic decisions.

HISTORICAL DEVELOPMENT OF STRATEGIC MANAGEMENT

Birth of Strategic Management

Strategic management as a discipline originated in the 1950s and 60s. Although there were numerous early contributors to the literature, the most influential pioneers were Alfred D. Chandler, Jr., Philip Selznick, Igor Ansoff, and Peter Drucker.

Alfred Chandler recognized the importance of coordinating the various aspects of management under one all-encompassing strategy. Prior to this time the various functions of management were separate with little overall coordination or strategy. Interactions between functions or between departments were typically handled by a boundary position, that is, there were one or two managers that relayed information back and forth between two departments. Chandler also stressed the importance of taking a long term perspective when looking to the future. In his 1962 groundbreaking work Strategy and Structure, Chandler showed that a long-term coordinated strategy was necessary to give a company structure, direction, and focus. He says it concisely, "structure follows strategy."

In 1957, Philip Selznick introduced the idea of matching the organisation's internal factors with external environmental circumstances. This core idea was developed into what we now call SWOT analysis by Learned, Andrews, and others at the Harvard Business School General Management Group. Strengths and weaknesses of the firm are assessed in light of the opportunities and threats from the business environment.

Igor Ansoff built on Chandler's work by adding a range of strategic concepts and inventing a whole new vocabulary. He developed a strategy grid that compared market penetration strategies, product development strategies, market development strategies and horizontal and vertical integration and diversification strategies. He felt that management could use these strategies to systematically prepare for future opportunities and challenges. In his 1965 classic Corporate Strategy, he developed the gap analysis still used today in which we must understand the gap between where we are currently and where we would like to be, then develop what he called "gap reducing actions".

Peter Drucker was a prolific strategy theorist, author of dozens of management books, with a career spanning five decades. His contributions to strategic management were many but two are most important. Firstly, he stressed the importance of objectives. An organisation without clear objectives is like a ship without a rudder. As early as 1954 he was developing a theory of management based on objectives. This evolved into his theory of management by objectives (MBO). According to Drucker, the procedure of setting objectives and monitoring your progress towards them should permeate the entire organisation, top to bottom. His other seminal contribution was in predicting the importance of what today we would call intellectual capital. He predicted the rise of what he called the "knowledge worker" and explained the consequences of this for management. He said that knowledge work is non-hierarchical. Work would be carried out in teams with the person most knowledgeable in the task at hand being the temporary leader.

In 1985, Ellen-Earle Chaffee summarized what she thought were the main elements of strategic management theory by the 1970s:

- Strategic management involves adapting the organisation to its business environment.
- Strategic management is fluid and complex. Change creates novel combinations of circumstances requiring unstructured non-repetitive responses.
- Strategic management affects the entire organisation by providing direction.
- Strategic management involves both strategy formation (she called it content) and also strategy implementation (she called it process).
- Strategic management is partially planned and partially unplanned.
- Strategic management is done at several levels: overall corporate strategy, and individual business strategies.
- Strategic management involves both conceptual and analytical thought processes.

Growth and Portfolio Theory

In the 1970s much of strategic management dealt with size, growth, and portfolio theory. The PIMS study was a long term study, started in the 1960s and lasted for 19 years, that attempted to understand the Profit Impact of Marketing Strategies (PIMS), particularly the effect of market share. Started at General Electric, moved to Harvard in the early 1970s, and then moved to the Strategic Planning Institute in the late 1970s, it now contains decades of information on the relationship between profitability and strategy. Their initial conclusion was unambiguous: The greater a company's market share, the greater will be their rate of profit. The high market share provides volume and economies of scale. It also provides experience and learning curve advantages. The combined effect is increased profits. The studies conclusions continue to be drawn on by academics and companies today: "PIMS provides compelling quantitative evidence as to which business strategies work and don't work" - Tom Peters.

The benefits of high market share naturally lead to an interest in growth strategies. The relative advantages of horizontal integration, vertical integration, diversification, franchises, mergers and acquisitions, joint ventures, and organic growth were discussed. The most appropriate market dominance strategies were assessed given the competitive and regulatory environment.

There was also research that indicated that a low market share strategy could also be very profitable. Schumacher (1973), Woo and Cooper (1982), Levenson (1984), and later Traverso (2002) showed how smaller niche players obtained very high returns. By the early 1980s the paradoxical conclusion was that high market share and low market share companies were often very profitable but most of the companies in between were not. This was sometimes called the "hole in the middle" problem. This anomaly would be explained by Michael Porter in the 1980s.

The management of diversified organisations required new techniques and new ways of thinking. The first CEO to address the problem of a multi-divisional company was Alfred Sloan at General Motors. GM was decentralized into semi-autonomous "strategic business units" (SBU's), but with centralized support functions.

One of the most valuable concepts in the strategic management of multi-divisional companies was portfolio theory. In the previous decade Harry Markowitz and other financial theorists developed the theory of portfolio analysis. It was concluded that a broad portfolio of financial assets could reduce specific risk. In the 1970s marketers extended the theory to product portfolio decisions and managerial strategists extended it to operating division portfolios. Each of a company's operating divisions were seen as an element in the corporate portfolio. Each operating division (also called strategic business units) was treated as a semi-independent profit centre with its own revenues, costs, objectives, and strategies. Several techniques were developed to analyze the relationships between elements in a portfolio. B.C.G. Analysis, for example, was developed by the Boston Consulting Group in the early 1970s. This was the theory that gave us the wonderful image of a CEO sitting on a stool milking a cash cow. Shortly after that the G.E. multi factoral model was developed by General Electric. Companies continued to diversify until the 1980s when it was realized that in many cases a portfolio of operating divisions was worth more as separate completely independent companies.

The Marketing Revolution

The 1970s also saw the rise of the marketing oriented firm. From the beginnings of capitalism it was assumed that the key requirement of business success was a product of high technical quality. If you produced a product that worked well and was durable, it was assumed you would have no difficulty selling them at a profit. This was called the production orientation and it was generally true that good products could be sold without effort, encapsulated in the saying "Build a better mousetrap and the world will beat a path to your door." This was largely due to the growing numbers of affluent and middle class people that capitalism had created. But after the untapped demand caused by the second world war was saturated in the 1950s it became obvious that products were not selling as easily as they had been. The answer was to concentrate on selling.

The 1950s and 1960s is known as the sales era and the guiding philosophy of business of the time is today called the sales orientation. In the early 1970s Theodore Levitt and others at Harvard argued that the sales orientation had things backward. They claimed that instead of producing products then trying to sell them to the customer, businesses should start with the customer, find out what they wanted, and then produce it for them. The customer became the driving force behind all strategic business decisions. This marketing orientation, in the decades since its introduction, has been reformulated and repackaged under numerous names including customer orientation, marketing philosophy, customer intimacy, customer focus, customer driven, and market focused.

The Japanese Challenge

By the late 70s people had started to notice how successful Japanese industry had become. In industry after industry, including steel, watches, ship building, cameras, autos, and electronics, the Japanese were surpassing American and European companies. Westerners wanted to know why. Numerous theories purported to explain the Japanese success including:

- Higher employee morale, dedication, and loyalty;
- Lower cost structure, including wages;
- Effective government industrial policy;
- Modernization after WWII leading to high capital intensity and productivity;
- Economies of scale associated with increased exporting;
- Relatively low value of the Yen leading to low interest rates and capital costs, low dividend expectations, and inexpensive exports;
- Superior quality control techniques such as Total Quality Management and other systems introduced by W. Edwards Deming in the 1950s and 60s.

Although there was some truth to all these potential explanations, there was clearly something missing. In fact by 1980 the Japanese cost structure was higher than the American. And post WWII reconstruction was nearly 40 years in the past. The first management theorist to suggest an explanation was Richard Pascale.

In 1981 Richard Pascale and Anthony Athos in The Art of Japanese Management claimed that the main reason for Japanese success was their superior management techniques. They divided management into 7 aspects (which are also known as McKinsey 7S Framework): Strategy, Structure, Systems, Skills, Staff, Style, and Supraordinate goals (which we would now call shared values). The first three of the 7 S's were called hard factors and this is where American companies excelled. The remaining four factors (skills, staff, style, and shared values) were called soft factors and were not well understood by American businesses of the time Americans did not yet place great value on corporate culture, shared values and beliefs, and social cohesion in the workplace. In Japan the task of management was seen as managing the whole complex of human needs, economic, social, psychological, and spiritual. In America work was seen as something that was separate from the rest of one's life. It was quite common for Americans to exhibit a very different personality at work compared to the rest of their lives. Pascale also highlighted the difference between decision making styles; hierarchical in America, and consensus in Japan. He also claimed that American business lacked long term vision, preferring instead to apply management fads and theories in a piecemeal fashion.

One year later The Mind of the Strategist was released in America by Kenichi Ohmae, the head of McKinsey & Co.'s Tokyo office. (It was originally published in Japan in 1975.) He claimed that strategy in America was too analytical. Strategy should be a creative art: It is a frame of mind that requires intuition and intellectual flexibility. He claimed that Americans constrained their strategic options by thinking in terms of analytical techniques, rote formula, and step-by-step processes. He compared the culture of Japan in which vagueness, ambiguity, and tentative decisions were acceptable, to American culture that valued fast decisions.

Also in 1982 Tom Peters and Robert Waterman released a study that would respond to the Japanese challenge head on. Peters and Waterman, who had several years earlier collaborated with Pascale and Athos at McKinsey & Co. asked "What makes an excellent company?". They looked at 62 companies that they thought were fairly successful. Each was subject to six performance criteria. To be classified as an excellent company, it had to be above the 50th percentile in 4 of the 6 performance metrics for 20 consecutive years. Forty-three companies passed the test. They then studied these successful companies and interviewed key executives. They concluded in In Search of Excellence that there were 8 keys to excellence that were shared by all 43 firms. They are:

- A bias for action — Do it. Try it. Don't waste time studying it with multiple reports and committees.
- Customer focus — Get close to the customer. Know your customer.
- Entrepreneurship — Even big companies act and think small by giving people the authority to take initiatives.
- Productivity through people — Treat your people with respect and they will reward you with productivity.
- Value-oriented CEOs — The CEO should actively propagate corporate values throughout the organisation.
- Stick to the knitting — Do what you know well.
- Keep things simple and lean — Complexity encourages waste and confusion.
- Simultaneously centralized and decentralized — Have tight centralized control while also allowing maximum individual autonomy.

The basic blueprint on how to compete against the Japanese had been drawn. But as J.E. Rehfeld (1994) explains it is not a straight forward task due to differences in culture. A certain type of alchemy was required to transform knowledge from various cultures into a management style that allows a specific company to compete in a globally diverse world. He says, for example, that Japanese style kaizen (continuous improvement) techniques, although suitable for people socialized in Japanese culture, have not been successful when implemented in the U.S. unless they are modified significantly.

Gaining Competitive Advantage

The Japanese challenge shook the confidence of the western business elite, but detailed comparisons of the two management styles and examinations of successful businesses convinced westerners that they could overcome the challenge. The 1980s and early 1990s saw a plethora of theories explaining exactly how this could be done. They cannot all be detailed here, but some of the more important strategic advances of the decade are explained below.

Gary Hamel and C. K. Prahalad declared that strategy needs to be more active and interactive; less "arm-chair planning" was needed. They introduced terms like strategic intent and strategic architecture. Their most well known advance was the idea of core competency. They showed how important it was to know the one or two key things that your company does better than the competition.

Active strategic management required active information gathering and active problem solving. In the early days of Hewlett-Packard (H-P), Dave Packard and Bill Hewlett devised an active management style that they called Management By Walking Around (MBWA). Senior H-P managers were seldom at their desks. They spent most of their days visiting employees, customers, and suppliers. This direct contact with key people provided them with a solid grounding from which viable strategies could be crafted. The MBWA concept was popularized in 1985 by a book by Tom Peters and Nancy Austin. Japanese managers employ a similar system, which originated at Honda, and is sometimes called the 3 G's (Genba, Genbutsu, and Genjitsu, which translate into "actual place", "actual thing", and "actual situation").

Probably the most influential strategist of the decade was Michael Porter. He introduced many new concepts including; 5 forces analysis, generic strategies, the value chain, strategic groups, and clusters. In 5 forces analysis he identifies the forces that shape a firm's strategic environment. It is like a SWOT analysis with structure and purpose. It shows how a firm can use these forces to obtain a sustainable competitive advantage. Porter modifies Chandler's dictum about structure following strategy by introducing a second level of structure: Organisational structure follows strategy, which in turn follows industry structure. Porter's generic strategies detail the interaction between cost minimization strategies, product differentiation strategies, and market focus strategies. Although he did not introduce these terms, he showed the importance of choosing one of them rather than trying to position your company between them. He also challenged managers to see their industry in terms of a value chain. A firm will be successful only to the extent that it contributes to the industry's value chain. This forced management to look at its operations from the customer's point of view. Every operation should be examined in terms of what value it adds in the eyes of the final customer.

In 1993, John Kay took the idea of the value chain to a financial level claiming " Adding value is the central purpose of business activity", where adding value is defined as the difference between the market value of outputs and the cost of inputs including capital, all divided by the firm's net output. Borrowing from Gary Hamel and Michael Porter, Kay claims that the role of strategic management is to identify your core competencies, and then assemble a collection of assets that will increase value added and provide a competitive advantage. He claims that there are 3 types of capabilities that can do this; innovation, reputation, and organisational structure.

The 1980s also saw the widespread acceptance of positioning theory. Although the theory originated with Jack Trout in 1969, it didn't gain wide acceptance until Al Ries and Jack Trout wrote their classic book "Positioning: The Battle For Your Mind" (1979). The basic premise is that a strategy should not be judged by internal company factors but by the way customers see it relative to the competition. Crafting and implementing a strategy involves creating a position in the mind of the collective consumer. Several techniques were applied to positioning theory, some newly invented but most borrowed from other disciplines. Perceptual mapping for example, creates visual displays of the relationships between positions. Multidimensional scaling, discriminant analysis, factor analysis, and conjoint analysis are mathematical techniques used to determine the most relevant characteristics (called dimensions or factors) upon which positions should be based. Preference regression can be used to determine vectors of ideal positions and cluster analysis can identify clusters of positions. Others felt that internal company resources were the key. In 1992, Jay Barney, for example, saw strategy as assembling the optimum mix of resources, including human, technology, and suppliers, and then configure them in unique and sustainable ways.

Michael Hammer and James Champy felt that these resources needed to be restructured. This process, that they labeled reengineering, involved organizing a firm's assets around whole processes rather than tasks. In this way a team of people saw a project through, from inception to completion. This avoided functional silos where isolated departments seldom talked to each other. It also eliminated waste due to functional overlap and interdepartmental communications.

In 1989 Richard Lester and the researchers at the MIT Industrial Performance Centre identified seven best practices and concluded that firms must accelerate the shift away from the mass production of low cost standardized products. The seven areas of best practice were:

- Simultaneous continuous improvement in cost, quality, service, and product innovation
- Breaking down organisational barriers between departments
- Eliminating layers of management creating flatter organisational hierarchies.
- Closer relationships with customers and suppliers
- Intelligent use of new technology

- Global focus
- Improving human resource skills.

The search for "best practices" is also called benchmarking. This involves determining where you need to improve, finding an organisation that is exceptional in this area, then studying the company and applying its best practices in your firm.

A large group of theorists felt the area where western business was most lacking was product quality. People like W. Edwards Deming, Joseph M. Juran, A. Kearney, Philip Crosby, and Armand Feignbaum suggested quality improvement techniques like Total Quality Management (TQM), continuous improvement, lean manufacturing, Six Sigma, and Return on Quality (ROQ).

An equally large group of theorists felt that poor customer service was the problem. People like James Heskett (1988), Earl Sasser (1995), William Davidow, Len Schlesinger, A. Paraurgman (1988), Len Berry, Jane Kingman-Brundage, Christopher Hart, and Christopher Lovelock (1994), gave us fishbone diagramming, service charting, Total Customer Service (TCS), the service profit chain, service gaps analysis, the service encounter, strategic service vision, service mapping, and service teams. Their underlying assumption was that there is no better source of competitive advantage than a continuous stream of delighted customers.

Process management uses some of the techniques from product quality management and some of the techniques from customer service management. It looks at an activity as a sequential process. The objective is to find inefficiencies and make the process more effective. Although the procedures have a long history, dating back to Taylorism, the scope of their applicability has been greatly widened, leaving no aspect of the firm free from potential process improvements. Because of the broad applicability of process management techniques, they can be used as a basis for competitive advantage.

Some realized that businesses were spending much more on acquiring new customers than on retaining current ones. Carl Sewell, Frederick F. Reichheld, C. Gronroos, and Earl Sasser showed us how a competitive advantage could be found in ensuring that customers returned again and again. This has come to be known as the loyalty effect after Reicheld's book of the same name in which he broadens the concept to include employee loyalty, supplier loyalty, distributor loyalty, and shareholder loyalty. They also developed techniques for estimating the lifetime value of a loyal customer, called customer lifetime value (CLV). A significant movement started that attempted to recast selling and marketing techniques into a long term endeavor that created a sustained relationship with customers (called relationship selling, relationship marketing, and customer relationship management). Customer relationship management (CRM) software (and its many variants) became an integral tool that sustained this trend.

James Gilmore and Joseph Pine found competitive advantage in mass customization. Flexible manufacturing techniques allowed businesses to individualize products for each customer without losing economies of scale. This effectively turned the product into a service. They also realized that if a service is mass customized by creating a "performance" for each individual client, that service would be transformed into an "experience". Their book, The Experience Economy, along with the work of Bernd Schmitt convinced many to see service provision as a form of theatre. This school of thought is sometimes referred to as customer experience management (CEM).

Like Peters and Waterman a decade earlier, James Collins and Jerry Porras spent years conducting empirical research on what makes great companies. Six years of research uncovered a key underlying principle behind the 19 successful companies that they studied: They all encourage and preserve a core ideology that nurtures the company. Even though strategy and tactics change daily, the companies, nevertheless, were able to maintain a core set of values. These core values encourage employees to build an organisation that lasts. In Built To Last (1994) they claim that short term profit goals, cost cutting, and restructuring will not stimulate dedicated employees to build a great company that will endure. In 2000 Collins coined the term "built to flip" to describe the prevailing business attitudes in Silicon Valley. It describes a business culture where technological change inhibits a long term focus. He also popularized the concept of the BHAG (Big Hairy Audacious Goal).

Arie de Geus (1997) undertook a similar study and obtained similar results. He identified four key traits of companies that had prospered for 50 years or more. They are:

- Sensitivity to the business environment — the ability to learn and adjust
- Cohesion and identity — the ability to build a community with personality, vision, and purpose
- Tolerance and decentralization — the ability to build relationships
- Conservative financing

A company with these key characteristics he called a living company because it is able to perpetuate itself. If a company emphasizes knowledge rather than finance, and sees itself as an ongoing community of human beings, it has the potential to become great and endure for decades. Such an organisation is an organic entity capable of learning (he called it a "learning organisation") and capable of creating its own processes, goals, and persona.

STRATEGIC CHANGE

In 1970, Alvin Toffler in Future Shock described a trend towards accelerating rates of change. He illustrated how social and technological norms had shorter lifespans with each generation, and he questioned society's ability to cope with the resulting turmoil and anxiety. In past generations periods of change were always punctuated with times of stability. This allowed society to assimilate the change and deal with it before the next change arrived. But these periods of stability are getting shorter and by the late 20th century had all but disappeared. In 1980 in The Third Wave, Toffler characterized this shift to relentless change as the defining feature of the third phase of civilization (the first two phases being the agricultural and industrial waves). He claimed that the dawn of this new phase will cause great anxiety for those that grew up in the previous phases, and will cause much conflict and opportunity in the business world. Hundreds of authors, particularly since the early 1990s, have attempted to explain what this means for business strategy.

In 1997, Watts Waker and Jim Taylor called this upheaval a "500 year delta." They claimed these major upheavals occur every 5 centuries. They said we are currently making the transition from the "Age of Reason" to a new chaotic Age of Access. Jeremy Rifkin (2000) popularized and expanded this term, "age of access" three years later in his book of the same name.

In 1968, Peter Drucker (1969) coined the phrase Age of Discontinuity to describe the way change forces disruptions into the continuity of our lives. In an age of continuity attempts to predict the future by extrapolating from the past can be somewhat accurate. But according to Drucker, we are now in an age of discontinuity and extrapolating from the past is hopelessly ineffective. We cannot assume that trends that exist today will continue into the future. He identifies four sources of discontinuity: new technologies, globalization, cultural pluralism, and knowledge capital.

In 2000, Gary Hamel discussed strategic decay, the notion that the value of all strategies, no matter how brilliant, decays over time.

In 1978, Dereck Abell (Abell, D. 1978) described strategic windows and stressed the importance of the timing (both entrance and exit) of any given strategy. This has led some strategic planners to build planned obsolescence into their strategies. In 1989, Charles Handy identified two types of change. Strategic drift is a gradual change that occurs so subtly that it is not noticed until it is too late. By contrast, transformational change is sudden and radical. It is typically caused by discontinuities (or exogenous shocks) in the business environment. The point where a new trend is initiated is called a strategic inflection point by Andy Grove. Inflection points can be subtle or radical.

In 2000, Malcolm Gladwell discussed the importance of the tipping point, that point where a trend or fad acquires critical mass and takes off.

In 1983, Noel Tichy recognized that because we are all beings of habit we tend to repeat what we are comfortable with. He wrote that this is a trap that constrains our creativity, prevents us from exploring new ideas, and hampers our dealing with the full complexity of new issues. He developed a systematic method of dealing with change that involved looking at any new issue from three angles: technical and production, political and resource allocation, and corporate culture.

In 1990, Richard Pascale (Pascale, R. 1990) wrote that relentless change requires that businesses continuously reinvent themselves. His famous maxim is "Nothing fails like success" by which he means that what was a strength yesterday becomes the root of weakness today, We tend to depend on what worked yesterday and refuse to let go of what worked so well for us in the past. Prevailing strategies become self-confirming. In order to avoid this trap, businesses must stimulate a spirit of inquiry and healthy debate. They must encourage a creative process of self renewal based on constructive conflict.

In 1996, Art Kleiner (1996) claimed that to foster a corporate culture that embraces change, you have to hire the right people; heretics, heroes, outlaws, and visionaries· The conservative bureaucrat that made such a good middle manager in yesterday's hierarchical organisations is of little use today. A decade earlier Peters and Austin (1985) had stressed the importance of nurturing champions and heroes. They said we have a tendency to dismiss new ideas, so to overcome this, we should support those few people in the organisation that have the courage to put their career and reputation on the line for an unproven idea.

In 1996, Adrian Slywotsky showed how changes in the business environment are reflected in value migrations between industries, between companies, and within companies. He claimed that recognizing the patterns behind these value migrations is necessary if we wish to understand the world of chaotic change. In "Profit Patterns" (1999) he described businesses as being in a state of strategic anticipation as they try to spot emerging patterns. Slywotsky and his team identified 30 patterns that have transformed industry after industry. In 1997, Clayton Christensen (1997) took the position that great companies can fail precisely because they do everything right since the capabilities of the organisation also defines its disabilities. Christensen's thesis is that outstanding companies lose their market leadership when confronted with disruptive technology. He called the approach to discovering the emerging markets for disruptive technologies agnostic marketing, i.e., marketing under the implicit assumption that no one - not the company, not the customers - can know how or in what quantities a disruptive product can or will be used before they have experience using it.

A number of strategists use scenario planning techniques to deal with change. Kees van der Heijden (1996), for example, says that change and uncertainty make "optimum strategy" determination impossible. We have neither the time nor the information required for such a calculation. The best we can hope for is what he calls "the most skillful process". The way Peter Schwartz put it in 1991 is that strategic outcomes cannot be known in advance so the sources of competitive advantage cannot be predetermined. The fast changing business environment is too uncertain for us to find sustainable value in formulas of excellence or competitive advantage. Instead, scenario planning is a technique in which multiple outcomes can be developed, their implications assessed, and their likeliness of occurrence evaluated. According to Pierre Wack, scenario planning is about insight, complexity, and subtlety, not about formal analysis and numbers.

In 1988, Henry Mintzberg looked at the changing world around him and decided it was time to reexamine how strategic management was done. He examined the strategic process and concluded it was much more fluid and unpredictable than people had thought. Because of this, he could not point to one process that could be called strategic planning. Instead he concludes that there are five types of strategies. They are:

- *Strategy as plan:* A direction, guide, course of action - intention rather than actual
- *Strategy as ploy:* A maneuver intended to outwit a competitor
- *Strategy as pattern:* A consistent pattern of past behaviour - realized rather than intended
- *Strategy as position:* Locating of brands, products, or companies within the conceptual framework of consumers or other stakeholders - strategy determined primarily by factors outside the firm
- *Strategy as perspective:* Strategy determined primarily by a master strategist

In 1998, Mintzberg developed these five types of management strategy into 10 "schools of thought". These 10 schools are grouped into three categories. The first group is prescriptive or normative. It consists of the informal design and conception school, the formal planning school, and the analytical positioning school.

The second group, consisting of six schools, is more concerned with how strategic management is actually done, rather than prescribing optimal plans or positions. The six schools are the entrepreneurial, visionary, or great leader school, the cognitive or mental process school, the learning, adaptive, or emergent process school, the power or negotiation school, the corporate culture or collective process school, and the business environment or reactive school.

The third and final group consists of one school, the configuration or transformation school, an hybrid of the other schools organized into stages, organisational life cycles, or "episodes".

In 1999, Constantinos Markides also wanted to reexamine the nature of strategic planning itself. He describes strategy formation and implementation as an on-going, never-ending, integrated process requiring continuous reassessment and reformation.

Strategic management is planned and emergent, dynamic, and interactive. J. Moncrieff (1999) also stresses strategy dynamics. He recognized that strategy is partially deliberate and partially unplanned. The unplanned element comes from two sources: emergent strategies (result from the emergence of opportunities and threats in the environment) and Strategies in action (ad hoc actions by many people from all parts of the organisation).

Some business planners are starting to use a complexity theory approach to strategy. Complexity can be thought of as chaos with a dash of order. Chaos theory deals with turbulent systems that rapidly become disordered. Complexity is not quite so unpredictable. It involves multiple agents interacting in such a way that a glimpse of structure may appear. Axelrod, R., Holland, J., and Kelly, S. and Allison, M.A., call these systems of multiple actions and reactions complex adaptive systems. Axelrod asserts that rather than fear complexity, business should harness it. He says this can best be done when "there are many participants, numerous interactions, much trial and error learning, and abundant attempts to imitate each others' successes". In 2000, E. Dudik wrote that an organisation must develop a mechanism for understanding the source and level of complexity it will face in the future and then transform itself into a complex adaptive system in order to deal with it.

INFORMATION AND TECHNOLOGY DRIVEN STRATEGY

Peter Drucker had theorized the rise of the "knowledge worker" back in the 1950s. He described how fewer workers would be doing physical labor, and more would be applying their minds. In 1984, John Nesbitt theorized that the future would be driven largely by information: companies that managed information well could obtain an advantage, however the profitability of what he calls the "information float" (information that the company had and others desired) would all but disappear as inexpensive computers made information more accessible.

Daniel Bell (1985) examined the sociological consequences of information technology, while Gloria Schuck and Shoshana Zuboff looked at psychological factors.

Zuboff, in her five year study of eight pioneering corporations made the important distinction between "automating technologies" and "infomating technologies". She studied the effect that both had on individual workers, managers, and organisational structures. She largely confirmed Peter Drucker's predictions three decades earlier, about the importance of flexible decentralized structure, work teams, knowledge sharing, and the central role of the knowledge worker. Zuboff also detected a new basis for managerial authority, based not on position or hierarchy, but on knowledge (also predicted by Drucker) which she called "participative management".

In 1990, Peter Senge, who had collaborated with Arie de Geus at Dutch Shell, borrowed de Geus' notion of the learning organisation, expanded it, and popularized it. The underlying theory is that a company's ability to gather, analyze, and use information is a necessary requirement for business success in the information age. In order to do this, Senge claimed that an organisation would need to be structured such that:

- People can continuously expand their capacity to learn and be productive,
- New patterns of thinking are nurtured,
- Collective aspirations are encouraged, and
- People are encouraged to see the "whole picture" together.

Senge identified five components of a learning organisation. They are:

- Personal responsibility, self reliance, and mastery — We accept that we are the masters of our own destiny. We make decisions and live with the consequences of them. When a problem needs to be fixed, or an opportunity exploited, we take the initiative to learn the required skills to get it done.

- Mental models — We need to explore our personal mental models to understand the subtle effect they have on our behaviour.
- Shared vision — The vision of where we want to be in the future is discussed and communicated to all. It provides guidance and energy for the journey ahead.
- Team learning — We learn together in teams. This involves a shift from "a spirit of advocacy to a spirit of enquiry".
- Systems thinking — We look at the whole rather than the parts. This is what Senge calls the "Fifth discipline". It is the glue that integrates the other four into a coherent strategy.

Since 1990 many theorists have written on the strategic importance of information, including J.B. Quinn, J. Carlos Jarillo, D.L. Barton, Manuel Castells, J.P. Lieleskin, Thomas Stewart, K.E. Sveiby, Gilbert J. Probst, and Shapiro and Varian to name just a few.

Thomas A. Stewart, for example, uses the term intellectual capital to describe the investment an organisation makes in knowledge. It is comprised of human capital (the knowledge inside the heads of employees), customer capital (the knowledge inside the heads of customers that decide to buy from you), and structural capital (the knowledge that resides in the company itself). Manuel Castells, describes a network society characterized by: globalization, organisations structured as a network, instability of employment, and a social divide between those with access to information technology and those without.

Stan Davis and Christopher Meyer (1998) have combined three variables to define what they call the BLUR equation. The speed of change, Internet connectivity, and intangible knowledge value, when multiplied together yields a society's rate of BLUR. The three variables interact and reinforce each other making this relationship highly non-linear.

Regis McKenna posits that life in the high tech information age is what he called a "real time experience". Events occur in real time. To ever more demanding customers "now" is what matters. Pricing will more and more become variable pricing changing with each transaction, often exhibiting first degree price discrimination. Customers expect immediate service, customized to their needs, and will be prepared to pay a premium price for it. He claimed that the new basis for competition will be time based competition.

Geoffrey Moore (1991) and R. Frank and P. Cook also detected a shift in the nature of competition. In industries with high technology content, technical standards become established and this gives the dominant firm a near monopoly. The same is true of networked industries in which interoperability requires compatibility between users. An example is word processor documents. Once a product has gained market dominance, other products, even far superior products, cannot compete. Moore showed how firms could attain this enviable position by using E.M. Rogers five stage adoption process and focusing on one group of customers at a time, using each group as a base for marketing to the next group. The most difficult step is making the transition between visionaries and pragmatists. If successful a firm can create a bandwagon effect in which the momentum builds and your product becomes a de facto standard.

Evans and Wurster describe how industries with a high information component are being transformed. They cite Encarta's demolition of the Encyclopedia Britannica (whose sales have plummeted 80 per cent since their peak of $650 million in 1990). Many speculate that Encarta's reign will be short-lived, eclipsed by collaborative encyclopedias like Wikipedia that can operate at very low marginal costs. Evans also mentions the music industry which is desperately looking for a new business model. The upstart information savvy firms, unburdened by cumbersome physical assets, are changing the competitive landscape, redefining market segments, and disintermediating some channels. One manifestation of this is personalized marketing. Information technology allows marketers to treat each individual as its own market, a market of one. Traditional ideas of market segments will no longer be relevant if personalized marketing is successful.

The technology sector has provided some strategies directly. For example, from the software development industry agile software development provides a model for shared development processes.

Access to information systems have allowed senior managers to take a much more comprehensive view of strategic management than ever before. The most notable of the comprehensive systems is the balanced scorecard approach developed in the early 1990s by Drs. Robert S. Kaplan (Harvard Business School) and David Norton (Kaplan, R. and Norton, D. 1992). It measures several factors financial, marketing, production, organisational development, and new product development in order to achieve a 'balanced' perspective.

THE PSYCHOLOGY OF STRATEGIC MANAGEMENT

Several psychologists have conducted studies to determine the psychological patterns involved in strategic management. Typically senior managers have been asked how they go about making strategic decisions.

A 1938 treatise by Chester Barnard, that was based on his own experience as a business executive, sees the process as informal, intuitive, non-routinized, and involving primarily oral, 2-way communications. Bernard says "The process is the sensing of the organisation as a whole and the total situation relevant to it. It transcends the capacity of merely intellectual methods, and the techniques of discriminating the factors of the situation. The terms pertinent to it are "feeling", "judgement", "sense", "proportion", "balance", "appropriateness". It is a matter of art rather than science."

In 1973, Henry Mintzberg found that senior managers typically deal with unpredictable situations so they strategize in ad hoc, flexible, dynamic, and implicit ways. He says, "The job breeds adaptive information-manipulators who prefer the live concrete situation. The manager works in an environment of stimulous-response, and he develops in his work a clear preference for live action."

In 1982, John Kotter studied the daily activities of 15 executives and concluded that they spent most of their time developing and working a network of relationships from which they gained general insights and specific details to be used in making strategic decisions. They tended to use "mental road maps" rather than systematic planning techniques.

Daniel Isenberg's 1984 study of senior managers found that their decisions were highly intuitive. Executives often sensed what they were going to do before they could explain why. He claimed in 1986 that one of the reasons for this is the complexity of strategic decisions and the resultant information uncertainty.

Shoshana Zuboff (1988) claims that information technology is widening the divide between senior managers (who typically make strategic decisions) and operational level managers (who typically make routine decisions). She claims that prior to the widespread use of computer systems, managers, even at the most senior level, engaged in both strategic decisions and routine administration, but as computers facilitated (She called it "deskilled") routine processes, these activities were moved further down the hierarchy, leaving senior management free for strategic decions making.

In 1977, Abraham Zaleznik identified a difference between leaders and managers. He describes leadershipleaders as visionaries who inspire. They care about substance. Whereas managers are claimed to care about process, plans, and form. He also claimed in 1989 that the rise of the manager was the main factor that caused the decline of American business in the 1970s and 80s. Lack of leadership is most damaging at the level of strategic management where it can paralyze an entire organisation.

According to Corner, Kinichi, and Keats, strategic decision making in organisations occurs at two levels: individual and aggregate. They have developed a model of parallel strategic decision making. The model identifies two parallel processes both of which involve getting attention, encoding information, storage and retrieval of information, strategic choice, strategic outcome, and feedback. The individual and organisational processes are not independent however. They interact at each stage of the process.

Reasons Why Strategic Plans Fail

There are many reasons why strategic plans fail, especially:

- Failure to understand the customer
  - — Why do they buy
  - — Is there a real need for the product
  - — inadequate or incorrect marketing research
- Inability to predict environmental reaction
  - — What will competitors do
    - » Fighting brands
    - » Price wars
  - — Will government intervene
- Over-estimation of resource competence
  - — Can the staff, equipment, and processes handle the new strategy
  - — Failure to develop new employee and management skills
- Failure to coordinate
  - — Reporting and control relationships not adequate
  - — Organisational structure not flexible enough
- Failure to obtain senior management commitment
  - — Failure to get management involved right from the start
  - — Failure to obtain sufficient company resources to accomplish task
- Failure to obtain employee commitment
  - — New strategy not well explained to employees
  - — No incentives given to workers to embrace the new strategy
- Under-estimation of time requirements
  - — No critical path analysis done
- Failure to follow the plan
  - — No follow through after initial planning
  - — No tracking of progress against plan

  - No consequences for above
- Failure to manage change
  - Inadequate understanding of the internal resistance to change
  - Lack of vision on the relationships between processes, technology and organisation
- Poor communications
  - Insufficient information sharing among stakeholders
  - Exclusion of stakeholders and delegates

Limitations of Strategic Management

Although a sense of direction is important, it can also stifle creativity, especially if it is rigidly enforced. In an uncertain and ambiguous world, fluidity can be more important than a finely tuned strategic compass. When a strategy becomes internalized into a corporate culture, it can lead to group think. It can also cause an organisation to define itself too narrowly. An example of this is marketing myopia.

Many theories of strategic management tend to undergo only brief periods of popularity. A summary of these theories thus inevitably exhibits survivorship bias (itself an area of research in strategic management). Many theories tend either to be too narrow in focus to build a complete corporate strategy on, or too general and abstract to be applicable to specific situations. Populism or faddishness can have an impact on a particular theory's life cycle and may see application in inappropriate circumstances.

In 2000, Gary Hamel coined the term strategic convergence to explain the limited scope of the strategies being used by rivals in greatly differing circumstances. He lamented that strategies converge more than they should, because the more successful ones get imitated by firms that do not understand that the strategic process involves designing a custom strategy for the specifics of each situation.

Ram Charan, aligning with a popular marketing tagline, believes that strategic planning must not dominate action. "Just do it!", while not quite what he meant, is a phrase that nevertheless comes to mind when combatting analysis paralysis.

7

Recruitment and Selection

RECRUITMENT

Definition Of Recruitment: Finding and Attracting Applications.

"Recruitment is the Process of finding and attracting capable applicants for employment. The Process begins when new recruits are sought and ends when their applications are submitted. The result is a pool of application from which new employees are selected."

Meaning of Recruitment

Recruitment is understood as the process of searching for and obtaining applicants for jobs, from among them the right people can be selected.

Though theoretically recruitment process is said to end with the receipt of applications, in practice the activity extends to the screening of applications so as to eliminate those who are not qualified for the job.

Purpose and Importance of Recruitment

- Determine the present and future requirements in conjunction with personnel planning and job analysis activities
- Increase the pool of job candidates at minimum cost
- Help increase success rate of selection process by reducing number of under-qualified or over-qualified applications.
- Reduce the probability that job applicants once selected would leave shortly
- Meet legal and social obligations
- Identify and prepare potential job applicants
- Evaluate effectiveness of various recruitment techniques and sources for job applicants.

Factors Governing Recruitment

- *External Factors:*
  - Demand and Supply (Specific Skills)
  - Unemployment Rate (Area-wise)
  - Labour Market Conditions
  - Political and Legal Environment (Reservations, Labour laws)
  - Image
- *Internal Factors*:
  - Recruitment Policy (Internal Hiring or External Hiring?)
  - Human Resource Planning (Planning of resources required)
  - Size of the Organization (Bigger the size lesser the recruitment problems)
  - Cost
  - Growth and Expansion Plans.

PREPARATION FOR RECRUITMENT

Before you think of inviting people to apply for a job you have to decide what types of persons are to be invited and what their characteristics should be. This calls for fixing the 'job specifications' which may also be called 'man specifications'. Job specifications are based on job description which is dependent upon the nature and requirements of a job. Thus, job specification will be different for each job.

Physical Specifications

For certain jobs some special physical features may be required. For example, for assembly of a TV set or some other electronic equipment good vision is required, for a typing job you need finger dexterity, for a heavy job you need a strong, heavy and thick-set body.

The particular physical abilities and skills necessary for a given job have to be specified. These may refer to height, weight, vision, finger dexterity, voice, poise, hand and foot coordination, motor coordination, colour discrimination, age-range, etc.

Mental Specifications

These include intelligence, memory, judgement, ability – plan, ability to estimate, to read, to write, to think and concentrate, scientific faculties, arithmetical abilities, etc. Different jobs require different degrees of such abilities and the more important ones should be specified.

Emotional and Social Specifications

These include characteristics which will affect his working with others, like personal appearance, manners, emotional stability, aggressiveness, or submissiveness, extroversion or introversion, leadership, cooperativeness, initiative and drive, skill in dealing with others, social adaptability, etc.

Behavioural Specifications

Certain management personnel at higher levels of management are expected to behave in a particular manner. These are not formally listed but have to be kept in mind during the process of recruitment, selection and placement.

Sources of Manpower

There are two categories of springs of supply of manpower:

1. *Internal springs*: These include personnel already on the pay-roll of the organization as also those who were once on the pay-roll of the company but who plan to return, or whom the company, would like to rehire. These include those who quit voluntarily or those on production lay-offs.
2. *External springs*: These springs lie outside the organization, like the new entrants to the labour force without experience.

These include college students, the unemployed with a wider range of skills and abilities, the retired experienced persons, and others not in the labour force, like married women. A policy of preferring people from within is advantageous as it improves the morale of the employees and promotes loyalty among them towards the organization.

This also helps employers as they are in a better position to evaluate those already with them and as these people require no induction. The policy of preferring internal candidates, however, suffers from some disadvantages. It may lead to inbreeding, discouraging new blood from entering an organization. If promotion is based on seniority, the real capable hands may be left out. Likewise, there are good and bad points about external springs. These springs provide a wide market and the best selection considering skill, training and education.

It also helps to bring new ideas into the organization. Moreover, this spring never 'dries up'. In respect of people selected under this system, however, one has to take chances with the selected persons regarding their loyalty and desire to continue. The organization has to make larger investments in their training and induction. You will realise now that dependence on just one of the springs is not in the interest of an organization. It must depend on both in a ratio to be fixed considering various factors:

- *Effect of the policy on the attitude and actions of all employees*: Employees, no doubt, feel more secure and identify their own long-term interest with that of the organization when they can anticipate first charge at job opportunities. The general application of the 'promotion from within' policy may encourage mediocre performance. The point to be considered here by the organization is, how important is the loyalty of the employees to it, balancing the risk of mediocre performance.
- *The level of specialization required of employees*: The principal spring in many organizations may be the ranks of the present employees who have received specialized training.
- *The degree of emphasis on participation by employees at all levels*: New employees from outside, with no experience in the firm, may not know enough about its service or product or processes to participate effectively, for some time at least.
- *The need for and availability of originality and initiative within the organization*: If the organization feels that it is training its people for these qualities it may prefer its own people; if not, new people with different ideas may be taken from outside.
- *Acceptance of seniority principle*: The policy or promotion from within will succeed only if management and employees accept the seniority principle with or without suitable modifications for promotion. If it is not accepted, selection may better be done on an open basis.

METHODS OF RECRUITMENT

All methods of recruitment can be put into three categories:

1. ***Direct Methods:*** Include sending recruiters to educational and professional institutions, employee contacts with public, manned exhibits and waiting lists.
   - *Schools and Colleges*: For clerical, labour and apprenticeship help, high schools can be extensively used. For technical, managerial and professional jobs, colleges, university departments and specialized institutes, like the IITs and IIMs, are used. These institutions usually have a placement officer a teacher-in-charge of placement, who normally provides help in attracting employers arranging interviews, furnishing space and other facilities and providing student resumes. The

companies maintain a list of such institutions, keep in touch with them, send their brochures indicating job openings, future prospects, etc. On the basis of these students who want to be considered for the given job(s) are referred to the company recruiter.

- *Employees' Contact with the Public*: The employees of the organization are told about the existence of particular vacancies and they bring this to the notice of their relatives, friends and acquaintances.
- *Manned Exhibits*: The organizations send recruiters to conventions and seminars, setting up exhibition at fairs, and using mobile offices to go to the desired centres.
- *Waiting Lists*: Many firms lean heavily on their own application files. These records list individuals who have indicated their interest in jobs, either after visiting the organization's employment office or making enquiries by mail or phone. Such records prove a very useful spring if they are kept up-to-date.

2. ***Indirect Methods:*** Cover advertising in newspapers, on the radio, in trade and professional journals, technical journals and brochures. When qualified and experienced persons are not available through other springs, advertising in newspapers and professional and technical journals is made.

   Whereas all types of advertisements can be made in newspapers and magazines, only particular types of posts should be advertised in the professional and technical journals; for example, only engineering jobs should be inserted in journals of engineering.. A well thought-out and planned advertisement for an appointment reduces the possibility of unqualified people applying. If the advertisement is clear and to the point, candidates can assess their abilities and suitability for the position and only those who possess the requisite qualifications will apply.

3. ***Third-Party Methods:*** Various agencies are used for recruitment under these methods. These include commercial and private employment agencies, state agencies, placement offices of schools, colleges and professional associations, recruiting firms, management consulting firms, indoctrination seminars for college professors, friends and relatives.

   Private Employment Agencies specialize in specific occupation like general office help, salesmen, technical workers, accountants, computer staff, engineers and executives, etc. These agencies bring together the employers and suitable persons available for a job. Because of their specialization, they can interpret the needs of their clients and seek out particular types of persons. State or Public Employment Agencies, also known as Employment or Labour Exchanges, are the main agencies for public employment. They also provide a wide range of services, like counselling, assistance in getting jobs, information about the labour market, labour and wage rates, etc.

Executive Search Agencies maintain complete information records about employed executives and recommend persons of high calibre for managerial, marketing and production engineers' posts. These agencies are looked upon as 'head hunters', 'raiders', and 'pirates'.

Indoctrination Seminars for College Professors: These are arranged to discuss the problems of companies to which professors are invited. Visits and banquets are arranged so that professors may be favourably impressed and later speak well of the company and help in getting required personnel. Friends and Relatives of Present Employees constitute a good spring from which employees may be drawn. This, however, is likely to encourage nepotism, *i.e.* persons of one's own community or caste may only be employed. This may create problems for the organization. Trade Unions are often called on by the employers to supply whatever additional employees may be needed. Unions may be asked for recommendations largely as a matter of courtesy and an evidence of goodwill and cooperation. Professional Societies may provide leads and clues in providing promising candidates for engineering, technical and management positions. Some of these maintain mail order placement services. Temporary Help Agencies employ their own labour force, both full-time and parttime and make them available to their client organizations for temporary needs. Casual Labour spring is one which presents itself daily at the factory gate or employment office. Most industrial parts rely to some extent on this spring. This spring, you will realise, is the most uncertain of all springs.

Deputation: Persons possessing certain abilities useful to another organization are sometimes deputed to it for a specified duration. Ready expertise is available but, as you can guess, such employees do not easily become part of the organization.

PROCESS OF RECRUITMENT

- *Recruitment Planning*:
  - Number of contacts
  - Types of contacts

- *Recruitment Strategy Development:*
  - Make or Buy Employees
  - Technological Sophistication
  - Where to look
  - How to look
- *Internal Recruitment*:
  - Present employees
  - Employee referrals
  - Transfers & Promotions
  - Former Employees
  - Previous Applicants
  - Evaluation of Internal Recruitment
- *External Recruitment*:
  - Professionals or Trade Associations
  - Advertisements
  - Employment Exchanges
  - Campus Recruitment
  - Walk-ins Interviews
  - Consultants
  - Contractors
  - Displaced Persons
  - Radio & Television
  - Acquisitions & Mergers
  - Competitors
  - Evaluation of External Recruitment
- *Searching*:
  - Source activation
  - Selling
  - Screening of Applications
- *Evaluation and Cost Control*:
  - Salary Cost
  - Management & Professional Time spent
  - Advertisement Cost
  - Producing Supporting literature
  - Recruitment Overheads and Expenses
  - Cost of Overtime and Outsourcing

  - Consultant's fees
- *Evaluation of Recruitment Process*:
  - Return rate of applications sent out
  - Suitable Candidates for selection
  - Retention and Performance of selected candidates
  - Recruitment Cost
  - Time lapsed data
  - Image projection.

RECRUITMENT PROCESS OUTSOURCING

Recruitment Process Outsourcing (RPO) is a form of business process outsourcing (BPO) where an employer outsources or transfers all or part of its recruitment activities to an external service provider.

To quote the Recruitment Process Outsourcing Association, "Recruitment Process Outsourcing is when a provider acts as a company's internal recruitment function for a portion or all of its jobs. RPO providers manage the entire recruiting/hiring process from job profiling through the on-boarding of the new hire, including staff, technology, method and reporting. A properly managed RPO will improve a company's time to hire, increase the quality of the candidate pool, provide verifiable metrics, reduce cost and improve governmental compliance."

On the other hand, occasional recruitment support, for example temporary, contingency and executive search services is more analogous to out-tasking, co-sourcing or just sourcing. In this example the service provider is "a" source for certain types of recruitment activity. The biggest distinction between RPO and other types of staffing is Process. In RPO the service provider assumes ownership of the process, while in other types of staffing the service provider is part of a process controlled by the organisation buying their services.

History

While temporary, contingency and executive search firms have provided staffing services for many decades, the concept of an employer outsourcing the management and ownership of part or all of their recruiting process wasn't first realized on a consistent basis until the 1970s in Silicon Valley's highly competitive high tech labor market. Fast-growing high tech companies were hard-pressed to locate and hire the technical specialists they required, and so had little choice but to pay large fees to highly specialized external recruiters in order to staff their projects.

Over time, companies began to examine how they might reduce the growing expenses of recruitment fees while still hiring hard-to-find technical specialists. Toward this end, companies began to examine the various steps in the recruiting process with an eye toward outsourcing only those portions that they had the greatest difficulty with and that added the greatest value to them. Initial RPO programmes typically consisted of companies purchasing lists of potential candidates from RPO vendors. This "search/research" function, as it was called, generated names of competitors' employees for a company and served to augment the pool of potential candidates from which that company could hire.

Over time, as business in general embraced the concept of outsourcing more and more, RPO gained favour among Human Resource management: not only did RPO reduce overhead costs from their budgets but it also helped improve the company's competitive advantage in the labor market.

As labor markets became more and more competitive, RPO became more of an acceptable option. Furthermore, through the advent in the 1980's and 1990's of human resources outsourcing (HRO) companies that began taking on the processes associated with benefits, taxes, and payroll, companies began recognizing that recruiting—a significant cost of HR—should also be considered for outsourcing. In the early 2000's more companies began considering the outsourcing of recruitment for major portions of their recruiting need.

There have been fundamental changes in the US labor market that serve to reinforce the use of RPO as well. The labor market has become increasingly dynamic: workers today change employers more often than in previous generations.

De-regulated labor markets have also created a shift towards contract and part-time labor and shorter work tenures. These trends increase recruitment activity and may encourage the use of RPO. It should also be noted that even in slower economic times or higher unemployment, RPO is still considered by companies to assist in an increasing need to screen through a larger candidate pool.

Benefits

RPO's promoters claim that the solution offers improvement in quality, cost, service and speed. RPO providers claim that economies of scale enables them to offer recruitment processes at lower cost while economies of scope allow them to operate as high-quality, specialists. Economies of scale and scope are said to arise from a larger staff of recruiters, databases of candidate resumes, and investment in recruitment tools and networks.

RPO solutions are also claimed to change fixed investment costs into variable costs that vary with fluctuation in recruitment activity. Companies may pay by transaction rather than by staff member, thus avoiding under-utilization or forcing costly layoffs of recruitment staff when activity is low.

Problems

If a company failed to define its overall recruitment strategy and hiring objectives, then any recruiting programme may fail to meet the company's needs. This is especially true for outsourced programmes like RPO. RPO can only succeed in the context of a well defined corporate and staffing strategy. As with any programme, a company must manage its RPO activities. A company must provide initial direction and continued monitoring to assure the desired results. Overall, providing guidance to external activities can present a significant management challenge. Outsourcing of company processes may fail or prove a poor organisational fit. Improperly implemented RPO could reduce the effectiveness of recruitment.

The costs charged for recruitment transactions may total more than the cost of the internal recruitment department.

RPO service providers may fail to provide the quality or volume of staff required by their customers.

Placing all recruitment in the hands of a single outside provider may discourage the competition that would arise if multiple recruitment agencies were used.

An RPO solution may not work if the company's existing recruitment processes are performing poorly. An RPO solution may not work if the service provider has inadequate recruitment processes or procedures to work with the client.

RPO may not resolve difficulties that organisations have hiring staff when the organisation is perceived negatively by potential employees. This will instead require improved branding and an adjustment of image. In fact, very few RPOs can successfully integrate their client's brand and therefore do not represent their client's brand as well as a retained search or internal recruiting resource may drive brand representation and or marketing.

Further, most RPOs perform their staffing functions and service offsite, further disconnecting the client's growth & recruiting strategy from the actual workforce within the client company. This is important because during a period of rapid recruitment growth, one of the many positive effects that a company typically enjoys is an increase in the workforce wellness or an overall workforce positivity of sentiment of optimism that comes with personnel additions... this may be lessened with an OFFSITE recruiting function.

Organisations with efficient hiring process that are viewed as employers-of-choice by potential staff may stand to gain negligible benefits from RPO.

SELECTION

Selection is the process of picking up individuals (out of the pool of job applicants) with requisite qualifications and competence to fill jobs in the organization. A formal definition of Selection is as under

Definition of Selection: Process of differentiating

"Selection is the process of differentiating between applicants in order to identify and hire those with a greater likelihood of success in a job."

Difference between recruitment and selection:

Recruitment:

1. Recruitment refers to the process of identifying and encouraging prospective employees to apply for jobs.
2. Recruitment is said to be positive in its approach as it seeks to attract as many candidates as possible.

Selection:

1. Selection is concerned with picking up the right candidates from a pool of applicants.
2. Selection on the other hand is negative in its application in as much as it seeks to eliminate as many unqualified applicants as possible in order to identify the right candidates.

PROCESS/ STEPS IN SELECTION

- *Preliminary Interview*: The purpose of preliminary interviews is basically to eliminate unqualified applications based on information supplied in application forms. The basic objective is to reject misfits. On the other hands preliminary interviews is often called a courtesy interview and is a good public relations exercise.
- *Selection Tests*: Jobseekers who past the preliminary interviews are called for tests. There are various types of tests conducted depending upon the jobs and the company. These tests can be Aptitude Tests, Personality Tests, and Ability Tests and are conducted to judge how well an individual can perform tasks related to the job. Besides this there are some other tests also like Interest Tests (activity

preferences), Graphology Test (Handwriting), Medical Tests, Psychometric Tests etc.

- *Employment Interview*: The next step in selection is employment interview. Here interview is a formal and in-depth conversation between applicant's acceptability. It is considered to be an excellent selection device. Interviews can be One-to-One, Panel Interview, or Sequential Interviews. Besides there can be Structured and Unstructured interviews, Behavioural Interviews, Stress Interviews.
- *Reference & Background Checks*: Reference checks and background checks are conducted to verify the information provided by the candidates. Reference checks can be through formal letters, telephone conversations. However it is merely a formality and selections decisions are seldom affected by it.
- *Selection Decision*: After obtaining all the information, the most critical step is the selection decision is to be made. The final decision has to be made out of applicants who have passed preliminary interviews, tests, final interviews and reference checks. The views of line managers are considered generally because it is the line manager who is responsible for the performance of the new employee.
- *Physical Examination*: After the selection decision is made, the candidate is required to undergo a physical fitness test. A job offer is often contingent upon the candidate passing the physical examination.
- *Job Offer*: The next step in selection process is job offer to those applicants who have crossed all the previous hurdles. It is made by way of letter of appointment.
- *Contract of Employment*: After the job offer is made and candidates accept the offer, certain documents need to be executed by the employer and the candidate. Here is a need to prepare a formal contract of employment, containing written contractual terms of employment etc.

Essentials of a Good Selection Practice

- Detailed job descriptions and job specifications prepared in advance and endorsed by personnel and line management
- Trained the selectors
- Determine aids to be used for selection process
- Check competence of recruitment consultants before retention
- Involve line managers at all stages

- Attempt to validate the procedure
- Help the appointed candidate to succeed by training and management development

Barriers to Effective Selection

- *Perception*: We all perceive the world differently. Our limited perceptual ability is obviously a stumbling block to the objective and rational selection of people.
- *Fairness*: Barriers of fairness includes discrimination against religion, region, race or gender etc.
- *Validity*: A test that has been validated can differentiate between the employees who can perform well and those who will not. However it does not predict the job success accurately.
- *Reliability*: A reliable test may fail to predict job performance with precision.
- *Pressure*: Pressure brought on selectors by politicians, bureaucrats, relatives, friends and peers to select particular candidate are also barriers to selection.

HIRING

General

Policies and procedures about hiring are designed to provide guidelines for filling a vacant position with the right candidate. The hiring decision is a major investment by an organisation and the policies around making this decision need to be clear. Hiring policies need to comply with human rights legislation through anti-discriminatory practices.

Hiring policies can be presented in many different ways.

Recruitment and Selection

Policies on recruitment and selection outline how recruitment will be done and provide guidelines for the selection process.

Recruitment is the process of gathering a group of qualified applicants. It includes tasks like writing a job description and job postings, and going through the steps of posting it internally (e.g. bulletin boards, intranet, e-mail notification), externally (e.g. newspaper ads, temp agencies, internet), or both. Selection is the process designed to determine the most qualified candidate from the group of applicants. It includes tasks like reviewing resumes, interviewing, work related testing, reference checks and the final employment offer. From the words in a job posting to the questions asked during an interview, it is necessary to be objective and to focus on the requirements of the job in order to avoid discriminatory practices. Consult applicable human rights legislation to ensure your recruitment and selection process complies with it.

Hiring — Offer of Employment

The offer letter begins the employment relationship and it is a good place to include the terms and conditions of employment.

An offer letter may include details on the start date, vacation and benefits entitlement, hours of work and overtime, whether the position is temporary or permanent (if short term include the last day of work) and probationary period. A fixed term contract should include the date on which it ends. Often the employee accepts an offer by signing the letter and it is placed in the employee personnel file.

Ensure that the offer letter is consistent with your policies and procedures, and compliant with applicable employment standards legislation.

Hiring — Probation

A period of probation:

- Allows for the process of conducting reviews and assessing employee performance prior to granting full employee status
- Can help avoid future problems by finding out early on if the person and the job aren't a good fit
- Is for a specific amount of time (it may include guidelines around possible extensions)

The probationary period as outlined in your organisation's policies should be stated in the letter of offer. The policy on probation may address performance reviews, details of communication, eligibility for benefits, the possibility of extending the probationary period, and termination. Termination during or at the end of the probationary period must be in compliance with employment legislation.

All jurisdictions allow for a period of time at the beginning of employment when no notice of termination is required. However, if an organisation has a probationary period that exceeds this period of time, notice or payment in lieu of notice is required. For example, in British Columbia, notice of termination is required after three months. Therefore an employer who decides to terminate an employee at the end of a six-month probationary period will have to give notice or payment in lieu in accordance with

British Columbia employment standards. It is important to sit down with the new hire to explain the details of the probationary period and to discuss expectations.

Hiring — Orientation

An effective orientation can have positive results for the organisation. Orientation helps the new hire understand what the organisation is all about and what the expectations are for her/him.

Policies on orientation provide guidelines for welcoming new employees and providing them with information about job requirements, the organisation, the people, and workplace policies and procedures.

Hiring — Employment of Relatives

A policy on the employment of relatives provides a useful framework for avoiding awkward and potentially difficult work situations.

The policy can be simple and straightforward. It often states whether hiring relatives is permitted or not. If hiring relatives is permitted, the policy sets out guidelines such as stipulating that an employee cannot be directly supervised by an immediate relative.

Hiring — Filling of Temporarily Vacant Positions

Temporarily vacant positions can arise when an employee takes a leave of absence (e.g. parental leave). During this time the organisation must fill the position until the employee is scheduled to return.

Polices define a temporarily vacant position and provide guidelines on how it will be filled (e.g., internal transfer or temporary external hire).

Holidays

Statutory or public holidays are days the government (federal and/or provincial) has designated as paid days off. Much of the content of your policy will be based directly on the law.

In addition to identifying statutory holidays, most legislation also governs:

- How holidays which fall on a regular day off are to be handled
- The rate of pay that must be paid to those who work the holiday
- How to calculate holiday pay for part-time employees

It is important to note that in most jurisdictions part-time employees are entitled to holiday pay whether or not the holiday falls on their usual work day. Your policy should identify the holidays that are provided by law and any other holidays that your organisation gives such as Remembrance Day or Easter Monday (if these days are not legislated in your jurisdiction). In all provinces and territories statutory holidays include two holidays based in the Christian faith: Christmas and Good Friday. As Canada has become more diverse, most jurisdictions, through their human rights legislation have made employers responsible for accommodating the religious holidays of other faiths within appropriate guidelines.

For example, in Ontario, an employer has a duty to accommodate an employee who practices another faith with two days of religious holidays - the same number of Christian-based holidays as provide for in the employment standards. These days are in addition to the statutory holidays legislated by the province. If an organisation gives its employees Easter Monday as a holiday, making three Christian-based holidays, then the duty to accommodate an employee of another faith would be three days. In this example, the onus is on the employee to request the religious accommodation.

The human rights legislation and the duty to accommodate religious holidays in the workplace are continuously evolving. Review the human rights legislation for your jurisdiction to ensure that your organisation is complying with the current laws.

SELECTION TESTS

A test is a sample of an aspect of an individual's behaviour, performance or attitude.

It can also be a systematic procedure for comparing the behaviour of two or more persons:

1. *Purpose of Tests*: The basic assumption underlying the use of tests in personnel selection is that individuals are different in their job-related abilities and skills and that these skills can be adequately and accurately measured. Tests seek to eliminate the possibility of prejudice on the part of the interviewer or supervisor. Potential ability only will govern selection decisions. The other major advantage is that the tests may uncover qualifications and talents that would not be detected by interviews or by listing of education and job expenence.
2. *Types of Tests*: The various tests used in selection can be put in to four categories:
   - Achievement or Intelligence Tests,
   - Aptitude or Potential Ability Tests,

- Personality Tests, and
- Interest Tests.

Achievement or Intelligence Tests

These are also called 'proficiency tests'. These measure the skill or knowledge which is acquired as a result of a training programme and on the job experience. These measure what the applicant can do. These are of two types:

1. *Test for Measuring job Knowledge*: These are known as 'Trade Tests'. These are administered to determine knowledge of typing, shorthand and in operating calculators, adding machines, dictating and transcribing machines or simple mechanical equipment. These are primarily oral tests consisting of a series of questions which are believed to be satisfactorily answered only by those who know and thoroughly understand the trade or occupation. Oral tests may be supplemented by written, picture or performance types.
2. *Work Sample Tests*: These measure the proficiency with which equipment can be handled by the candidate. This is done by giving him a piece of work to judge how efficiently he does it. For example, a typing test would provide the material to be typed and note the time taken and mistakes committed.

Aptitude or Potential Ability Tests

These tests measure the latent ability of a candidate to learn a new job or skill. Through these tests you can detect peculiarity or defects in a person's sensory or intellectual capacity. These focus attention on particular types of talent such as learning, reasoning and mechanical or musical aptitude. 'Instruments' used are variously described as tests of 'intelligence', 'mental ability', 'mental alertness', or simply as 'personnel tests'. These are of three types:

1. *Mental Tests*: These measure the overall intellectual ability or the intelligence quotient (I.Q.) of a person and enable us to know whether he has the mental capacity to deal with new problems. These determine an employee's fluency in language, memory, interction, reasoning, speed of perception, and spatial visualisation.
2. *Mechanical Aptitude Tests*: These measure the capacity of a person to learn a particular type of mechanical work. These are useful when apprentices, machinists, mechanics, maintenance workers, and mechanical technicians are to be selected.

3. *Psychomotor or Skill Tests*: These measure a person's ability to do a specific job. These are administered to determine mental dexterity or motor ability and similar attributes involving muscular movement, control and coordination. These are primarily used in the selection of workers who have to perform semi-skilled and repetitive jobs, like assembly work, packing, testing, inspection and so on.

Personality Tests

These discover clues to an individual's value system, his emotional reactions, maturity and his characteristic mood. The tests help in assessing a person's motivation, his ability to adjust himself to the stresses of everyday life and his capacity for interpersonal relations and for projecting an impressive image of himself.

They are expressed in terms of the relative significance of such traits of a person as selfconfidence, ambition, tact, emotional control, optimism, decisiveness, sociability, conformity, objectivity, patience, fear, distrust, initiative, judgement, dominance, impulsiveness, sympathy, integrity, and stability. These tests are given to predict potential performance and success for supervisory or managerial jobs.

The personality tests are basically of three types:

1. *Objective Tests*: These measure neurotic tendencies, self-sufficiency, dominance, submission and self-confidence.
2. *Projective Tests*: In these tests, a candidate is asked to project his own interpretation onto certain standard stimuli. The way in which he responds to these stimuli depends on his own values, motives and personality.
3. *Situation Tests*: These measure an applicant's reaction when he is placed in a peculiar situation, his ability to undergo stress and his demonstration of ingenuity under pressure. These tests usually relate to a leaderless group situation, in which some problems are posed to a group and its members are asked to reach some ceases without the help of a leader.

Interest Tests

These tests are designed to discover a person's areas of interest and to identify the kind of work that will satisfy him. The interest tests are used for vocational guidance, and are assessed in the form of answers to a well-prepared questionnaire.

Bibliography

Ajit Kumar Ghosh: *Human Resource Management : With Cases*, Manas, 2006.

Anuradha Sharma and Aradhana Khandekar: *Strategic Human Resource Management : An Indian Perspecitve*, Response Books, 2006.

Bach, S.: *Managing Human Resource: Personnel Management in Transition*, Blackwell, Oxford, 2005.

Bandura, A.: *Social Learning and Personality Development,* New York, Holt, Rinehart, and Winston, 1963.

Bhatia, S K : *International Human Resource Management : A Global Perspective : Practices and Strategies for Competitive Success*, Deep and Deep, 2005.

Bhola, Ajay: *Modern Human Resource Management : Principles and Techniques*, Regal Pub, 2008.

Damon, William: *Social and Personality Development: Infancy through Adolescence,* New York, Norton, 1983.

Deenabandhu Das: *Human Resource Development in Public Sector Undertakings*, Mohit, Delhi, 2003.

Denhardt, R. B.: *Managing Human Behavior in Public & Nonprofit Organizations,* Thousand Oaks, Sage, 2002.

Dileep Kumar M: *Organisational Behaviour, Human Resource Management and Management*, Serials Publications, 2010.

Gupta, Sachin : *Human Resource Development : Concepts and Practices*, Deep and Deep Pub, Delhi, 2005.

Gurpreet Randhawa: *Education and Human Resource Management*, APH, Delhi, 2007.

Hacking, Ian: *Rewriting the Soul : Multiple Personality and the Sciences of Memory,* Princeton, Princeton University Press, 1995.

Hemant Wagdre: *International Human Resource Management*, Adhyayan, New Delhi, 2007.

Hopkins, D. : *Personal Growth Through Adventure*, London, David Fulton Publishers, 1993.

Jayant Kumar Chakraborty: *Human Resource Management : For Public Sector Undertakings*, Satyam Pub, 2009.

Kathleen V.: *Real People : Personal Identity without thought Experiments*, Oxford, Clarendon Press, 1988.

Kelly, G.A.: *Theory of Personality : The Psychology of Personal Constructs.* New York, W.W. Norton, 1955.

Kohlberg, L.: *The Philosophy of Moral Development: Moral Stages and the Idea of Justice,* New York, Harper & Row, 1981.

Legge, K.: *Human Resource Management, Rhetorics and Realities,* Macmillan, London, 1995.

Levin, David Michael: *Pathologies of the Modern Self,* New York, NYU Press, 1988.

Mahler, Margaret: *The Psychological Birth of the Human Infant,* New York, Basic, 1975.

Maslow, A.: *Motivation and Personality,* New York, Harper and Row, 1987.

Metti, Ajay: *Human Resource Management in the Hotel Industry,* Anmol, 2008.

Mohiadeen, P.M. Meera : *Personnel and Human Resource Management,* ABD, 2003

Piyush Kanti Mahapatra: *Human Resource Management in Libraries,* Ess Ess, 2002.

Rakesh Hooja and Girish K. Srivastava : *Managing Change, Organisational Behaviour and Human Resource Development,* Rawat, Meerut, 2008.

Redman, T. and Wilkinson, A.: *Contemporary Human Resource Management,* Pearson, London, 2008.

Rishma Vedd: *Management Accounting and Strategic Human Resource Management,* Deep and Deep, 2003

Sachin Gupta : *Human Resource Development : Concepts and Practices,* Deep and Deep Pub, Delhi, 2005.

Schuster, C.: *The Process of Human Development,* Boston, Little, Brown & Co., 1980.

Sperling, Michael: *Attachment in Adults: Clinical and Developmental Perspectives,* New York, Guilford Press, 1994.

Srivastava, M.P. : *Introspection of Plan Priorities Human Resource Development Programmes and Sectoral Activities (1951-1997),* Manak, Meerut, 1998.

Sugan C Jain: *New Trends in Human Resource Management,* RBSA Pub, 2007.

Suresh Vyas: *Human Resource Development in Business,* Mangal Deep, Kolkata, 2005.

Suri, R.K. and S.L. Gupta: *Case Studies in Human Resource Management,* Pentagon Press, 2007.

Tapomoy Deb: *Human Resource Development : Theory and Practice,* Ane Books India, Delhi, 2006.

Wiggins, Jerry: *The Five Factor Model of Personality: Theoretical Perspectives,* New York, Guilford Press, 1996.

Wilkinson, A.: *Contemporary Human Resource Management,* Pearson, London, 2008.

Index

P

R

S

❑❑❑

www.ingramcontent.com/pod-product-compliance
Lightning Source LLC
Chambersburg PA
CBHW050524240926
51846CB00003B/686
9789383263523